GUEST PARKING 2:
Ian Wolfe
Carl Laemmle Jr.
Alan Napier
David Manners

BY RICK ATKINS

Published in the USA by:

BearManor Media
P O Box 71426
Albany, Georgia 31708
www.bearmanormedia.com

ISBN: 978-1-59393-955-7
BearManor Media, Albany, Georgia
Printed in the United States of America
Book design by Robbie Adkins, www.adkinsconsult.com

CONTENTS

DEDICATION

This book is dedicated to the loving memory of my parents, Faye and Dewey.

I am also inspired and extend this dedication to the memories of Adela Rogers St. Johns, Ruth Friedland Regis, Edward "Eddie" Regis, Josephine Simeur, Doug Surber, JoAnn Simeur Surber, David Marowitz, and Ruth Chernoff.

Acknowledgements

Without the help of the following guests, this book could not have been written; David Simeur, for his invaluable help and guidance; my brother, Dean, who selflessly supported this project, and my sisters, Martha and Kathy, for your continued moral support. I love you.

Additional thanks go to those of whom *guest parking* allotments have expired: Meryl O'Loughlin, a thoughtful casting director from 1976; Wendayne and Forrest J Ackerman, friends and mentors who inspired me greatly; Max Laemmle, Lillian Borteck, Ian and "Beth" Wolfe, their love and devotion for each other exemplified who they were to others. I love them forever; Carl Laemmle Jr., his loyalty to me was astounding—and my promise to him has come to fruition; Elise Nisse, her kindness remains touching; Alan Napier, his charm and modesty is remembered greatly especially at teatime; Stanley Bergerman, an unforgettably kind and impressive human being; Fay Bergerman, the second wife of Stanley Bergerman. I admired her honesty and humor. She was truly a lovely lady; Carol Laemmle Bergerman, who later adopted spelling her name "Carole," I loved her unique personality; Bill Bixby, a generous and talented actor/director; Evelyn Moriarty, an original. I cherish our eleven-year friendship; Elizabeth "Liesel" Adler (niece of Laupheim sculptor and artist Friedrich Adler), a dear lady with a kind heart, who traveled from her home in London to join a number of us in Laupheim, Germany in the summer of 1999; David Manners, during his final year of life, met with me after years of written correspondence. I'll never forget his gentle spirit, his honesty and his broad smile; Carla Laemmle, a true blue friend is a gift to cherish forever. We lived nearly eighteen years of history together, along with our friend Dr. Udo Bayer of Baden Württemberg Laupheim, Germany, a scholar and author who contributed greatly to this book. It is my feeling that all of these individuals spiritually live on in some way.

Extended thanks must go to the following individuals; my publisher Ben Ohmart, Angela "Anji" Holtzman, Jane E. Moore, Arnold

Stern, Burt Alexander, Jennifer Nichols, Lupita Tovar Kohner, Gabriele Bayer, Elizabeth Lincke; Jeff Pirtle (NBCUniversal Archives & Collections); Zachary Zito, Hali Helfgott, Neil Lipes, Philip J. Riley, Gregory William Mank, John Norris, and Dan Van Neste.

Last, but not least, I must thank our beloved bichon, Kefer, a true Godsend. Mr. Kefer's unconditional love, patience and his presence helped to pave the way to better health for me.

PREFACE

As it stands with all of my friends, including Zita Johann, we agreed that *Guest Parking* is a place in which life is precious yet temporary. When one stops to think about it, we really are only guests, alluding, of course, to our very temporal mortal existence here on earth.

The following stories are true and written without guile. Research was derived from personal letters, working notes and audiotape quoted in whole or in part, acknowledgments of participants, alongside photographs from the author's collection and other credited contributors. My disclaimer is simple. I make no claims on any book authored by me, which may fall under the "*Guest Parking*" title as being biographies; authorized or not. Three of the four gentlemen featured in this book were actors of the stage and movies. Two of them also worked in radio. One was a motion picture producer.

My earliest memories began as a five-year-old living with my family in Chicago during the 1960s. It was first television and later what our Mom called the "big treat," going to the movies with my two sisters for entertainment. Eventually, I grew passionate about actors in the performing arts and brought my younger brother into it as well. Over the years, I became entranced with a diverse variety of music, first over the radio, record player, and, of course, at the movies. The musical memories never completely faded from my consciousness.

During my teenage years, I had little in common with contemporaries. I began making trips to the downtown library in Chicago, where I could do plenty of research and compose letters to my choice correspondents. When I began receiving replies from them, my parents became concerned. They eventually accepted and encouraged me in my endeavors. In my fifteenth year, I began traveling to meet some of these people after which numerous return trips were made.

I am since honored to have authored books: *Let's Scare 'Em!* (*Grand Interviews and a Filmography of Horrific Proportions*,

1930-1961); McFarland and Company Publishers published it in August 1997, and *Among the Rugged Peaks: An Intimate Biography of Carla Laemmle,* published by Midnight Marquee Press in February 2009. In the fall of 2006, I was inspired to write *Guest Parking: Zita Johann* (with an Afterword by Liesl Ehardt), which BearManor Media Publishers published in April 2011. I thought this book would be my last.

Soon before its publication, I was diagnosed with cancer. Aggressive medical treatments followed with difficult side effects had me questioning my own mortality. With these thoughts, I felt that I needed to get busy on something else to write. I had more to share and the thought of writing again was inevitable. After five years, the best news is there is no cancer.

When writing resumed on this current book in 2011, which was shelved in 2002, I felt there was something lacking. I pondered and questioned it. 'Where is the energy in bringing multiple subjects together in another book?' My love for music rekindled after unearthing varieties of music recordings, which helped as moral support and inspiration setting forward an awakening writing process. It was sometimes downright whimsical!

Ultimately, the "powers that be" took charge of my pondering and whom to write about. I preface that I am not the child of a celebrity, nor am I related to anyone in the entertainment industry. As one friend said of me, "He's just a pleasant peasant!"

The summer of 1979, in Los Angeles, California, was a momentous time in my life. Before the ever-popular GPS (Global Positioning System) road navigation devices were invented, this twenty-year-old "Chicago boy" relied (as most people did) upon printed maps or directions given to me by others. I recall most of the popular music then being broadcast over my rental car radio. My first stop was Sherman Oaks, California where I first rented a motel room and later arrived at the home of veteran character actor, Ian Wolfe.

Ian Wolfe was one of the few American-born actors who developed a formative array of characters with varied dialects. He skillfully demonstrated them on the stage, in motion pictures, radio and television. He was a great listener and advisor. He had a positive influence on me about life and living it. His quick wit and charming nature added to this delightful man. With years gone by, I continue to re-read his notes and letters to me. Ian bestowed loving and zestful names on me such as, "Lad," "Riki-Tiki-TavO," "Snot-nose" and "Grandson." He once wrote the following, "Dear Lad: Your little note sounds good. Hang in there! ... Let the music find its own tune. ... Down life's road, follow suit, but not have the suit follow you!"

After spending two days with Ian and his lovely wife Beth, our last dinner night was memorable. When arriving back to their home, Ian gave me map directions to the Beverly Hills home of the former movie producer, Carl Laemmle Jr., where I would be going the next day. To this day, I can still distinctly remember Ian saying to me, *"Now lad ... you must follow your map. Do not go a-r-o-u-n-d the mountain. Go ... over it!"* That I did!

As for Carl Laemmle Jr., his most prestigious effort as a movie producer was *All Quiet on the Western Front*. It earned him motion picture's highest honor from the Academy of Motion Picture Arts and Sciences for Best Picture of 1930. By the time he was twenty-eight-years old, Junior's motion picture accomplishments were numerous. He is best remembered for early 1930s horror movies that he produced during his tenure at Universal Pictures Corporation. Universal City Studios was his father's brainchild. It opened to the public in March 1915.

Junior and I shared a three-year correspondence, and he was always encouraging me to visit him. Between the covers of this book is the more extensive chapter regarding my story about "Junior" Laemmle, one of Hollywood's most neglected figures. My first story about him, "A Son to the House of Laemmle: Carl Laemmle Jr." was published by McFarland and Company in my first book, *Let's Scare 'Em!*

Immediately following my visit with Junior Laemmle, I headed to the Pacific Palisades where I met another veteran character actor, Alan Napier, at his home which sat high above the Oceanside. What many people may not know about Alan Napier is that he began his career on the stages of England in 1924, and later appeared in motion pictures there before immigrating to America in 1939 where he swiftly resumed his career.

Alan's career spanned fifty-seven years. He never wanted to be typecast, but it all changed for him in the late 1960s. He is best remembered as playing Alfred the butler on the 1960s *Batman* TV series. Alan was a well-educated, delightful, caring, but modest man. His youthful spirit will be with me always. An earthly bonus for many of we "fans" is catching Alan Napier in television reruns. He gets my immediate attention. I am proud that he considered me his friend. Every time I have tea, I think of him.

The final subject of this book is the former Hollywood actor David Manners. I was eleven years old when I first saw him in a television rerun of the 1931 Universal horror movie, *Dracula*, starring Bela Lugosi. To me, David's appeal on screen was his gentleman-like qualities. His good looks certainly did not hurt him either.

Between 1929 and 1936, David Manners played a variety of roles before turning his back on Hollywood at the age of thirty-six. His first major role was as the soldier Raleigh in *Journey's End* (1930 with Colin Clive; directed by James Whale); he also played the blind young man John Carson in *The Miracle Woman* (1931 with Barbara Stanwyck), and the dashing Kit in *A Bill of Divorcement* (1932 with Katharine Hepburn) just to name a few of David's thirty-nine motion pictures.

I got to know David Manners after we began corresponding with each other beginning in 1975 for his seventy-fifth birthday. His kind letters and insightful writings continued for over twenty years. Some of his writings grace the final chapter of this book.

David was great support to me through an earlier round of cancer treatment during the 1990s. When we finally met. David swooned and said, "You look great, Rick. I'm surprised that I still have *my* hair too." To which I said, "You look grand!" This garnered his ageless familiar smile.

At Universal Pictures, producer and general manager, Carl Laemmle Jr., cast David Manners in *Dracula*, with Bela Lugosi. Soon after, David appeared in the following Laemmle productions: *The Mummy* (1932 with Boris Karloff and Zita Johann), *The Black Cat* (1934 with Jacqueline Wells, later known as Julie Bishop, Boris

Karloff and Bela Lugosi), and *Mystery of Edwin Drood* (1935 with Douglass Montgomery, Claude Rains and Heather Angel, from the unfinished novel by Charles Dickens). A lesser-known film, *Moonstone*, released by Monogram Pictures in 1934, was one of my favorites.

The film appearances of all actors and producers will live on by way of motion pictures, television, cable television, revival movie houses, DVD, and the Internet. They encouraged me to practice the lively art of writing and trusted that I would follow through effectively. Their lives continue to inspire me.

Finally, my dear friend, Carla Laemmle, a former dancer and actress of the 1920s and 1930s (and the niece of Universal City Studios founder, Carl Laemmle) agreed to contribute to this book. Having read the countless opus drafts over time, Carla said, "Rick, I would be honored to write anything before my *guest parking* privileges are revoked!"

When we were not together, Carla and I talked constantly by telephone over the years. A few days before she passed, we shared a near forty-five minute telephone conversation. We began talking about past moments in our lives. Carla asked me, "Would you go back?" I said, 'No.' She said, "Yes and no. There's good and bad in everything. Life is never perfect. Yes. I would go back to when I first met Ray Cannon while I was living at Universal."

Then I asked Carla about the "no" in her answer. She quipped and laughed: "Well, I've already done that!" Carla ended the call by not saying her usual and musical ... "I love you!" Instead, her tone changed as she said, "Rick, always remember that I love you." To which I replied, 'I love you Carla.' She wrote the following in a letter to me in June 2000.

"Dear Rick, ...I was thinking when I read your last letter regarding feeling someone's spiritual presence. Why—oh—why, I have never been able to feel Ray's presence. I have desired it so very much. I talk to him all the time and ask him to give me a sign but I have not been able to lift the veil that separates us. But I have no doubt that my love, our love, is a lasting bond that will bring us together again and again in whatever planes of manifestation might be. I have always known that he was far along on the Path and perhaps even halted the course to help me. I learned so much of goodness and beauty from him.

Yesterday, as usual, I had the radio on and something they were playing inspired me to get up and dance. But it was much more than that—I had the urge to get Ray's picture and dance with him! I held it before me as I—we - danced - tears just streaming down my face. It was truly a spiritual moment in time. I thought afterwards, what would anyone think of such a scene?

But it seemed so natural to me - and I was not ninety-years-old. I was <u>young</u> and expressing my love. Anyway, I know you will understand. As a matter of fact, I thought what a heart-tugging scene it would make in a movie - and I was doing it in <u>real</u> <u>life</u>!"

Carla Laemmle danced her way into many hearts where she will forever remain. She passed from our world June 12, 2014, at the youthful age of one hundred and four, but not without leaving the reader with her written epilogue.

Without further adieu, we present *Guest Parking 2: Ian Wolfe, Carl Laemmle Jr., Alan Napier and David Manners.*

Carla Laemmle and the Author at the California Club in Los Angeles, October 19, 2011, the evening before her 102nd birthday. Photo credit: Hali Helfgott.

Ian Wolfe as the mortician Mr. D'Amato in the 1989 film Checking Out
(HandMade Films and Warner Brothers). Photo courtesy of Ian Wolfe.

CHAPTER 1
IAN WOLFE: THE CHARACTER MAN

Throughout his seventy-one-year career, Ian Wolfe was one of the few American born actors who played hosts of characters with various dialects, first on the stage, later in motion pictures, over radio, and television. He made over nineteen hundred appearances in the entertainment world: two hundred and twenty-one appearances in Hollywood movies, which includes several short films; fifteen hundred on-stage performances between 1919 and 1970; three dozen radio broadcasts, and one hundred and seventy-five aired television appearances between 1949 and 1987.

Ian Wolfe had other outstanding accomplishments: he was a husband and father of two daughters. He and his wife, Elizabeth, better known as Beth, were married for sixty-eight years. She was the awe-inspired feminine side to Ian. He wrote the following note to this writer:

> It was love at first sight. Beth and I remember that day quite well. I helped break up a physical feline fight as we were separately leaving an Esoteric and Perennial Wisdom class. I jumped in to scatter them. Beth and I were married about a year later, Christmas Eve, 1923. I was directing some theatre at the Pasadena Playhouse at the time we met. After we were married, we first resided in Oceanside, California until 1936.
>
> It will be sixty-nine years this next Xmas Eve that Beth and I were married. The way I feel now ... I don't think I'll reach it!

The couple celebrated sixty-eight years of marriage, Christmas Eve, 1991. Not making it the following year, Ian was called to (what he referred to as) "The Great Divide," January 23, 1992 at age ninety-five years, two months and twenty days. Beth followed her husband in death one year and one week later, January 30, 1993. Their enduring love and devotion for each other remains an inspiration to the many lives that they touched. Ian and Beth knew that my love for them was never abandoned. A framed picture of the couple sits nearby. Another of my favorite inscribed photographs of my honorary "Gramps," is close by, in which he is pictured wearing a special wristwatch that he later gave me as a gift.

Among the most memorable times for this author was having the opportunity to see Ian actually work in a studio. Other pleasures with Beth and Ian were going to the movies, first to see Ian's appearance in the Bette Midler movie, *Jinxed* and later delighted in their company seeing the movie, *E.T. the Extraterrestrial.* In April 1983, I invited my sister, Kathy, to travel with me to spend a week in California to meet some friends. As a gift for Kathy's birthday, Beth and Ian treated us to a day at the Universal Studios. These were only some of the dear memories!

On the earthly occasion of Ian Wolfe's one hundred and fifteenth birthday, November 4th, 2011, this author began re-reading cards, notes and letters written over a sixteen-year period by Ian and Beth Wolfe. One of the first mailings I ran across was the following by Ian, which has been carried out by this author.

Do justice with Gramps whatever you decide literarily. And blessings go with it-- for the rescue of the unfinished manuscript --whether you do anything more with it or not -- if they would in fact become two separate stories. Best to re-title the separate story "The Character Man." I would like that, and that is what I am!

Start from the beginning about how you first contacted me. Do you and me a favor; stick to the credits that we worked on together, which includes my stage credits and any anecdotes regarding people associated with the stage and films that may follow.

Finally Lad, You'll be writing enough about me as it is. I advise only a tally of my professional film credits. If you do indeed find them all, please <u>do</u> <u>not</u> list every doggone one! Besides, I wasn't keen about a good number of them. Ay?

It all began one evening in Chicago at home in 1975 watching the *Phyllis* television sit-com pilot, starring Cloris Leachman, when I spotted the familiar face of Ian Wolfe playing a Minister. (1)

Inscribed photo from Ian Wolfe to the author, in the fall of 1976. It was the first of many inscribed by the actor of a then current headshot made in the spring of 1976.

It was hard to believe that Ian Wolfe was the same actor who appeared in the 1946 motion picture *Bedlam*, starring Boris Karloff and Anna Lee. In comparison, the thirty years that separate the two acting appearances seemed to make this man look ageless. Since, "Ian sightings" became popular among friends and family. (2)

Ian Wolfe sent this photo and inscribed, "a very poor arabesque" to the author for Christmas 1979. He wrote on the reverse side, "Rick—Me at exactly 21, a laugh for you...In front of an old bit of sheeting in dancing school. What a foolish young fellow!! Then I realized (after a stint in the Army Medical) that I was a character actor and not a dancer. I went to the Dramatic School in N.Y._Ian."

As the "sit-com" concluded, this seventeen-year-old took notice of the casting director's name in the closing credits. I later wrote to her for an address for Ian Wolfe. Meryl O'Loughlin graciously replied with a forwarding address for the actor. (3) Following through, I wrote to Ian Wolfe. He was seventy-nine then. Within a couple of weeks, Ian replied. His letter began, "Such enterprise must deserve an answer! ..." (4) For the next three years we continued a written correspondence before we met the afternoon of July 3, 1979 in Sherman Oaks, California.

This writer arrived promptly at three o'clock pm to the modest and cozy ranch home of Ian Wolfe.

After a rap, tap, tap on the front door knocker, Ian came to the door quickly with a hearty welcome followed by a sheepish grin,

"Come in! Come in! It is so good to finally meet you. I'm the Big-Bad Wolf!" His was followed by his wife's voice. She began lovingly scolding Ian for startling me. Once inside, Ian introduced me to Beth. She was such a darling lady! She offered iced tea, which was accepted.

Over the next couple of hours in the confines of their cozy living room, the three of us talked through an array of subjects. Ian said that he and Beth had lived at their Noble avenue address since 1936. I would spend the next two days in their company having rented a nearby motel room. Beth insisted that I walk over to share breakfast the next day and after.

Beth was a talented artist. She had a passion for painting landscapes and still life. One room in the home was her art room. Beth was modest about her work, but one could see a sense of pride wash over her when she talked about her artworks. I felt that some of her pieces could have been publicly displayed. All of her works demonstrated her artistic evolution. One particular piece was her rendition of a French neighborhood. I swooned. She was awestruck by my knowledge of Ian's work and was always encouraging. During later visits, Beth also had a knack for delectable home cooked meals and fresh desserts.

Undoubtedly, Beth was most proud of was being married to Ian. In her naturally feminine and soft-spoken beautiful Australian voice Beth said the following.

Ohhh! Don't let anyone kid you. It isn't easy in the early years of marriage . . . and it's work after that. We have been fortunate having raised two daughters and managed to live comfortably because of Ian's line of work. However, I wouldn't recommend it to anyone.

There have been ups and downs. The exciting times that come with it is that we have had the good fortune of traveling together to places in this country, and abroad, because of various jobs that require filming on locations rather than in the studios. I am from Australia, and was used to moving around. Therefore, I was well suited for travel. It's never ceases to be exciting.

Ian Wolfe as Harry Bevan in the Broadway production of "The Barretts of Wimpole Street" (1931) compared to his Hollywood look as the same character in the 1934 film version at MGM produced by Irving Thalberg. Photos from the author's collection.

As a matter of fact, we are going to London in a couple of weeks. Ian is appearing in a film for Warren Beatty, entitled, *Reds*. Warren is directing and starring in it. After that Ian will be on location in Salina, Kansas near where he was brought up in Kansas City, Kansas. He will be traveling solo. That will be a nice little trip for him.

We were surprised when the clock displayed five-thirty pm and no formal interview had yet started. Beth and Ian invited me out for dinner. Ian said to me, "You must be famished? It may be best that we begin the interview after we eat?" We all agreed. We returned from dinner around seven-thirty pm, and began the interview while Beth served hot tea and dessert. Ian ended the interview by saying: "It's not often that I sit up until nearly one a.m. with someone like you. You can call me Gramps." Gramps he would be. Understandably, Beth remained "Beth."

After this initial meeting, a mutual trust was established between us. Our friendship collectively span over the next dozen years. I made numerous return visits to the happy home on Noble Avenue. Written correspondences and monthly phone calls continued. Ian began supplying me with more information regarding his long life and acting career in addition to condensed facts regarding his family history. He also kept me up to date on his forthcoming television and movie parts. Ian's other interests were a life-long comprehensive study of religions and philosophies, writing poetry since the age of fifteen, and mountain climbing. Ian wrote the following.

I have no religious affiliations. I find Zen beautiful and fascinating as a Way of Life, not really a religion. There are many and varied, perhaps inner-related paths up "The Mountain" towards Wholeness and Oneness – toward the eventual unity of All Mankind.

My lifelong hobby is my own personal study of comparative religions and philosophies especially Oriental ones, though I was raised a Baptist and my father was a Railroad YMCA Secretary and was a sort of a lay minister in various Protestant churches.

My wife and I, we are dedicated to the United Nations. We are healthy, down to earth (I hope) Esoteric and Perennial Wisdom students, with no fixed "ties."

It was at one of these student meetings in the spring of 1923 when I met Elizabeth Wolfe. She came from prominent pioneer stock in Australia, near Perth, coincidentally with nearly the same racial lines as myself English, German and Irish, except that she traces a bit of French in her family instead of my bit of Welsh.

In 1979, Ian Wolfe shared some of his family background and humble professional beginnings. He later said. "You may bore your readers to tears with all of this? Whatever you decide to choose is fine with me, Lad."

The Wolfe ancestors immigrated to Illinois from a general area of northwest New Jersey (then known as New Caesarea) not far from Delaware Water Gap, in 1731 traveling from Vermont, upper New York State and West Virginia when it was all Virginia.

My mother, Abigail (Thomas) was born near Canton, Illinois. Her family's first recorded settlers to America were in 1640.

Ian Wolfe as he appeared in The Mighty Barnum *(Twentieth Century Fox, 1934) as the Ambassador, Mr. Kent. Photo courtesy of Ian Wolfe.*

My mother was known for her work with animals. She and my father were quite strict, maybe a little overly religious when they were younger. They were practical and unusually kind and helpful to relatives and friends, in many ways!

I was born November 4, 1896 around 7:03 am, in Canton, Illinois (Fulton County) of very early Colonial-American stock, all jokingly spoken of by me as, "Thoroughly bred."

I am one of three children born to Mary "Rose" Wilson Wolfe and Marcus Aurelius Wolfe (known as Mark or M.A. Wolfe). I got the Marcus as a middle name; used the M. rarely. My parents had moved around to various locals such as Grand Island, Nebraska where I entered the first grade, Council Bluffs, Iowa, Ellis Kansas, and later Kansas City, Kansas.

At twenty-one, after a stint as a Volunteer Medical Sergeant in the first World War, I wasn't on active duty, but I know that I didn't want to stay in the service. So, I told them that I was a dancer. I loved pantomime. The eurhythmic gestures of expressing one's self with the entire body fascinated me! After I got out of the army, I was living in Kansas City, Kansas at the time. I traveled to New York by train where I studied dance and pantomime under the direction of Ruth St. Denis and her husband, Ted Shawn. They were two very well-known performers in their days. I was twenty-one and really started out to be a dancer, but learned more pantomime. I also took courses at the Academy of Dramatic Arts where I studied for about two years. I was twenty-three and finding my way, as it were.

In the fall of 1919 (right after the big actor's strike), I was working on the road in a morality play called *"Experience,"* and believe me, it was!" I played two parts, "Style," a very dressed up British fellow in fashion, high-styled dress clothes; and in a gambling scene I played quite an opposite character. Once I had to go on and play the "Youth" in it, which was the male lead.

The original lead "Youth" got lockjaw on the train as we were approaching Philadelphia, Pennsylvania. And at a moment's notice, before I had time to rehearse the play sufficiently, I had to go on.

I believe that is why to this day, I have a bit of stage fright especially with something that is live.

I didn't know in those days if you hadn't had sufficient re-hearsals you can refuse to go on. But I did go on and it saved everyone's salaries. So, I was a hero from then on. At any rate, the acting bug had bitten me.

At nearly eight-three, I still have the ability to do fairly commanding things. I still have good study. I still have good command of character and yet I'm just playing crap mostly. I do feel fortunate to have my faculties. Not all old actors have command of their faculties or can let alone act. I think the only sin, the only real sin is jitters, but I fight it off.

I loved the theatre, where so many of us got our start. As motion pictures became the craze, film producers were looking to so many of the stage performers. Many of them had immediate jobs. Studying the arts was a great way to meet people then. Along this route was Lionel Barrymore.

In October 1921, Ian Wolfe made his Broadway debut in Henn Bernstein's *"The Claw."* It opened at the Broadhurst Theatre. Arthur Hopkins directed it. Lionel Barrymore was the star. Ian Wolfe played the part of a servant. It ran over 100 performances. It closed in January 1922. Ian remembered the following of Lionel Barrymore.

He liked actors. I remember when we were "on the road" by train, and how he would be sitting with the men from the cast, or anyone else who would listen to him for that matter, in the smoker, telling old yarns about the theater.

After I came out to Hollywood, I did two or three pictures with him. Lo and Behold, I also worked with him on several radio broadcasts of "Mayor of the Town." Lionel was a very wonderful man to work with.

In Short Hills, New Jersey during Ian Wolfe's "salad days" he tried his hand at writing a play, which he entitled, *"Children of Thunder"* (*The Brontes of Wuthering Heights*). Ian laughed while mentioning it to this writer.

Oh, here I was going to be a playwright, another Eugene O'Neill, I thought? The play was a tragedy, a comedy and a fantasy with a prologue rolled into three acts. I'm sure with

Ian Wolfe as the Swedish Consul in Clive of India *(Twentieth Century Fox, 1935). Ian remembered the British actor and fellow cast member Colin Clive, with whom he worked with in two films. Photo courtesy of Ian Wolfe.*

the audiences of today that it would be a go! I shelved the thing long ago and never looked at it since. (5) Once a friend reminded me, "You're a character actor." And that's what I have been. I resigned myself to the fact that I wouldn't be a star or even a leading man.

Ian Wolfe (as the apothecary) and Leslie Howard (as Romeo Montague) in a scene from Romeo and Juliet *(MGM, 1935). Photo courtesy of Zach Zito.*

I suppose, in a strange perverted sort of way, I'm a success [as he laughs] because I've done so damn many things and such a variety of things. That's what I set out to do after I realized what my friend had said was true. I also realized that my voice is what was preferred in parts. I did many radio broadcasts in my day.

For several years, during Ian's early theatre work and on into his film work, Ian Wolfe went through varied professional name changes. Ian said, "It was my agent's idea. He thought that by changing my name, it would gain more recognition to my career. We changed it more than once." The following names were applied, Ian M. Wolfe, Ian Van Wolfe, Ien Wulf, Ian Wulf, Ien Wul, Ian Vulff, and Ian MacWolfe. Ian commented, "That was the biggest mistake that I ever made professionally."

Ian Wolfe as "Herbert" the mean jailer in Marie Antoinette *(MGM, 1938). Photo courtesy of Ian Wolfe.*

Ian Wolfe was thirty-seven when the film *The Barretts of Wimpole Street* was his "big introduction" to motion pictures. He had originally played it on the stage with Katharine Cornell on Broadway and it toured for fifty-five weeks during the 1931-32 season.

Irving Thalberg brought me out to Hollywood in the spring of 1934 to recreate the part of Harry Bevan (a British fop),

The Wonderful Wizard of Oz *radio series ran between September 1933 and March 1934 over the NBC network. Pictured here are young Nancy Kelly as Dorothy and Ian Wolfe as the Wizard. Photo courtesy of Neil*

and played it in the film to Norma Shearer. Although, I was devoted to Katharine Cornell, I thought that Norma Shearer played a lovely Elizabeth Barrett. Norma Shearer was married to Mr. Thalberg, as you may know. Irving Thalberg and Sidney Franklin got me started in the movie business.

Thalberg first sent me over to RKO and they put me in a picture that is now as obscure as the character that I played in it [he frowns followed with a smile]. It was called *The Fountain*. John Cromwell, a veteran Broadway and Hollywood actor directed it. I remember appearing in this and a later film of his, *Abe Lincoln in Illinois*. The reasoning behind me going to another studio was that Mr. Thalberg thought it would be best not to put me under contract. This is how I would go along throughout my career. It was really to my advantage. I could go anywhere for work.

Then I was sent to Twentieth Century Fox in *The Mighty Barnum* [1934] and *Clive of India* [1935].

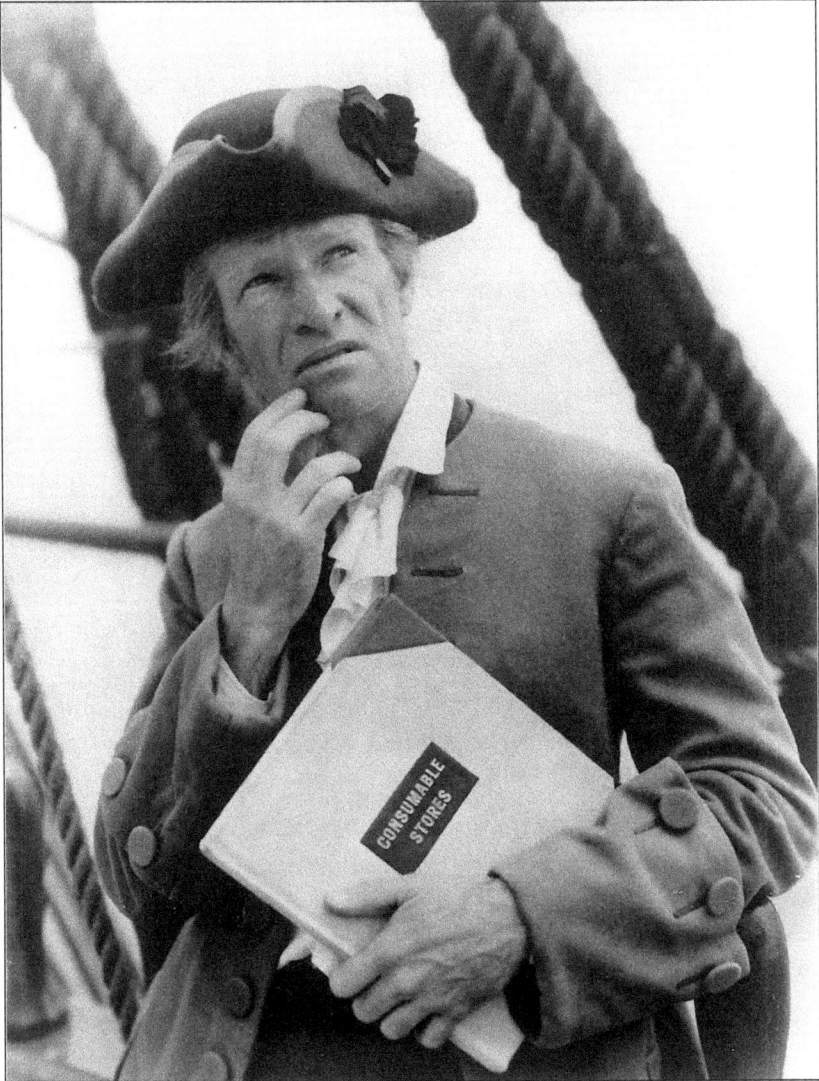

Ian Wolfe as Maggs the storekeeper in Mutiny on the Bounty (1935).
About his character, Ian said, "Thalberg saw that I could play a
meanie. Some say meaner than the Captain Bligh character. I feel that
it was my most important part... It always looked good on a resume."
Photo courtesy of Ian Wolfe.

I do recall the fine British actor Colin Clive was in the
latter. The only other thing I remember about the movie
outside of Colin Clive was my outfit, which you see in that
photo you are holding. Under Thalberg, was The Barretts of

Ian Wolfe, Clark Gable, DeWitt Jennings, Charles Laughton, Alec Craig, and Wallis Clark in a scene from Mutiny on the Bounty. *Photo courtesy of Ian Wolfe.*

Wimpole Street [1934], *Mutiny on the Bounty* [1935], *Romeo and Juliet* [1936]; I played the apothecary who sold Romeo (played by Leslie Howard), the deadly potion; The last two films Thalberg never lived to see. He had a weakened heart from what I understand. He was one of the "greats" in production in Hollywood. He was so ill then, but so nice to me. I was never really close to him though. I think he needed all the peace that he could get. I never bothered him.

Sidney Franklin, who directed *The Barretts*, later cast me in *On Borrowed Time* [1939]; I had a small memorable scene with Lionel Barrymore. Sidney Franklin also cast me in *Mrs. Miniver, Random Harvest* [both in 1942], *The White Cliffs of Dover* [1944], and *Young Bess* [1953].

In looking back to his radio days, Ian Wolfe remembered that before his motion picture debut and several years before the MGM classic movie, a fifteen-minute radio series "The Wizard of

Ian Wolfe (left) as "Robert" the butler in a scene with Bob Cummings in Alfred Hitchcock's Saboteur *(Universal Pictures, 1942). Photo from the author's collection).*

Oz," was broadcast three times a week during September 1933 through March 1934 over the NBC network. Ian played the Wizard and the twelve-year-old actress Nancy Kelly played Dorothy Gale (6).

Wolfe, the talented actor supplied other voices to characters throughout the radio series. Among other radio broadcasts of the times with Ian Wolfe were such programs as, "School of the Air" and "March of Time." His voices ranged from a variety of derelicts to vegetables such as, a string bean, mushroom, carrot and a head of cabbage. (7)

I rolled with the tide during radio spots and early film days. And then another assignment! This time it was at Old Universal. It was my first job there. I played a supporting part alongside the top "horror stars" ... Boris Karloff and Bela Lugosi! *The Raven* was my fifth film.

Ian Wolfe, a suave and deft delineator of villainous roles gives another as "James" the butler in Nightmare *(Universal Pictures, 1942). Photo courtesy of Ian Wolfe.*

The following is one of Ian Wolfe's favorite anecdotes from an experience at Universal Studios when he and Boris Karloff met for the first time during the making of *The Raven.*

He was pacing around. I was usually early. And because of his terrific makeup Mr. Karloff was always early. And apparently he had a fight with Old Universal. I didn't know that.

Ian Wolfe as "Caleb" the gardener in Her Primitive Man (Universal Pictures, 1944). Photo courtesy of Ian Wolfe.

And I was in dress clothes and nervous. I was pacing the floor and needed to go to the men's room. The place was so strange to me and I didn't know where to go. So we came on with our good mornings, and as I say later, I learned that he was a real pussycat and even then he saw the funny side of it after he said it, but I said, 'Mr. Karloff, can you direct me to the men's room? Is there a toilet around here?'

And with his face twisted to one side and one eye all faked, and his mouth twisted, Mr. Karloff said, "The whole damn studio is a toilet." And we both roared with laughter! I don't remember how I found where the bathroom was. Apparently, he said it's out this door and to the left. Boris Karloff later was a founding member of the Screen Actors Guild.

Mr. Karloff was a prince among men and liked actors. He didn't play tricks on them. I didn't know a great deal about his personal life. I did something in live television in New York with him, a pilot a thing that didn't go, a series that he tried out for where he played a small town lawyer. But it never got beyond the pilot. Bela Lugosi, I really wasn't acquainted with or really knew him at all on *The Raven* set. I barely remember him or myself for that matter in *Zombies on Broadway*, but that's the thing. Sometimes, you just go and do your lines, chalk it up and go home.

However, Beth and I did know Lugosi's last wife Hope [Lininger]. She turned up one day when I was in the office of my agent. This was after he [Lugosi] had publicly admitted to drug addiction. She was a charming and sweet person. She worked as a private secretary at a hotel in the Hawaiian Islands where we visit. We occasionally exchange Christmas cards. A few chance meetings. That would be all. (8)

After *The Raven*, I was cast in a small part alongside Colin Clive. It was a rather menacing part. The title escapes me [MGM's *Mad Love*]. I'd forgotten it, but as a result of that film, Irving Thalberg (bless his memory) saw, somehow, that I was far from restricted to comedy, or to light roles; he started quite a run of "meanies." The first was *Mutiny on the Bounty* that surely changed the course of my so-called ca-

Ian Wolfe as "Joseph" in The Moon is Down *(Twentieth Century Fox, 1943). Photo courtesy of Ian Wolfe.*

reer in Hollywood! It not only saved me professionally, but also allowed my family of four to exist physically and financially! I feel that it was my most important part. The film won the Best Picture Academy Award of 1935, and is considered a Hollywood classic. It always looked good on my resume. My menacing character Maggs (called "Mr. Samuel" in the book), the storekeeper aboard the ship who some consid-

Sherlock Holmes in Washington (Universal Pictures, 1943). This was the first of four appearances made by Ian Wolfe in the super-sleuth series, pictured with Basil Rathbone. Photos courtesy of Ian Wolfe.

Lobby card from The Scarlet Claw *(Universal Pictures, 1944), in which Ian Wolfe is pictured. This was his favorite part played in the Sherlock Holmes movies. Photo from the author's collection.*

er was meaner than Captain Bligh, undisputedly played to perfection by the incomparable Charles Laughton.

Down the road, it [*Mutiny*] brought me a great variety of work, even if small roles. I was acquainted professionally with Mr. Laughton over the years. We were in several films together. I remember his charming wife Elsa Lanchester, being of great wit, humor and energy. I recently read in the newspaper that Elsa will be appearing in another film.

Mutiny on the Bounty, I am proud to have been a part of it, although I don't like to see myself on film most of the time. [As told to this author in 1979...] There are a few of us old-timers living from the film. In recent years, I've been asked to attend events honoring the movie. Those sorts of things tend to make me nervous with live audiences. However, I did attend one. Everyone involved with arranging it was very kind and helpful, but I never realized all the hoopla involved. After *Mutiny*, I started playing a string of menacing roles. Usually, I do not prefer seeing myself in movies or on television. If I am playing characters way away from myself as possible or what they call "the straight roles," I like it.

I do enjoy characters that are entirely different or have different speech, an elaborate makeup or a historical thing, that I enjoy. There are many of my things that I haven't seen and wouldn't!

Many times, fans question me, "What was it like to work with Greta Garbo?" Well, the truth of the matter is, I wouldn't know. There are some cases one may see the back or far shot of someone in the camera. That may actually be a "double" or "stand-in." It's a clever way of 'shooting around,' primarily, the star when the star is not available.

You may have a scene in which you are in the same room with the star and it appears to be but really is not. That is one of the magical things about Hollywood filmmaking. I never met Greta Garbo. I never saw her, was never in a scene with her, although it appears that way in the film *Conquest*. And sometimes we haven't scenes together with other actors and our scenes are shot separately and one goes home. I remember most actors whom I have worked with.

On the other hand, I have occasionally get asked questions from very young fans who look to me as God for answers and I play along. That is one of the reasons why I dread formal interviews. I usually just don't do them. They want to talk about every film and don't give you much room edgewise. You are the chosen one, dear boy.

That reminds me of a scene completed sliced from *The Silver Chalice*. There was a scene between my character and the young boy [later played as an adult by Paul Newman, his first film], who I had sold for his new life. It was a tender scene. I still have a part in the movie, but not much of one.

On the other hand, there are times that I was cut completely from films like *Captain Blood, The Sea Hawk* and *The Song of Bernadette*. There was much brouhaha with the casting of over five thousand for *The Song of Bernadette*.

The producers changed the star and many in the cast before arriving with Jennifer Jones as its star. The upside to it all is that I still got paid. Hurrah! Perhaps I played in too many things.

I've been hesitating in the retelling of the following story. It makes me feel as if it all happened just yesterday. It was fifty years ago. It was during the shooting that Greta Garbo movie, *Conquest*. I had on this elaborate costume. The story took place in the days of Napoleon Bonaparte. Charles Boyer played Napoleon.

I was having a hard time after my fitting with this elaborate costume with the ruffles and all. We were all on the set, but Garbo. I took the closest available mirror that I could find to adjust my wear.

Suddenly, I hear several men (gaffers and grips) yelling at me from high in the rafters ... "Get the hell out of Miss Garbo's mirror!" I saw no harm in it. There was no one using it.

It not only frightened me hearing the sudden voices from above, it embarrassed the hell out of me and that same humiliation is there to this day when I tell it. Can you imagine?

One of Ian's hopeful roles would have been the High Lama in director Frank Capra's *Lost Horizon* [1937]. Ian explained.

Professionally, that would have helped me. The news around town at the time was that Frank Capra knew whom he wanted to play that role. Sadly, the actor was gravely ill and died before they could cast him. I wished to have tested for that role, but the news had already hit the trade papers that Capra cast Sam Jaffe in the role. One recent publication made it sound as if I was fighting Sam Jaffe for the role. I never tested for it. It was wishful thinking on my part—and that's how the fortune cookie crumbles, baby!

Ian Wolfe later appeared in two of Frank Capra's pictures, *You Can't Take It with You* (1938) and *Here Comes the Groom* (1951), both which the director also produced. Ian said of Frank Capra, "He was an actor's dream come true, a filmmaking genius!" Ian Wolfe also talked about his experience appearing in Sherlock

Lobby card from The Pearl of Death *(Universal Pictures, 1944), the third appearance made by Ian Wolfe in the Sherlock Holmes series. Photo from the author's collection.*

Holmes movies, which starred Basil Rathbone and Nigel Bruce. Ian first explains crediting in motion pictures.

For starters, if one were a mere character actor you had an option of being credited in a film, if you chose 'yay,' a very small percentage of pay was taken. I chose 'nay' a great deal of the time in and around the Holmes films. Lo and behold, I have been told that my name is in *Saboteur, Nightmare, Her Primitive Man and The Moon Is Down*. As the years and the parts rolled on, one sees me credited more and more. Once residuals came into play for movies those options were dropped. Any motion picture made after 1960 paid residuals and you were credited depending on the size of your role. Of course, the stars sold the product and rightly so.

Nowadays, I notice that more young people are concerned with the director of a film as a consideration. Some television residuals began paying in the early 1950s through SAG [Screen Actors' Guild], for which I remain a member.

Nigel Bruce (Dr.Watson), Ian Wolfe (Amos Hodder), Evelyn Ankers (Naomi Drake) and Basil Rathbone (as Sherlock Holmes) in a scene from The Pearl of Death *(Universal Pictures, 1944). Photo courtesy of Ian Wolfe.*

I've also been a member of AFTRA [American Federation of Television and Radio Artists] and AEA [Actor's Equity Association]. It's all union policy. More lucrative television residuals were paid to actors in the 1970s by SAG [Quick laugh and sighs] ... now you see why I hadn't the sense to give it up?

Yes, I was in four of the fourteen Sherlock Holmes films [made between 1939 and 1946], as you have them so handy here, Lad. I will read them. *Sherlock Holmes in Washington* [1943], *The Pearl of Death* [1944], *The Scarlet Claw* [1944] and *Dressed to Kill* [1946]. I remember the director, nice guy to work with, Mr. [Roy William] Neill. He directed many of them as I remember. The experience was fun and interesting to me because I was able to play a good range of characters and dialects. Mr. Neill knew exactly what he wanted out of

Publicity poster from Dressed to Kill *(Universal Pictures, 1946), Ian Wolfe's fourth and final appearance in the Sherlock Holmes series. He played the Commissioner of Scotland Yard (pictured in lower left). Photo from the author's collection.*

a scene. He also had expertise regarding [Sir Arthur] Conan Doyle's super sleuth, which made it easier for we actors.

I think that's one thing, which keeps me going. I can work with young directors, with very different ideas or the older ones. It doesn't bother me. I like direction and I have directed in civic theaters myself.

If I could get what they want it's almost as much fun as achieving what I want. What was fun for me in the Sherlock Holmes or in any other films for that matter was playing way-and-away from myself with dialects of those characters. If it is entirely different and if I have different speech especially in the old days, I would change my way of speaking and an elaborate makeup and in a historical thing. That I enjoyed. Otherwise, I don't usually like seeing myself if it's what you call a straight part. No... That would include any of the films that I played that way. There have been many things that I've never seen. I know whether it is good or bad. There's a funny line about Ethel Barrymore. I don't think she ever saw herself on film. And they asked her, 'why not?' She said, "I never saw myself in the theatre!" But when I see myself on television or a video in some things, I say, OH! Take that thing away! I don't want to see that! How did they ever cast me in that? Sometimes it almost destroys me.

Basil Rathbone liked actors and he was grand to work with. He was a trained professional theater actor from the old school. At that time, he and his wife were much the head of the British colony here. They were very social. I'm rarely social. So we didn't know them outside of working.

I also did some radio with Basil Rathbone. As I told you, Nigel Bruce, and I were in other films separate from Sherlock Holmes. He was a "dear ol' chap" with a great sense of humor. I remember hearing him at the end of an address he once gave. Was about the only part you could hear because of his mumbling and finished with, 'Never forget your British ... and-there-you-ARE!'

Ian Wolfe remembered working with Alfred Hitchcock, the grand master of suspense in two of the director's motion pictures, *Foreign Correspondent* (United Artists, 1940) and *Saboteur* (Universal Pictures, 1942).

"Hitch" as he was called was a perfectionist in the true sense of the word. I always addressed him as Mr. Hitchcock. He was always on cue and had an eye better than the camera. I had the opportunity to work with him twice. Both films were successes, but which Hitchcock film isn't? I played a butler in each one. Personally, if I had my druthers, I preferred the butler Robert, the role I played in *Saboteur* rather than the one played in *Foreign Correspondent*. I had more to do in that film and was a bigger meanie with just a pinch of humor per se. In one scene, I had to hit the star, Bob Cummings. "Hitch" knew exactly what he wanted out of his actors and you'd doggone better know what is going on and you better be good at it. Mr. Hitchcock handpicked most of the actors he cast in his pictures.

In his television series, I've seen a few of them; his prologues really sold the show. If you missed his epilogues you would have lost the ultimate ending. I don't know why I wasn't in any of them; but I won't hold that against anyone. I see that he was still working a few years ago. To have worked with Alfred Hitchcock was privilege enough.

Acting is not all the glamour that one would think especially in the early days. It's been hard. There were times with our children when I had to borrow money to keep us eating. I eventually paid it all back.

There have been some terrible times and there have been some wonderful times too.

I declare lightly, but seriously, that my main claim to fame and my greatest accomplishment (from Theatre, Films, Radio and Television) is that my wife and I, and our two daughters survived!! I see the love in the whole thing now, but then I hated myself. I agree with the young people of today. You have to love yourself. Well, not in the sense of kissing yourself per se, but I understand where they are coming from.

Ian Wolfe shared with this author the following "PROFESSION-AL BIOGRAPHY," written in autumn of 1977.

I have now played character roles, some featured, a few co-starred or guest starred (others too small), in something over two hundred so-named theatrical motion pictures.

To date, I have done some one hundred and thirty-five television things (live film, and tape), appearing in some major series more than once such as, *Star Trek, Bonanza, Gunsmoke*, etc.

Recently my wife and I went to Hawaii, where I played opposite our admired Helen Hayes in the television series *Hawaii 5-O*. Beth and I were devoted to Helen both as an actress and a person. In the summer of 1960, for a "Strawhat" tour of New England, I played opposite Helen Hayes in *"The Chalk Garden."*

Helen's son, James MacArthur, and Jack Lord were the stars of *Hawaii 5-O*. I appeared with Jack Lord in his previous series *Stoney Burke*; first met him during the filming of *The Court-Martial of Billy Mitchell*, in which I played President Calvin Coolidge; had a part in a television episode of John Newland's *One Step Beyond*.

I have recently played delightfully with Archie Bunker (Carroll O'Connor), on *All in the Family*, and was helped by him, as well as warmed up by the graciousness of Jean Stapleton.

I have played a few ministers and priests. Someone said I should start my own church! I have lately played a Monsignor in the forthcoming controversial TV series "Soap."

In motion pictures, I was the minister in *Johnny Belinda*, in which Jane Wyman won the Oscar. I also appeared with Jane Wyman briefly (where I didn't play a minister) in *Here Comes the Groom* and *Pollyanna*. (9)

I was the minister in *Seven Brides for Seven Brothers*, a trailblazer of a musical success although I never sang (saved the film)! I had a long friendship with Norma Shearer, who was then retired from acting.

Norma Shearer invited me up to Sun Valley, Utah where location shots were made for the film. Shearer and her ski instructor husband, Martin Arrouge, took me high on the mountain 'cause I'm very agile, having done mountain climbing. I loved that and have never forgotten it.

I was a priest in *The Terminal Man* with George Segal. I will soon be in the motion picture *Mean-Dog Blues*, in which I play a devilish Oklahoma-Texas prejudicial judge -- one of many I have played of various varieties.

In all sorts of character parts I have supported many stars, of both genders, sometimes not much more than the dust that made them twinkle. I have worked with many great directors successfully -- and with some of the worst.

In a lighter vein, but the comedy being welcome to the gods, I also stood on my hands on the summit (geodetically registered at the height of) fourteen thousand, four hundred and ninety-six feet, beside the cairn of rocks piled up there by my hands. This was to establish my own personal "Damphool Club" – those few having gone highest by "Shanks' Mare"(one's own walking feet –an old country expression from my family – maybe New England) instead to a full fifteen thousand feet altitude in the United States.

It is a small and exclusive club – as most people would not be damned fool enough to even think of it!! But it has a few members – mostly friends. I was later flown over the summit of Mt. Whitney by a skilled aviator.

As to the mountains, literally, I have been a trail-climbing addict. Though not recommended, I have climbed quite a few high peaks alone – some by moonlight. Last, at age 71, the highest in Southern California, San Gorgonio ("Old Greyback") at eleven thousand, five hundred and two feet.

On Mt. Whitney, earlier (highest in U.S. proper) (in 1954, at age fifty-eight). I was alone up there some thirty-six hours, due to a severe storm, for which I was equipped.

On the summit, though earlier trained in singing but experienced mostly in the bathroom, I had thrills singing The

Lord's Prayer and The Star Spangled Banner and chanting mantras toward global ONENESS.

Another interest of mine is an extended (mostly personal) addiction to poetry; very little published; rarely tried. * Recent craze: HAIKU, short Japanese poems of 17 syllables in 3 lines. I would be proud to do just one that lived!

Ian Wolfe spoke to this author about several professional experiences. One such experience follows while appearing with Shelley Winters in director George Stevens' A Place in the Sun.

One of the better films and memorable parts that I played was the kindly doctor [Dr. Wyeland] in George Stevens' A Place in the Sun [1951]. I liked Mr. Stevens. He was a big name in Hollywood. I didn't have to work hard on that character, because I basically played myself, although I'd rather enjoy playing characters furthest from myself. But if you want to see plain ol' me, for a few minutes, this film is it.

When you are an a-c-t-o-r, one must be able to take direction well whether it is on the stage, movies, radio or television. When actors ad-lib a line or receive physical direction from a director, there may be some considerations.

However, the director is in charge and I really couldn't argue with that. I believe that the mistake with many of the young actors today, they do not take direction well.

As I may be repeated myself, but many moons ago, I did a little stage-managing and also some directing, mostly in Civic Theatres, seasons in Santa Barbara, Ca., a little summer stock at the Pasadena Playhouse here in California; Tacoma, Washington and briefly with the New York Theatre Guild School.

Having that experience is when I knew that I'd remain an actor [he grimaces and then smiles]. I have the utmost respect for directors.

For instance, when I was working on A Place In the Sun, the director, George Stevens, was having a difficult time with Shelley Winters, especially in the scene that she played with me. I played the part of a kindly doctor, who is paid a visit by

Shelley Winters' character [Alice Tripp]. Shelley's character has come to me to discuss the possibilities of abortion, a word that was never in movies in those days. It was a taboo subject. Anyway, Shelley's character was to cry, but Mr. Stevens couldn't stand her blubbering and crying her tears.

Take after take and nothing was resolved. Mr. Stevens called for a break. I asked him if I could talk with her. He said, "Yes, Mr. Wolfe, anything but that blubbering!" I took Shelley aside and we talked about general subjects kindly.

Once she was relaxed, I told her, 'I think that if you fought back your tears and delivered your lines on that level, it may work to everybody's advantage. I know dear, we actors can cry at the drop of a hat.' That produced a hearty laugh from her.

When shooting resumed, Shelley and I delivered our lines. She sustained the emotion beautifully! Mr. Stevens yelled, "Cut! Print!" Then Mr. Stevens turned to me and asked, "What did you do to her Mr. Wolfe?"

Instead of going into explanation, I simply told Mr. Stevens that I took Shelley for a cup of coffee, which garnered some laughter on the set and put us at ease [Ian in glee].

In retrospect, I don't think that I did anything more for Shelley than what Mr. Stevens would have gotten from her. We were working into the wee hours of the morning. I gave her a gentle push, if you will.

Lo and behold! After all of the years since the film, Shelley Winters recently made mention of me in her "tell-all" book. I am honored that she remembered me. Friends sometimes tease me about it unmercifully! But I take most of it in good humor. That was an important role for Shelley. It earned her an OSCAR nomination. However, the award ultimately went to Elizabeth Taylor, who was nominated for the same movie. As you and the rest of the world know, they are both fine actresses. (10)

Among other favorable parts in motion pictures for Ian Wolfe was portraying two United States Presidents; James K. Polk in *California* (1947) with Barbara Stanwyck, Ray Milland and Barry

Fitzgerald; and President Calvin Coolidge in *The Court-Martial of Billy Mitchell* (1955). It starred Gary Cooper and Charles Bickford.

During our initial meeting, Ian remembered director Nicholas Ray and the three films in which they worked together, *They Live By Night* (1949), *On Dangerous Ground* (1952), and *Rebel Without a Cause* (1955).

> First of all, I must say there is this huge grapevine that grows in this business. One job connects to another, then another through producers, casting agents or directors. That's when the telephone begins to ring.
>
> My first job with Nick Ray came through John Houseman (an actor), who started out as a producer. *They Live By Night* was his film. I did several films for John Houseman, including "*Julius Caesar.*" It was because of Mr. Houseman that I also worked with Nick Ray in *On Dangerous Ground*.
>
> The last time I ever worked with Nick Ray was in *Rebel Without a Cause*. Nick called my agent. I was the astronomer, Dr. Minton, who gave the lecture at the planetarium and befriended James Dean's character. That was actually shot up at the Griffith Observatory in Los Feliz, an area here in Los Angeles. It is quite an attraction for tourists from all over the world. What a production it turned out to be. Then with the tragic loss of its star, James Dean at only twenty-four years of age, *Rebel* became an enormous success, as you know. Nick and I always got along well. Sadly, Nick Ray passed away not even a month ago; I read it in the newspaper.

When this author once asked Ian the following question, 'Since you won't name a bad director, did you ever know of any performers who made a director's job more difficult?' Mr. Wolfe answered with the following.

> I really shouldn't answer that question because I really see no good or bad. I am fairly confident that I got along well with most everyone. I didn't kiss anybody's ass in this business. There are only a few who really come to mind, Hedy Lamarr, (a very young) Lana Turner, George Sanders and Natalie Wood.

Ian Wolfe, Cary Grant and Myrna Loy in a scene from Mr. Blandings
Builds His Dram House *(RKO 1948). My character in the film didn't give
them such a wonderful experience," snickered Wolfe. Photo from the
author's collection.*

All treated me kindly, but I surely felt sympathy for those
directors. Who knows? Someone could be saying the same
about me? Time *is* money, you know!

Ian Wolfe was proud of his association with having appeared in
Best Picture Academy Award winning films and nominated Best
Picture films by the Academy of Motion Picture Arts and Scienc-
es over the years. They are listed as follows. Best Picture: *Mutiny
on the Bounty* [1935], *You Can't Take It with You* [1938], and *Mrs.
Miniver* [1942].

Nominated for Best Picture: *The Barretts of Wimpole Street*
[1934], *Romeo and Juliet* [1936], *You Can't Take it With You* [1938],
Foreign Correspondent [1940], *Random Harvest* [1942], *The Song
of Bernadette* [1943], *Wilson* [1944], *Johnny Belinda* [1948], *A Place
In the Sun* [1951], *Julius Caesar* [1953], *Seven Brides for Seven
Brothers* [1954], *Witness for the Prosecution* [1957], and *Reds* [1981].

The following are other motion pictures that Ian Wolfe mentioned noteworthy to him, in which he appeared.

The Son of Monte Cristo [1940], I played a German meanie henchman to George Sanders' character. Again, it was a character far from me. I enjoyed those parts.

Mr. Blandings Builds His Dream House [1948], "I liked the part very much. It gave me some recognition. Cary Grant and Myrna Loy were wonderful to work with and very good to me on and off screen. In the movie, I was the realtor who sold them their dream house. Yah. Hah!

The Judge Steps Out [1949] "During my early days in New York, I once took a job as a stenographer. Little did I know that experience would later have me appearing with Alexander Knox, an excellent theatre actor who unfortunately made the Hollywood blacklist."

Colorado Territory [1949] "I played a railroad conductor. Had a pleasant experience on that film. The director, Raoul Walsh, was a great director, very well known in Hollywood. Some years later, as my wife and I rode the Narrow Gage from Durango, Colorado to Silverton, we were delighted to reminisce with the real conductor, still working, who had coached me!

They Live By Night [1949] "It was my first experience working under director Nicholas Ray. The youths in the film were Farley Granger and Cathy O'Donnell. I played the marriage broker. The film has become a small classic on television here."

The Great Caruso [1951], "I worked with the director once before and had respect for him. It was also a moving motion picture, in both respects. And to hear Mr. Lanza sing was one of the highlights of the entire experience. I remember Alan Napier was in it. Mr. [Richard] Thorpe was the director. He was known for his long shots. I shared one with Mr. Napier. The darling of the successful MGM film was Ann Blythe. She played Caruso's wife. This was one that Beth and I enjoyed seeing recently."

Houdini [1953], "I remember the part of a fellow magician. The director asked for me having had worked together once before. Tony Curtis and his wife, and co-star, Janet Leigh were such kind people. But that was one part I didn't much care for. The movie wasn't much of a success."

Scene from Witness for the Prosecution *(MGM, 1957); pictured in a courtroom, Charles Laughton, Ian Wolfe and Elsa Lanchester (Laughton's wife). Billy Wilder directed the film that was nominated for an Academy Award. Photo from the author's collection.*

Sincerely Yours [1956] "Liberace starred in this, his only starring film role. I played his speech therapist with more screen presence than most character men [From the original 1979 interview with this author]. I remember as we were rapping up the film, Lee (as he liked to be called) got the cast together one evening and gave each of us something to remember him. It was a lovely black lacquered, serving tray, lined on the edges in gold and on its face the lovely artwork carved into it of a grand piano along with his signature etched in the tray spelling 'Sincerely yours, Liberace.' Lee, as he preferred to be called is a talented, delightful, intelligent and generous man."

Witness for the Prosecution [1957] "I played Charles Laughton's valet, as it were, to add a bit of scenery. I had the idea of turning my own collar up and just tying the tie around to look more the part. Billy Wilder, the director, approved. Elsa Lanchester was always attentive to her beloved Charles, on set, much as you see them in the movie."

Ian Wolfe as Mr. Loomis in director Larry Yust's 1974 cult movie,
Homebodies *(AVCO Embassy Pictures). Photo courtesy of Ian Wolfe.*

All in a Night's Work [1961] "Some more screen presence here. I played Dean Martin's Irish chauffeur, accent and all, with Shirley MacLaine. I still hear about that one through fan mail."

Homebodies [1974], "This was a rather strange film going nowhere. It's about a group of old people living in a building. Then murder takes place! I played the owner and the janitor of the building. It's now become a little cult classic."

Reds [1981] "This film took Beth and I all the way to London for two weeks. Warren Beatty was the director, writer, producer and star, which was quite a feat for anyone to succeed. Warren and I established a good rapport. Beth and I were happy to see him win the Academy Award for Best Director of the film. I played a doddering old man, hard of hearing. Bessie Love played my wife. Several years later, Warren Beatty phoned me direct to cast me as the Forger in *Dick Tracy*. Of course, I accepted."

Ian Wolfe agreed to his comments regarding fantasy, thriller and/or horror movie appearances of his, "with no harm done." In his first letter to this author, Ian wrote, "I hadn't realized I had been in many "horror movies, but on second thought, most *all* of them seem horrible [to which Ian drew a smiley face]!"

Mad Love [1935, MGM]: "I didn't know that Peter Lorre was in it. That might explain that strange get up. I do remember Colin Clive though. I was his very mean stepfather. Unfortunately, within a couple years of that movie, Mr. Clive died rather young. "

The Raven [1935, Universal]: "It was my first job at Universal. I've already told you that story."

On Borrowed Time [1939, MGM]: "That was a small part. My character's name was Charles Wentworth. I loved that film and the play too. I didn't appear in the play."

The Return of Dr. X [1939, Warner Brothers]: "Yes. I played a caretaker of some cemetery. Had you not told me, I wouldn't have known that it starred Humphrey Bogart. I can't recall having any scenes with him."

Flesh and Fantasy [1943, Universal]: "I played a Librarian in it, briefly! The stories were rather fast paced, but one I never cared to watch it through. A local channel runs a lot of the old films. I may have been cut from it. Forgive me, *me boy!*"

Murder in the Blue Room [1944, Universal]: "That's the thing that was made at Universal. That photograph, I autographed to you, is from that film. I don't think it was very scary, more of a comedy thing. I remember I played a scared butler in it. But a real horror movie has got to have a scare to it."

The Invisible Man's Revenge [1944, Universal]: "My only memory of that film was my friend, Lester Matthews. We shared many

Ian Wolfe (pointing) as Sidney Long in a scene with Boris Karloff from Bedlam (RKO, 1946), which became one of the actor's personal crowning glories. Bedlam was directed by Mark Robson and produced by Val Lewton. Photo courtesy of Ian Wolfe.

films and television things. The actor, Jon Hall, later became a resident of our community here in Sherman Oaks."

Strange Confession [1945, Universal]: "Another one of my bleak butler parts, but memorable in a sense that my agent was putting me to work frequently. Lon Chaney's son was in that one. That's about all I remember there."

Zombies on Broadway [RKO, 1945]: "You've tried to get me to remember that one. But I do not remember it, Lad. Send me to the gallows!"

Bedlam [RKO, 1946]: "I was a mad, loony, psychotic lawyer. *Bedlam* was the story of the St. Mary of Bethlehem Hospital that was converted into an asylum that took place in 1761. It was notoriously known for the brutal treatment of inmates. I was Sidney Long ... "Crown S-o-l-i-c-i-t-o-r!" Anna Lee was also in the film. What a lovely lady. As I said, I don't usually like seeing myself ... oooh! I enjoyed that one though."

Ian Wolfe (as Herr Gruber) and Lawrence Harvey (as Wilhelm Grimm)
in The Wonderful World of the Brothers Grimm *(MGM, 1962). Filmed*
in Germany by directors Henry Levin and George Pal. Photo from the
author's collection.

Moonfleet [1955, MGM]: "Fritz Lang was the director. Our friend Lester Matthews had also been cast in the film. The producer John Houseman cast me in it. Fritz Lang was a cerebral director, who didn't mull. He was precise. It was an interesting experience working with him, but the film fleeted! "

The Lost World [Twentieth Century Fox, 1960]: "Yes. I was that bearded blind man in the cave, Rick [Ian smiles]! I looked like Father Time! That was another small part and I got killed off in that one. I died rather well in some of those pictures [Ian again smiling]."

The Wonderful World of the Brothers Grimm [MGM, 1962]: "This was filmed on location in and around Rothenberg, Germany. It was a fantasy film. I played Herr Gruber, another meanie. It starred Lawrence Harvey. It wasn't an A grade film, but it did take me to Germany."

Diary of a Madman [United Artists, 1963]: "I was butler (or valet) to Vincent Price in this. I don't remember much about it, but I do receive a ridiculously small residual from it just at or after tax time and it throws off our books."

Games [1967, Universal]: "I remember James Caan in it. During a break we have many of those in his business, Caan and I had a rather long and involved conversation about life and living. He is highly intelligent and a smart young whippersnapper of a man. He's achieving success even now. The film was rather successful as far as thrillers go. The director was Curtis Harrington, who made a name for himself in Hollywood.

THX 1138 [1971, Warner Brothers]: "It was a highly unusual and futuristic film. If anything, it will go down as director George Lucas' first feature film."

Dick Tracy [Buena Vista Pictures, 1990]: "It was my last film. I was happy to end with that film rather than the one preceding it entitled, *Checking Out*. It crumbled fiercely! Although I did rather humor in my far-out character, Mr. D'Amato, the undertaker. So be it! My swan song is *Dick Tracy*, playing the Forger. And I'll be sending you a few pictures, Lad.

Over the years, Ian Wolfe shared further thoughts and professional information either by written letters, telephone calls, or what he told this writer during other live visits. He had one photograph that he was puzzled by. He gave it to this writer with the inscription, "Maybe you can find what I am!"

Lad: It was always of great interest for me to watch directors from all facets of entertainment. Seriously, to me, one

Inscribed photo from Ian Wolfe asking, "Maybe you can find what I am!" It came from the long running television series You Are There, *hosted by Walter Cronkite, in which historical events were reenacted. The ninth episode of the first season entitled,* The Witch Trail at Salem, Massachusetts *(August 1692) finds Ian Wolfe as the Judge. The thirty-minute episode aired March 29, 1953. Photo courtesy of Ian Wolfe.*

of the faults in films always has been that it's so easy to get sidetracked.

Because pieces fit together like a Chinese puzzle and it takes a great director and great producer to get a continued theme. Most of the movies are mish-mash and I believe it's getting worse.

I worked with a great many actors. Most of them were strictly professional acquaintances. There were only a few mutual friendships that I had with actors.

There was Sam Hinds. He came up through the community theater in Pasadena. He was a dedicated actor and one hell-of-a nice guy. Also, Lester Matthews was at the Pasadena Playhouse.

Later when I toured in Hochhuth's "The Deputy," in New York for forty weeks and then did it for the Center Theatre Group. There was Lester playing in it. And then we toured for another sixteen weeks, thus playing the featured role of The Father General, head of the Jesuits in Rome, five hundred times.

So, Lester and I got to know each other better, he and his wife and mine. He died a few years ago. And I'd say he got what he wanted. His wife, after the emotional wore off, I'd say about two or three weeks after his death we all got an invitation to come to the house and have a cocktail and we all brought food. His son was there and tapped on a glass and said, 'this is what my father wanted -- friends.' And we drank a toast to Lester. Instead of having a funeral and all that weepy stuff, after it was all over, Lester's last wish was granted. Eventually, I'll be sending you my lists, in no particular order.

Dear Lad, Here is the long awaited memorable nods from yours truly. Acquainted only professionally during plays, movies, radio or television aside from others who may have already been mentioned ...before I hang up my boots. As ever, Me...

Directors:

Edwin L. Marin, W.S. Van Dyke, Frank Lloyd, Jean Negulesco, Robert Z. Leonard Mervyn LeRoy, George Cukor, Henry Potter (better known as H.C.), Richard Rosson, Herman Shumlin, William Spier (radio producer and director), Henry King, William Wyler, Mark Robson, Joseph L. Mankiewicz, Raoul Walsh, Richard Thorpe, Henry Levin, Robert Altman, Charles Lamont, Herman Shumlin, Lewis Milestone, Clarence Brown, Stanley Donen, George Pal, Otto Preminger, George Lucas, Larry Yust, Lee Philips, Warren Beatty and Tim Hutton.

Producers:

Arthur Hopkins, Harold Rosson (brother of director Richard Rosson), Jean Negulesco, John Houseman, Frank Lloyd, David O. Selznick, Val Lewton, and Arthur Hornblow Jr.

Actors:

(Ladies first:) Lillian Gish, Bette Davis, Myrna Loy, Linda Darnell, Nancy Kelly, Teresa Wright, Marlene Dietrich, Jean Simmons, Lauren Bacall, Lorraine Day, Greer Garson, Anna Lee, Merle Oberon, Janet Leigh, Lucille Ball, Jeanette Nolan, Virginia Gregg, Ellen Corby, Jean Stapleton, Sally Struthers, Kate Jackson (who also directed me in a television episode) and Ann Jillian.

(Gentlemen:) Walter Abel, Franchot Tone, Clark Gable, John Barrymore, David Niven, Errol Flynn, Tyrone Power, Ronald Colman, Walter Pidgeon, Paul Muni, Ralph Bellamy, Howard De Silva, Cedric Hardwicke, Vincent Price, Claude Rains, Otto Kruger, Sydney Greenstreet, Farley Granger, Robert Mitchum, James Dean, Corey Allen, Jeff Corey, Gary Cooper, George Sanders, Tom Conway (Sander's brother), Will Geer, Lawrence Harvey, "Duke" John Wayne, James Caan, Burgess Meredith, Peter O'Toole, Warren Beatty, Bill Bixby, Jeff Daniels, and Andrew McCarthy.

There were some very talented character actors of whom I worked with professionally. I was acquainted with Hans Conreid, Reginald Owen, Una O'Connor, Maria Ouspenskaya (referred to as the first lady of the Russian Theatre),

Victor Kilian, John Abbott, Henry Daniell, Laird Cregar, Gino Corrado, Frank Puglia, Miles Mander, J. Carroll Naish and Nigel Bruce (I appeared in several others films with him aside from his Dr. Watson character in Sherlock Holmes.)

Oh yes, and Alan Napier. Over the years, I remember him showing up on sets with small dogs. The dogs would change with time, but not their size. Alan was a pleasant and kind human being, a professional actor, in the highest regard. We'd have some pleasant chats. (We were in a number of the same films too.)

Aside from Lionel Barrymore, Sam Hinds (Samuel S. Hinds) in the early days, and Lester Matthews, there was Peter Brocco, an actor. He has been a dear friend of ours for many years. My family life and my other interests would keep me away from much of the Hollywood brouhaha. I prefer it that way.

Ian Wolfe's thirty-eight-year television career began with the first TV episode of The Lone Ranger. It was shot in Hollywood and aired on ABC television in November 1949.

Regarding his popular television appearances on Gene Roddenberry's science-fiction series, *Star Trek*, in the late 1960s, Ian Wolfe said the following.

I did two of those. Previously, Bill Shatner and I did a couple of live shows in New York, so I was already acquainted with him. But he was marvelous about this scene in "All Our Yesterdays," where he had to wrestle me, an old man, to the floor!

He knew just how to do it and gave me all the holds to get me to the floor and knock me around. I was a librarian, Mr. Atoz. I think it turned out pretty well. There was a little thing to that.

I had some sort of elaborate Chinese or Mongolian boots and costume. Well, I looked down into one of these boots and on a tag inside read... Ronald Colman. They were the boots from the wardrobe department at Paramount, where we were shooting. Ronald Colman! I hoped he had worn the

Ian Wolfe (left) as Septimus in "Bread and Circuses," the first of two Star Trek television appearances (Paramount Television, Episode 55: March 15, 1968). He later appeared in Star Trek (Episode 79: March 14, 1969) as Mr. Atoz in "All Our Yesterdays." Photo courtesy of Ian Wolfe.

boots in the Lost Horizon. I still joke that this was as close to *Lost Horizon* that I was going to get.

The other one was called "Bread and Circuses." I was the head of a sect, Septimus, who lived in a cave. It was a much better part when it was written, but they had to take a lot of it out so we wouldn't offend God knows whom?

So the part was sliced way down, but I was in it. I get some fan mail about those programs.

Mr. Wolfe made one hundred and sixty-four additional appearances on popular TV programs. Among them were: "*Playhouse 90, 77 Sunset Strip, Studio One in Hollywood, The Invaders, Twilight Zone, Bonanza* (four episodes, two of which were directed by Robert Altman), *Perry Mason, Petticoat Junction, The Andy Griffith Show, Ironside, The Partridge Family, The Mary Tyler Moore Show, Phyllis, Alice, Flo, This Is the Life* (Long running film series from 1952-1988: episode in 1980, "*Independence and '76* " (Produced by the International Lutheran Laymen's League); *Barney Miller, Cheers, Remington Steele, Scarecrow and Mrs. King, The Facts of Life,* and *Amazing Stories* ("Grandpa's Ghost," directed by Tim Hutton). He also had a recurring part in *WKRP in*

Cincinnati as Hirsch, Mrs. Carlson's butler. He also auditioned for television commercials, over the years, two of which were briefly aired during the early 1980s for Coca-Cola and Lincoln-Mercury.

The best times for this author were being out with Ian when it was just the two of us. To see when people would recognize him was fun. Sometimes he'd ham it up! Ian told me, "They'll recognize my face, but not my name. Everyone is so friendly about it. They are always kind and never want to take much of my time." Ian once shared the following incident.

I was at the market the other day and was rather surprised hearing someone calling out my name. I heard him over my shoulder coming closer and as I turned around, there he was, DeForest Kelley. As you know, he became most popular in the *Star Trek* television series.

We became acquainted several years before on the set of another television series, in which we both appeared. By this time, DeForest had been appearing in the *Star Trek* motion picture sequels.

He and I had quite a little conversation right there in the market. He asked me if I'd be interested in appearing in any of them. I told him kindly that I didn't think the producers would want to reprise any of the old-timers.

I usually don't meet up with fellow actors, just everyday people and I'm happy about that. I began to shift the conversation telling him about my other interests in poetry and entering Haiku contests, which seemed to interest him greatly. (11)

One of the most memorable opportunities for this author was watching Ian Wolfe work. I had the great opportunity to assist Ian at the Burbank/Warner Brothers Studios in California. In the fall of 1982, shooting began on a mid-season replacement over CBS television for their 1983 season. It was a fantasy/sitcom called *Wizards and Warriors* (originally titled, *Greystone's Odyssey*). (12)

For four consecutive days, I watched veteran Hollywood make-up artist Tom Tuttle, transform Ian into the Good Wizard, adding forty pounds of extra weight to his 150-pound frame. The costume made it difficult for the spry actor, then eighty-six, to be too mobile during the long hours of shooting in full makeup. On

Ian Wolfe as the finished Good Wizard Traquil with the author (October 1982). One of two photographs lifted from actual film footage taken at the Warner/Burbank Film Studios. Photo courtesy of Bill Bixby.

the first day of shooting, Ian had to be transported to and from the set on a flatbed cart until he was comfortable enough to walk around on his own. This author was keeping good company with Gramps by running lines of dialogue and happily gophering for him. The episode was entitled "The Unicorn of Death." The experience was magical and unforgettable.

This author celebrated a birthday on the fourth day of shooting. A still photographer was buzzing around the set all afternoon clicking away. I was hoping to have a photo taken with Ian in costume. Suddenly the photographer was gone having left for the day. The director was actor Bill Bixby, a kind man and talented director. He had a quick and easy remedy. Mr. Bixby shot footage of interaction between Ian and I, as the cast and crew sang "Happy Birthday" to both of us. (Ian's birthday falls two weeks later.) The studio technicians later lifted two still photographs off the footage. (13)

*Mr. and Mrs. Ian Wolfe and their beloved Russian Blue Feline "Joey,"
with the author at their home (April 13, 1983). Photo from the author's
collection.*

During this time, in his eighty-sixth year, Ian Wolfe took this author desert hiking to an area running along the San Andreas fault
in Lancaster County, Ian gave me the tour of foliage among the
sage bush, great pine trees and desert rose. Ian knew more about
botany than anyone I knew.

At one point, we were walking under several great pine trees.
The pinecones were the size of baseballs. I told Ian that I had never seen pinecones that big. Ian said, "Ah, those? Those are small.
Wait until next season. I'll send you one." I jokingly referred to
him as Euell Gibbons. We laughed. Ian said, "Mr. Gibbons made a
name for himself before leaving with his cereal commercial!" (14)

The following Christmas, this author received a huge pinecone
in the mail about the size of a soft ball! On the cone were still
fresh traces of sap on its points. (15) The Wolfes decorated it with

colorful jellybeans along with an enclosed Christmas card from them signed "Mr. & Mrs. Big-Bad."

This author lovingly remembers "Gramps" and Beth. The best advice Ian and Beth gave to this friend and author in finding one's own way was to be you wherever in life one travels. My parents were also supportive of that important advice.

A cherished note from Beth follows.

> Thank you Rick for the cheery note. We all need them at times when tensions pop up. The card is lovely as I look at it. I believe it is from a painting of the French artist, Camille.
>
> Parts of the painting I incorporated into one of my own paintings several years ago that you remembered. Not being entirely original I didn't sign it. Well! I do remember the boy in his new grey suit and tie in 1979, with his sporty car; so very bright and peppy. Much love, Beth.

Less than two years before Ian Wolfe passed away, he developed pulmonary fibrosis. Ian felt that in his ninety-third year that he probably wasn't going to make it another year.

About six weeks before Ian's death (at age ninety-five), I received a note from him. I phoned and Beth answered. She asked me not to keep him on but for a short time. Ian also wanted to talk to my mother, which they did shortly.

Ian gently spoke to me and said, "Lad, I feel that I have done my best for you. I love you. When I go, shed one tear and then rejoice! Do not grieve. I will always be with you." Beth later informed me by telephone that Ian passed away. Later, Beth mailed card stock copies of the following Haiku written by Ian. (16)

> *EPITAPH OF AN ACTOR (by Ian Wolfe)*
> *If employers call*
> *tell them I'm "on location"*
> *in some other world.*

Beth and this author remained in touch. The last following note from her is dated January 6, 1993.

Professional head shot taken of Ian Wolfe (inscribed to the author in 1988, at age ninety-two). Photos courtesy of Ian Wolfe.

"Dear Rick,

Please excuse my tardiness. Thank you for your grand Christmas gift. Unfortunately, I have developed a heart condition and need someone with me 24 hours a day. I'm not bed ridden, but many activities are curtailed much to my annoyance. Trust all is well at your home. Your love over the years has been treasured. Deep regards for your Mom. All the Best for 93. Love always, Beth"

Ian Wolfe (as Professor Brauer) and Peter O'Toole (as Dr. Harry Wolper) in a scene from Creator *(Universal Pictures, 1985). The inscription reads, Professor in "Creator" to Rick from Ian Wolfe." Photo courtesy of Ian Wolfe.*

I was later informed in a letter from Debra Winger that Beth had passed away. Eva Elizabeth Moreton Schroder Wolfe was ninety-three when she passed away January 30, 1993.

In October 2011, thirty-three years after this author first walked through the Wolfe's front door; this fifty-three year old paid a visit to their Sherman Oaks neighborhood. Sadly, the only familiar spot at the Noble Avenue address was the huge old oak tree, which remains strong and bold along the common walk. Next to it is a newly built home that stands where the Wolfes once lived. With love, I planted a big hug on that old oak tree. Their spirits live on!

In the introduction to his unpublished poetic manuscript entitled, *Forty-four Scribbles and a Prayer,* Ian Wolfe wrote the following:

> These rhyming ballads and lyrics were mostly written rather recently by me as examples of long experience in fooling with words and verses in various forms for many years. I am soon to be ninety-two. The efforts are not sacrosanct and can be changed to suit — if and when they find friendly collaboration.
>
> My father, Marcus-Aurelius Wolfe was a Protestant "lay" minister and Railroad YMCA secretary. All during my high school years we lived within a short block (in Kansas City, Kansas) of two African-American Protestant churches across the street from each other.
>
> Our neighbors were largely African-American. I was accustomed to hearing beautiful singing and I know quite a few learned "Spirituals." Though I was born in a small town in Illinois and some of my ancestors came to America right after The Mayflower (probably in a row-boat) I know many of the speech patterns of various peoples and countries.
>
> I have played quite a few strictly British parts with all-British casts . . . though I was born in Illinois. I played more legitimate British parts than any other American actor now living . . .
>
> If I don't <u>think</u> about it, my speech is "Standard English" or Eastern Seaboard (sometimes called "Middle Atlantic"). But I know well the various speech patterns. I am also versed in Haiku and have won prizes, although one might not think so from this *jabber wacky!*

Ian Wolfe wrote the following poem. It is part of his unpublished manuscript, *Forty-Four Scribbles and A Prayer (Lyrics and Ballads by Ian Wolfe).* I know that he would want to share this particular page with the reader.

A PRAYER FOR LOVE

There are many kinds of friendship
And all types of love
Yet any sort is better far, than none
Some are merely handshakes.
A few become too serious - -
Others only comical and fun.
There are many charming blossoms
Along the traveled road
Waiting the promise of Spring
and scented air,
They signify a sacred joy, and plentitude
from jeweled, inner realms beyond compare.
LOVE is the answer
the mystic answer
The final thing that we can ever know
LOVE IS the answer
the ONLY answer
So search its cave and hide-out;
let it grow, grow, grow ...
Search and find it soon - -
And let it GROW

Ian Wolfe as the "Forger" with his playful inscription to this author from his final film "Dick Tracy" (Touchstone and Buena Vista Pictures, 1990). Photo courtesy of Ian Wolfe.

Carl Laemmle Jr., general manager of productions at Universal Pictures from 1929 through 1936. Photo courtesy of Neil Lipes.

CHAPTER 2
CARL LAEMMLE JR.... IT'S A GREAT BIG PICTURE!

Carl Laemmle Jr. was best known in Hollywood as "Junior" or "Junior Laemmle," although his given name was Julius Laemmle, born in Chicago, Illinois and raised in New York City. He became the first executive actually born into the business of motion pictures, instead of coming into it after beginning his career in some other line of work. He was the only son of a blue-eyed adventuresome visionary, a Bavarian Jew from Laupheim, Württemberg, Germany known as Carl Laemmle, later known as "Uncle Carl." One of the first American film pioneers, many considered him "The Papa of 'em all." He ultimately became one of the most illustrious and beloved movie producers of his time and an unsung humanitarian of monumental deeds, who stood a mere five-feet-two inches tall.

Carl Laemmle first employed his fifteen-year-old son as a part-time production assistant at Universal City Studios in California. During that particular summer away from his schooling in New York City inspired Julius. When he became sixteen, he legally had his name changed to Carl Laemmle Jr. before he, his father and sister moved to California. Junior Laemmle began as a writer and later followed in his father's

"Julius Laemmle, 417 Riverside Drive" (age three and a half) dressed as a Prussian soldier, New York City, Halloween 1911. Photo courtesy of Udo Bayer.

The Universal Film Manufacturing Company was celebrating seven years of business in 1919. Carl Laemmle Jr. was eleven, as seen here with his father who by that time became president of the company. Photo from the author's collection.

footsteps playing an integral role as a motion picture producer. He stood an inch taller than his father.

Father and son will remain associated with the Universal Film Manufacturing Company (now Universal Pictures Corporation) and Universal City Studios (now Universal Studios Hollywood) leaving a lasting legacy of fine artistic products. It was a long time plan to meet Junior Laemmle. A written correspondence between us began in March 1976, which lasted until August 1979. The first of several letters dated March 30, 1976:

Dear Mr. Atkins:

I am in receipt of your letter of March 18 and am interested in your project. If there is anything I can do to help your research, call me when you come to Hollywood and I should be pleased to talk with you. My phone number is CR-----.

Very truly yours,

Carl Laemmle Jr.

The morning of July 6, 1979 has remained a vivid memory to this author especially after revisiting the Junior Laemmle address in October 2011. A deluge of specifics came quickly to mind remembering first the excitement turned to anxiety after phoning Junior Laemmle's home. The gentleman who answered the telephone identified himself as Jerry, Junior's nurse. Jerry was devoted to Junior's care for many years. He said, "Mr. Laemmle has not been well for many years."

This writer was unaware of the nature of Mr. Laemmle's illness until arriving at his home that day. Jerry did not say much else over the phone, but was kind in giving me directions to the Tower Grove address. He ended the call by saying that Mr. Laemmle would be expecting me in the afternoon at 2:30 p.m. Before leaving Sherman Oaks, Mr. and Mrs. Wolfe confirmed the road directions with me to Beverly Hills.

The drive to Junior's home felt like an eternity with all the twists and turns along the mountain road. Progressively gaining height to the destination along Benedict Canyon, then a sudden sharp curve from out of the blue seemed as if the car was on automatic pilot! Finally, the Tower Grove street sign appeared. Driving past several homes, Junior's address was the last house at the top of Tower Grove Drive with the address painted at the foot of his driveway. I arrived safely and on time. The spacious grounds around the handsome one level home were beautiful and well-kept with a Japanese garden in plain sight. It was a welcoming sight. (1)

Jerry previously said in our conversation that someone would be waiting outside the carport for me at the end of the driveway, and there was. The gentleman introduced himself as Louie. He was a quiet and friendly man of Filipino descent. Louie walked with me to the front door. I rang the doorbell and looked at my wristwatch. It was exactly 2:30 pm! With anticipation, I thought that Junior might be coming to the door. Instead, a short brawny lady in a white uniform, wearing orthopedic shoes and cat-eyed bifocals, opened the door. She was very kind and greeted me with her thick German brogue, "Come in, Mister Atkins. Welcome! I am Elise." (2)

Elise walked me through a narrow corridor of portable wall sections located to the left side of the foyer. The foyer was adorned with paintings, custom-made theater masks and sculptures. Junior's autograph collection was proudly displayed on the sectioned walls, many which were passed down to him by his father. Among some of the notable autographs displayed were Albert Einstein, Thomas Mann, Sinclair Lewis, Edsel Ford, Henry Ford II, Herbert Hoover, Franklin D. Roosevelt, George Gershwin, Frank Lloyd Wright, in addition to an original etching to Junior that was a gift from Salvador Dali. The collection ended at the living room where Elise offered me cold refreshment. She told me that Mr. Laemmle was in his bedroom and would be available soon. His bedroom was located just off the living room. I asked Elise if Mr. Laemmle was going to come into the living room. She gave me no answer, instead excused herself.

Sitting patiently on the sofa near the coffee table with lemonade, I noticed an attractive dark varnished wooden box. On its lid, sealed in clear shellac was a photograph of a young Mr. Laemmle standing with a gentleman unknown to me. Many years later, I learned that the unknown gentleman in the photograph with Junior was the boxer Jack Dempsey, a friend of the Laemmle family. Both were pictured dressed in suits and hats. The occasion was young Laemmle's Bar Mitzvah, April 28, 1921. The item was a custom-made cigar box lined with cork, which Junior had several made and given as gifts to namely poker buddies and friends. (3)

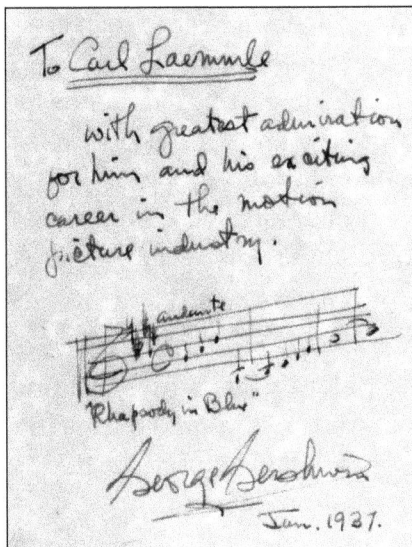

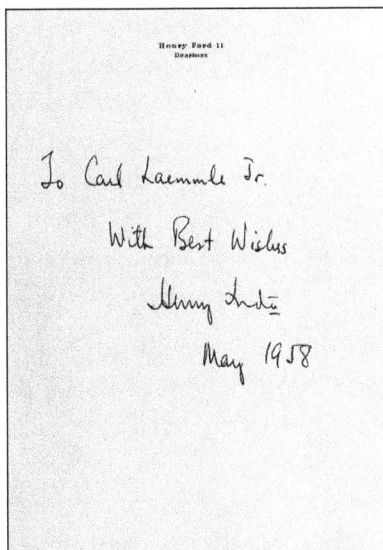

Part of the Laemmle autograph collection consisted of the following inscriptions, George Gershwin to Carl Laemmle, January 1937; Edsel Ford to Carl Laemmle, May 4, 1938; and Henry Ford II to Carl Laemmle, Jr., May 1958. Photos courtesy of Udo Bayer.

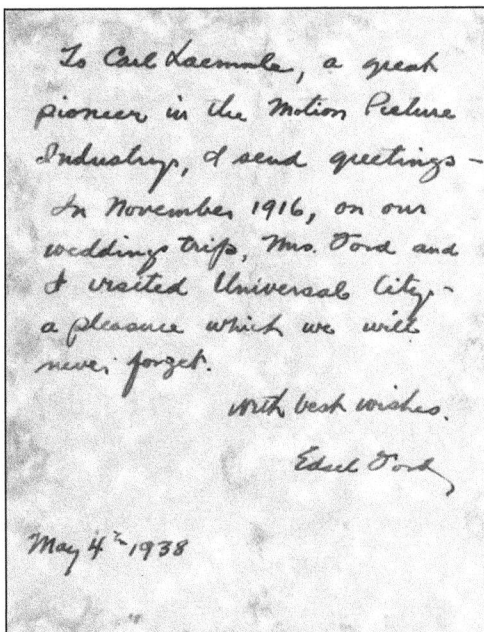

Elise returned to the living room. I became suspicious and asked Elise if we could step outside to discuss the nature of Junior's illness and if he had family nearby. Elise told me:

Multiple sclerosis. He was diagnosed when he was fifty. Mr. Laemmle has not been well for many years.

His niece lives nearby, but she is in Hawaii right now. His sister died many years ago. His brother-in-law visits him frequently. He also receives visits from some of his old friends.

Books, the Hollywood trade papers and fan letters are read to him. He always loves a good story. Young people like you, who write to him, always impresses Mr. Laemmle. He has been looking forward to your visit, Mr. Atkins. We go back inside. I do not keep you both waiting.

The diversion with Elise gave me a chance to catch a second wind and learn more about Junior before collecting myself and returning to the bedroom. Elise escorted me there where the former movie producer was lying in his bed. His body was turned to one side. His right arm appeared partially paralyzed.

Jerry introduced himself as he was tucking blankets in and around Mr. Laemmle. Jerry must have noticed my shock and asked me to move my car, which was blocking his car under the carport. Jerry said that he would be leaving for the rest of the afternoon. During the course of the visit, Mr. Laemmle rang the buzzer for Elise at least three times when I was asked to leave the room. Elise alerted me earlier that Mr. Laemmle would tire easily and have to be tended to. At one break, she reassured me, "He is having good day today. He does not do this for just anybody. He likes you, Mr. Atkins."

An indelible impression was made on this writer that day as we exchanged formalities. After being seated in a chair beside of his bed, Mr. Laemmle began speaking in a distinct but weakened voice. (4)

CLJ: I am happy to meet you, Mr. Atkins.

RA: I am happy to finally meet you, Mr. Laemmle.

CLJ: It is my pleasure. We've been writing letters for a while. What is your age now?

RA: Twenty, sir.

CLJ: When will you be twenty-one?

RA: October.

CLJ: Welcome to California and an early Happy Birthday to you, Mr. Atkins.

You can call me Junior, and I will call you Atkins.

The interview became Mr. Laemmle's last. According to Elise, it was his first formal interview, "in about thirty years." The following is the interview contents in its entirety. This writer made a promise to Junior that an extensive story would be written along with the interview. Junior's following remarks and suggestions to that promise are now realized.

> I would like that Atkins. When you write your story, do bring my father's history into it. His story makes for better reading than mine. It's a great big picture, Atkins.
> It's a small world that you live near where my father opened his first theatre.
> You and I also have in common being born in Chicago. You are interesting and a persistent young man. Keep up your studies, Atkins. It CAN be done. And like me, you know too much. That's a great start.

Since Junior Laemmle's death, this writer developed close friendships with some Laemmle family members and friends. By turning back the clock, historical successions of discourse come full circle. Accordingly, this allows the story to begin and to also honor Junior's request. This chapter may shed new light on one of Hollywood's much-neglected figures.

Long before Carl Laemmle virtually handed the reigns of Universal Studios over to his son, he hired friends, family members, and friends of family, eventually fellow Laupheimers as well. Humorist Ogden Nash, best known for his light verse poetry once wrote: "Uncle Carl Laemmle - Has a very large faemmle." With time, several dozen of these people were on his payroll some who jested to co-workers that they were getting pay for being a relative. The joke was certainly not on Mr. Laemmle. He would deem every employee worthy of his or her services. Isadore Bernstein was Mr. Laemmle's first west coast general manager. He was not a Laemmle relative.

By March 1914, Carl Laemmle had covered much ground in his new career in a relatively short period of eight years. He was thirty-nine when he started as a film exhibitor in Chicago with a successful nickelodeon business in February 1906. He was now his own boss, yet always remained humble regarding his dozen years of work within the confines of the Continental Clothing Company in Oshkosh, Wisconsin, which he left behind a few months prior.

Before the end of his first year in business, Laemmle had opened another theatre in Chicago. His success was considered by contemporaries of his day as coming late in life. This did not stop Mr. Laemmle. He simultaneously rented another storefront becoming a film distributor. Within another year his business was touted "the largest film renter in the world."

By the summer of 1909, he founded his own film production company, the Independent Motion Picture Company (IMP) with an office in New York and a film studio in New Jersey. Subsequently, he moved his operations west to California where he purchased a small studio and leased another location he called Universal City, which eventually was deemed by Laemmle as unsatisfactory. He wanted to own land on more space.

Isadore Bernstein, Mr. Laemmle's west coast general manager sent a wire to his boss in New York about an exclusive site for sale in California's Lankershim Township. Laemmle instructed Bernstein to insure the purchase ($165,000) for the sprawling former Taylor Ranch. Under Bernstein's supervision, construction began immediately to transform the land to a community solely dedicated to the making of motion pictures. Universal City remains the oldest and largest motion picture studios in the world still in operation. It was the parent company to the Universal Film Manufacturing Company that produced the actual celluloid product from which motion pictures were projected.

It was a Monday, March 15, 1915 when Carl Laemmle, the founder and president of Universal City Studios, opened it to the public. Universal City Studios is located approximately ten miles from the heart of Los Angeles, California and five miles north of the Hollywood Hills on the old El Camino Real, halfway between the missions of San Gabriel and San Fernando. The property that Carl Laemmle originally purchased consisted of 230 acres. Between 1914 and 1928, Universal City's output of motion pictures was tremendous.

Universal City has evolved over the years changing ownership numerous times since 1936 when Carl Laemmle sold and retired. Universal Studios Hollywood presently consists of 391 acres. The conglomerate celebrated their centennial in 2015. (5)

The Universal Film Manufacturing Company was formed in New York City, April 30, 1912, prior to the founding of Universal City. It was a joint effort with several independent moving picture producers on board. Carl Laemmle and his early IMP (Independent Moving Pictures) Company was one. Pat Powers, William Swanson, Mark Dintenfass, David Horsley, Charles Baumann, Adam Kessell, Charles Jourjon, and Jules Brulatour were others with combined interests. Mr. Laemmle started out as their treasurer. In a few months, he became the company president.

By their seventh year in business (1919), Carl Laemmle made the company one of the most powerful factors in the film world. The extent of the film company's growth by then argued well for its policy of giving the exhibitor every cooperation and first consideration. This was something that Mr. Laemmle prided himself from his past experience as an exhibitor.

The Universal Film Manufacturing Company was renamed Universal Pictures Corporation in 1922. The corporation celebrated their centennial in 2012. Between 1912 and 1915, the Universal Film Manufacturing Company churned out multitudes of film dramas, epic adventures, comedies, and varieties of serials as rapidly as Carl Laemmle could hire general managers. Next came relatives.

Nepotism was a fixed tradition at Universal City Studios. The first Laemmle relative to achieve early success there was Edward Laemmle, a nephew to Uncle Carl. Edward became a leading director at Universal. He got his start in 1916 and worked through 1935 with innumerable pictures to his credit. Ernst Laemmle was another of Carl's nephews. He directed a variety of dramas and short western films at Universal between 1924 and 1930.

Other family members who came out to Universal City were Abe and Julius Stern, Carl's brothers-in-law. The Stern brothers founded the Century Film Studios, Inc. They became popular producers of successful "Century Comedies" and "LK-O (Lehrman's Knock-Out) Comedies," which originally were being made at Universal City and released by Universal before Century Studios. The Stern Film Corporation produced over five hundred films between 1917 and 1929.

William Wyler was a cousin brought to America by Laemmle in 1920. He was first hired as an office boy. Wyler worked his way to assistant director by 1922. Wyler later achieved topnotch success as one of Hollywood's finest directors winning three Academy Awards and earning twelve Academy Award nominations during his long and prestigious career.

Perhaps the most notable general manager during Universal City's early days was the young and highly intelligent Irving Thalberg, to whom Laemmle saw great promise. It was Recha Laemmle (Mrs. Carl Laemmle) who was an acquaintance of Irving's mother Henrietta regarding the connection. After Carl met young Irving Thalberg, he hired him as his personal secretary in 1918 at the Universal Film Manufacturing Company New York office. Carl Laemmle felt a strong kinship towards the stridently independent young man fascinated by the business of motion pictures.

In the winter of 1918, Recha Laemmle became seriously ill. The forty-three-year-old wife and mother succumbed to influenza on the Monday morning of January 13, 1919, at their apartment located at 365 West End Avenue, four days short of her husband's fifty-second birthday. She had fallen victim to a pandemic that had claimed the lives of twenty million people around the globe over the previous year. Mrs. Laemmle's last wish for her family was to take care of each other. She was buried in a grave at Salem Fields Cemetery in Brooklyn, New York January 15, 1919. In addition to her husband, their seventeen-year-old daughter and ten-year-old son survived her.

Irving Thalberg assisted Mr. Laemmle through personal matters and business delays over several difficult months that followed. Thalberg accompanied Mr. Laemmle to Universal City in California in 1919. Once they arrived, Carl Laemmle went abroad and left Irving Thalberg in charge of studio management.

After Carl Laemmle obtained complete ownership of the Universal Film Manufacturing Company March 16, 1920, he appointed Thalberg as Universal's general manager, just weeks before his

Irving Thalberg (Vice-President of Metro, Goldwyn & Mayer) as seen during the 1930s. Thalberg left Carl Laemmle and Universal Pictures in 1923 to work for Louis B. Mayer. He remained there until his death at age thirty-seven in 1936. Photo from the author's collection.

twenty-first birthday. The young man was soon given all creative privileges in motion picture production by which he gained experience and advantage. Three major Universal Pictures produced under Irving Thalberg's supervision was, *Foolish Wives, Merry-Go-Round,* and *The Hunchback of Notre Dame.*

Irving Thalberg left Universal Pictures, February 23, 1923 to join producer Louis B. Mayer before the consolidation of Metro Gold-wyn and Mayer (MGM) on April 17, 1924.

It was no secret in Hollywood of the courtship between Irving Thalberg and Carl Laemmle's daughter, Rosabelle. It began in 1922 when she was twenty-one and continued after Thalberg's departure from Universal City. It was believed that Irving Thalberg would become Carl Laemmle's son-in-law. According to Rosabelle's daughter Carole Laemmle Bergerman, Rosabelle Laemmle kept several letters written between her and Irving Thalberg,

As their relationship seemed to get serious, it ended. Mutual love was not in the scenario, nor was Mr. Thalberg's heart condition. In the end, no promises were made to Miss Laemmle. Their courtship officially ended in February 1926 coinciding with Carl Laemmle's highly publicized twentieth anniversary for his service to the motion picture industry.

Rosabelle Laemmle became her father's steady companion. She also took a lively interest in art, welfare work and continually aided her father in most public events and charitable activities. Her keen foresight and her sound judgment were recognized throughout the film world. Her father sought her consul as to all questions and she inspired many of the progressive moves of the Laemmle organization.

Julius Bernheim, a nephew to Carl Laemmle became Irving Thalberg's successor at Universal City. Bernheim was born in Laupheim, Germany, the son of Jacob Bernheim and Carl's sister, Karoline Laemmle Bernheim. He was the first of the Laemmle nephews hired in Chicago, beginning as an office boy with the Laemmle Film Service in 1909. Bernheim moved to New York in 1911 and worked as a film editor and then to three other Laemmle exchanges before 1922 when he was hired at Universal City as a second director. Julius Bernheim had served under Irving Thalberg as unit business manager in 1923. Bernheim's tenure as general manager was one year 1924 through 1925. He left the position due to illness, but later returned to work as an associate producer for Universal Pictures as well as for German versions of Universal films between 1925 and 1935. Other general managers

Julius Bernheim (left) was named the new general manager at Universal after Thalberg's departure. Uncle Carl Laemmle is pictured here with his real life nephew (son of his sister Karoline) in 1923. Photo courtesy of Carla Laemmle.

Anna (Stern) Fleckles, sister of Mrs. Carl Laemmle as seen in 1938. Photo courtesy of Udo Bayer.

who followed Julius Bernheim were, John Griffith Wray, Raymond Schrock and Henry Henigson, all non-Laemmle relatives.

Carl Laemmle began grooming his son, Carl Jr. as the heir apparent early on. From the age of six, the boy traveled frequently with his father. He eagerly followed his father around always asking questions. Carl Laemmle indulged his son in creative projects. The boy learned how to write plays when he was eight. The experiences fascinated him.

As quickly as Julius Laemmle became Carl Laemmle Jr., he was known as "Junior," the name he wasn't fond of in the beginning.

Anna's husband Maurice Fleckles, long-time business partner to Carl Laemmle. Photo courtesy of Carla Laemmle.

During this time, the transient Mr. Laemmle traveled on business matters while his sister-in-law, Anna Stern Fleckles (the late Mrs. Laemmle's sister) and husband, Maurice Fleckles, shared the same New York apartment house on West End Avenue. The Laemmle children stayed with Mr. and Mrs. Fleckles until Junior completed his high school education. (6)

Carl Laemmle receives a royal welcome home from his public after the family returned to New York City. Their four-month long trip to Europe started in June after which Mr. Laemmle was taken ill. He recuperated after surgery in a London hospital. The family eventually made it to their destined Laupheim, Germany in August and home to the USA in October 1926. Photo from the author's collection.

Carl Laemmle had wished that his son would go to college. Instead, the fervent seventeen-year-old writer put his college prep courses on hold as the Laemmles relocated to California in late 1925.

In June 1926 as part of the twentieth anniversary celebration in the motion picture business, Carl Laemmle and his children boarded the Steamship Berengaria en route to Europe. During the voyage, Laemmle Sr., suffered a severe appendicitis attack. His life was in the balance. He was kept alive by constant medical advice via radio between his physicians in New York as the great ship neared England. Once in London, he underwent a serious appendicitis operation. Carl Laemmle literally fought his way back to health. Six months later, Mr. Laemmle returned to the States where he received a royal welcome when he reached New

Laupheim, Germany, September 1924: Julius Laemmle (age sixteen) with his father and two of his uncles, Siegfried Laemmle (left) and Joseph Laemmle (background) in Laupheim, Germany soon after Julius legally had his name changed to Carl Laemmle Jr. in Laupheim, Germany (September 1924). Photo courtesy of Carla Laemmle.

York City complete with a parade. New York City officials and heads of the film industry also gathered to meet him along with his children.

Junior never resumed his education. At eighteen, he became a successful writer at Universal, winning the title of production supervisor for two-reel featurettes released as *"The Collegians."* The first episode of the series, *Benson at Calford* was released in the United States November 8, 1926. At the age of twenty he became an associate producer, which entailed an exhaustive course of training by his father in all branches of motion picture production. Laemmle, Sr. is quoted:

> The second generation of the movies is growing. With this generation should come a change in the industry. One of its faults in the past has been amateurish leadership, too often, and mismanagement. The leaders and executives in so intricate and involved an industry as ours, in order to succeed, must have a vast store of information and knowledge concerning everyone in the many departments which function in the studio and in the huge organization of distribution. This knowledge can only come through training and experience.

From every department of the studio, Junior not only learned the intricacies of successful film production from the standpoint of the executive, but from the standpoint of the director, the actor and the technician as well. He was attached to one of the units at Universal City as an assistant to the director to learn the actual making of motion pictures on the sets. Early examples illustrate the family traveling to Europe. In early 1927, no longer wanting to live in hotels with his children, Carl Laemmle bought a Beverly Hills mansion for $650,000.00 that once belonged to the late actor-director Thomas Ince, a former employee of Laemmle. Ince's widow sold Laemmle the thirty-five-room home known as "Dias Dorados." Rosabelle Laemmle organized and acted as the hostess for most of the personal dinner parties and events at the mansion and at Universal City on behalf of her father. (7)

Father and son Laemmle in 1927 standing near the Ulm Cathedral (which took over five hundred years to complete) in Germany. Ulm is a neighboring city to Laupheim. Carl Laemmle made other trips to Europe (namely Switzerland) as late as 1938, but not to his homeland after 1927. Photo courtesy of Udo Bayer.

The fall of 1927 was an unforgettable and sad time for the Laemmle family. Junior and his father traveled to Laupheim, Germany. It was an annual trip taken with pride by Mr. Laemmle for many years. Junior was still known as Julius in the European province. Clara Einstein was an attractive girl. She was acquainted with Julius from earlier childhood. When the two reunited after a few years, the mature young lady that Clara became took Julius. Clara confided to a friend that Julius had become "a most handsome young man." We will never know what were to transpire from the flirtation. Due to further European political unrest, neither Carl Laemmle nor his families were welcomed back to Laupheim. It was the last trip made by any family member to the homeland until May 25, 1988 when the City of Laupheim welcomed back forty-six former Jewish residents as a goodwill gesture.

Among the attendees were Ruth Friedland Regis and her husband Edward Regis, of Kingsbridge Heights, Bronx, New York.

Ruth Friedland Regis, visiting Laupheim, Germany, July 1999. Photo by the author.

Ruth was the daughter of Max Friedland and Irma Jette Bernheim Friedland, and sister to Trudy Friedland. Ruth Friedland was born in Biberach, Germany in 1921 and lived in Laupheim with her family until 1933 when the family moved to Paris due to the Anti-Semitism in Germany. Ruth was a great niece to Carl Laemmle. She and her husband "Eddie" Regis returned to Laupheim in July 1999 where this author befriended them.

After the Laemmles returned to America, a former Hungarian stage director had achieved newfound success in America as a filmmaker. His name was Dr. Paul Fejos (Pál Fejös). The enterprising young man received his M.D. at Budapest before arriving to America in 1923. The following year, Fejos, was employed at the Rockefeller Institute in New York City, as a laboratory technician

LONESOME

A LAEMMLE SUPER SPECIAL

story by MANN PACE

with GLENN TRYON and BARBARA KENT

A PAUL FEJOS PRODUCTION

Lonesome (1928) was director Paul Fejos' first film for Universal Pictures. It was praised for its simplicity and fine directing of a well-acted boy meets girl story. Photo from the author's collection.

Film director Paul Fejos and associate producer Carl Laemmle, Jr. with actress Merna Kennedy, one of their stars of Broadway, which met with mixed reviews due to its excellent stage predecessor (Universal Pictures, 1929) Photo from the author's collection.

Members of the Western Motion Picture Advertisers with host Carl Laemmle Jr. have so far named six of the thirteen WAMPAS Baby Stars of 1928 (from left); Molly O'Day, Audrey Ferris, Alice Day, Dorothy Gulliver, Gwen Lee and Flora Bramley. Photo courtesy of Carla Laemmle.

and staff bacteriologist. After arriving in California in 1926, Fejos was given an opportunity as a filmmaker where he made his first American feature film *The Last Moment* (1927), which is today a "lost film." Critics praised it as an interesting but unusual film. A second film would follow as Fejos began shopping a new film project around to the Hollywood studios, including Universal.

After a few recurring visits to Universal City, Fejos established rapport with both Senior and Junior Laemmle. Dr. Paul Fejos found a suitable deal there. Fejos was as interested in directing motion pictures as Junior was in preventing the spread of germs. A contract was signed between him and Universal Pictures in December of 1927. *Lonesome* became Fejos' second picture. Released in 1928 by Universal Pictures, it became a big success for him and the studio, which was followed by *Broadway*, another "great big picture!" Junior's brother-in-law, Stanley Bergerman told this author the following.

Junior was gullible to the point of obsession with medical advices from Paul Fejos. Needless to say, Carl Laemmle protected his son and had first believed that their association was good business. After Junior was put in charge of the studio, Fejos began to pick apart at his renewed contract. That eventually led to a parting of ways for Fejos and Universal. (8)

A turn of events occurred within the Carl Laemmle family between May 1928 and June 1929. Carl Laemmle appointed Robert E. Welsh as Universal City's general manager in May 1, 1928. Junior was busy on the social circuit during this time. Among several events, he hosted was helping name several of the WAMPAS BABY STARS of 1928.

On the evening of January 2, 1929, Carl Laemmle Jr. was the best man at his sister's wedding. Rosabelle Laemmle had married (Mark) Stanley Bergerman at the Laemmle mansion in Beverly Hills. Mr. and Mrs. Bergerman's union produced a daughter and a son. Junior Laemmle's twenty-first birthday came April 28, 1929. It was celebrated with a banquet. Among the guest speakers were Charles "Charlie" Chaplin whom Junior greatly admired. After one year of service, Robert E. Welsh resigned his post as general manager. On May 1, 1929, Carl Laemmle Jr. was appointed "general manager in complete charge of production" at Universal City.

Carl Laemmle Presents - A Universal Picture - Produced by Carl Laemmle Jr. was a typical screen credit shared in numerous films produced between the mid-1920s through the mid-1930s. The ongoing question from theatergoers of the times: "Were they the same person?" With time, Junior would have his own identity. Excerpts from Universal publicity director John LeRoy Johnston's "Biographical Resume of Carl Laemmle Jr." follows.

By 1929 he had so thoroughly mastered the details of the motion picture industry that he was appointed general manager of the Universal Pictures Corporation. He became the first of a new generation in the film industry.

At this time the advent of talking pictures was producing a revolutionary effect on the business, and young Laemmle found himself not only in a new job, but also in a job that was entirely new to everyone in the industry.

Alice Day (Jacquiline Alice Newlin, 1905-1995). Photo from the author's collection.

His father was in Europe on an extended vacation, so the young man was forced to apply himself unaided to the new problems, which had arisen. ...

Marceline Day (Marceline Newlin, 1908-2000). Photo from the author's collection.

Like his father, Carl Laemmle Jr., was quiet and unassuming. His demeanor would never give an inkling of the fact that he is the executive head of a thirty million dollar corporation. He maintains his headquarters at Universal City, and is in constant touch with every production on the "lot," and is the

Sue Carol (Evelyn Jean Lederer, 1906-1982). Photo from the author's collection.

most indefatigable workers in the studio. He ... has dark brown eyes, black hair and weighs 130 pounds. He is unmarried."

Over the years, the exceptional finely dressed producer was photographed flashing his ever-present toothy Laemmle smile with young starlets of the times. He had an advantage over any layman to stake visits on most any young actress on set of a picture. Junior's personal life however was rarely covered unless

Dorothy Gulliver (Dorothy Kathleen Gulliver, 1908-1997). Photo from the author's collection.

possibilities of marriage were alleged. Sadly, these courtships ended with differences and difficulties, ultimately leaving Carl Laemmle Jr. an unmarried man. His first publicized flirtation was with actress Alice Day (sister of actress Marceline Day) in the fall of 1925. His cousin, the director Ernst Laemmle, introduced them. Junior was seventeen and she nineteen. Miss Day was not associated with Universal Pictures then. His flirtation with Miss Day became a steady relationship. It ended in 1928. (9)

Subsequently, Alice Day was hired by Ernst Laemmle to star in one of his Universal comedies *Phyllis of the Follies*. Concurrently,

Constance Cummings (Constance Halverstadt, 1910-2005). Photo from the author's collection.

the actress Sue Carol was also working on a picture at Universal. Junior became smitten with Sue Carol, who was then in the midst of a divorce. The ingénue (who later became Mrs. Alan Ladd) and Junior Laemmle remained longtime friends.

Film actress Sidney Fox (Sidney Leiffer, 1911-1942). Another lovely life cut short by tragedy. Photo from the author's collection.

Dorothy Gulliver was a bit player in motion pictures during the 1920s. Junior Laemmle chose her to star as June Maxwell in his serial *The Collegians*. Junior was attracted to Miss Gulliver, but advised early on, not to date women who would be working at the studio.

There was no romantic involvement between Junior Laemmle and Miss Carol, or Dorothy Gulliver. Much to Junior's embarrassment, he never wooed on set again. It is interesting to note that

Stanley Bergerman and the author, Brentwood Country Club, Los Angeles, October 20, 1996. Photo from the author's collection.

when the WAMPAS Baby Stars of 1928 were named, three of thirteen were Alice Day, Sue Carol and Dorothy Gulliver. (10)

In 1931, Junior Laemmle and a lovely newcomer named Constance Cummings were introduced at a party given by Myron Selznick. Junior had recently seen her on the screen in Columbia Pictures' *The Criminal Code*. The two began dating and Junior eventually proposed to Miss Cummings. A string of events took place after the engagement. The press had alleged that with Junior Laemmle being Jewish and Miss Cummings not, that a wedding would not be in order.

Rumors of Laemmle Sr., calling it off were only rumors. The family embraced Miss Cummings who later called off the engagement. Subsequently, Junior attended the 1932 Summer Olympics in Los Angeles where he met the eighteen-year-old Olympic swimmer, Eleanor Holm, whom he referred to as the love of his life. (11)

During this period, any press regarding Junior Laemmle and his courtships was overshadowed by an undisclosed truth. According

Benn W. Levy (Benn Wolfe Levy, 1900-1973) married Constance Cummings in 1933. Photo from the author's collection.

to Junior's niece, Carole Bergerman from what her uncle had told her:

I wouldn't say that she [Constance Cummings] called it off exactly. My uncle told me that before he would marry her, he went to his doctor for tests. He learned that he was sterile and vowed he'd never marry anyone. And he didn't.

Clärle "Clara" Einstein (1913- 1933). A lovely life cut short by tragedy.
Photo courtesy of Liesle Adler.

Rumors also circulated over a romantic involvement between Junior Laemmle and the ingénue Sidney Fox. Stanley Bergerman, told this writer the following in 1996.

This was far from the truth. The only thing that she [Sidney Fox] and Junior had between them was kindness and talent.

Junior discovered the young lady on Broadway and put her in the movies. He loaned her out to other studios to make pictures. She later married. Her tragic end [accidental overdosing on sleeping pills] was most unfortunate. Junior was in the army when he learned of the news and most saddened.

In July 1933, Constance Cummings married screenwriter Benn W. Levy and moved to England. Matters further escalated after Junior received news from Europe about the death of Miss Clara Einstein, August 12, 1933. Liesle Adler, niece of sculptor and former Laupheim resident, the late Frederich Adler, was a close friend of the late Miss Einstein. In 1999, Liesle Adler told this writer the following in Laupheim, Germany.

Clärle Einstein was my dear friend. We practically grew up together. We went to school together and got a job in the same place together at a Café here in Laupheim.

I learned of her fear of lightening, which was so great that when we girls got together for embroidery, if it was thunder storming, she would ask us to refrain from touching the needles until the lightening stopped.

So what happened to her? She went on vacation with her parents and her brother, Siegfried, to a summer place atop a nearby mountain retreat. She was outside along the hilltop when suddenly without warning a bolt of lightning struck her and threw her down the hillside into a ball of fire. She had no chance of survival.

To this day, I see her in the coffin covered with many flowers. It was so hard losing my best friend. The tragedy that surrounded her death at nineteen is a strange and very sad tale. I will send to you a picture of her. (12)

(from left) Julius Bernheim, Stanley Bergerman, Dale Van Every, Richard Schayer, Carl Laemmle Jr., Carl Laemmle, E.M. Asher, and Felix Young all at the helm of film productions released by Universal Pictures between 1929 and 1935. Photo from the author's collection.

Counsellor at Law, *(Universal Pictures, 1933).*

The Laemmles found their star in John Barrymore, the actor who came with a steep price in Counsellor at Law, which became one of the big successes of 1933. Photo courtesy of Neil Lipes]

Subsequently, Eleanor Holm married musician, Art Jarrett, in September 1933 after which, Junior, absorbed himself in work. He hired John Barrymore to star in *Counsellor at Law*, from the play by Elmer Rice. Junior said of Barrymore, "He came with a hefty price, but we accommodated him and it paid off." William Wyler, Junior's cousin

James Whale, the prolific director at Universal Pictures. He and Junior Laemmle made eleven motion pictures together between 1931 and 1936. Photo from the author's collection.

directed *Counsellor at Law*, which was a big success. Universal had an impressive group of associates during this time.

Junior also resumed his fantastic film projects and worked closely with director, James Whale, to finish *The Invisible Man,*

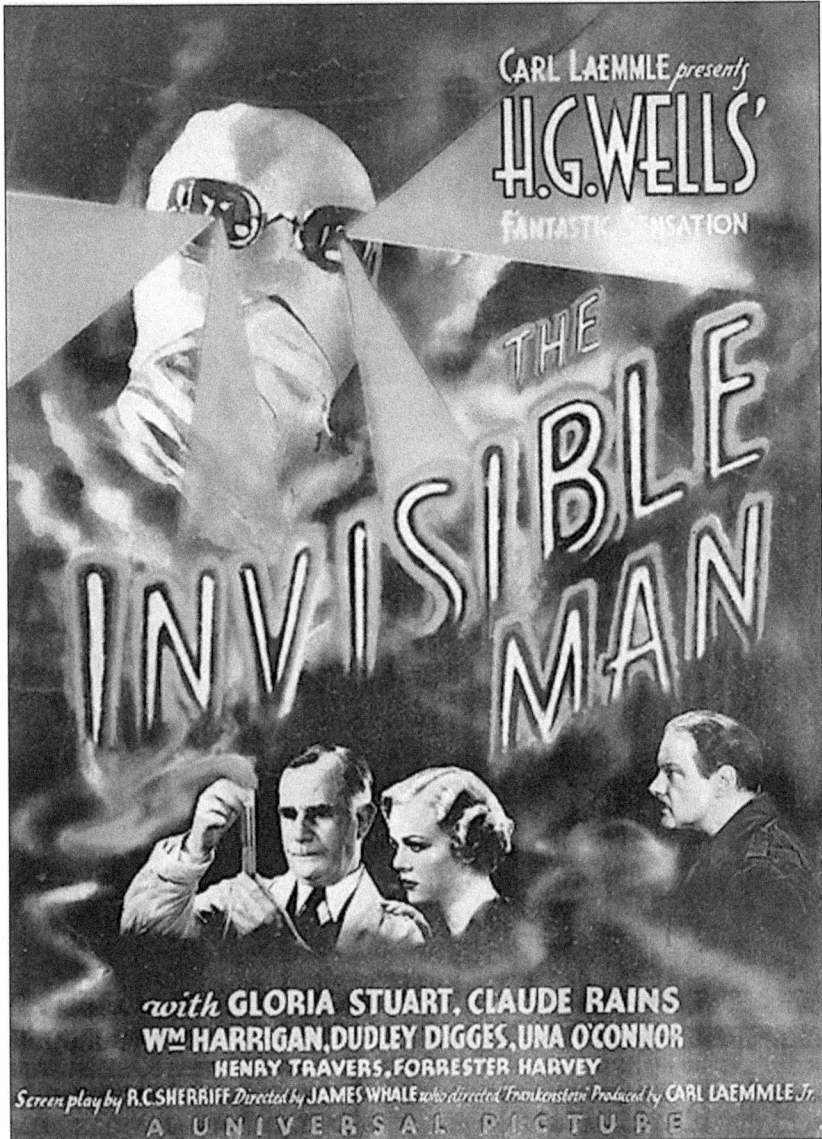

The Invisible Man *became one of the ten best pictures of 1933, and Junior Laemmle's favorite as he told this author in 1979. Photo from the author's collection.*

which became a huge moneymaker for the studio. When Junior was asked to name his favorite movie, without hesitating, he answered.

Carl Laemmle Jr. arrives in New York aboard the Santa Rosa after a seventeen-day trip, which included a stop in Havana, Cuba where he interviewed Colonel Fulgencio Batista (November 1933). Photo courtesy of Neil Lipes.

The Invisible Man. Whale and I cast a then unknown, Claude Rains, in his first film. I had a bit more to do with that [and with *Bride of Frankenstein* [probably one of the best Hollywood movie sequels ever made].

I worked closely with Whale and then again to make [Bride] an effective sequel. We had fun.

Before the end of 1934, *Universal Weekly* (Vol. 35/No. 22, Pgs. 5 and 28) from November 10, 1934 reported the following.

Carl Laemmle Jr., after a seventeen-day trip on the Santa Rosa of the Grace line arrived in New York on Election Day preparatory to his three months' trip to Europe.

At the present moment, he plans to sail on the Conte de Savoia on the twenty-third of November. He will put in the intervening two weeks in seeing the plays in New York, interviewing authors, directors, and scouting for screen material.

The only incident, which broke the monotony of the seventeen-day trip, was a stop in Havana where G.R. Naylor, Universal's representative, had arranged an interview [between] Mr. Laemmle and Colonel Batista. Colonel Batista [was] one of the most carefully guarded persons in world. The Colonel, though a very urbane and democratic appearing gentleman, is one of the most difficult in the world to meet, and Carl Laemmle Jr. is the first film official ever to have an interview with him or to be photographed with him.

The interview had to do with moving pictures in the Island of Cuba; also the possibility of a film to be made in Havana. Carl Laemmle Jr. [was] considering the purchase of a novel [having] a Havana background.

Harry Zehner, his assistant, Polan Banks, the novelist, and Archie Gottler, the songwriter, accompanied Mr. Laemmle.

The 1934-1935 season at Universal Pictures was Junior's busiest. He previously hired the following assemblage of screenwriters: Nina Wilcox Putnam, Dale Van Emery, Tom Reed, Edwin H. Knopf, Gladys Lehman, John Huston, Garrett Fort, P.J. Wolfson, Allen Rifkin, Pat Kearney, Martin Mooney, Gilbert Emery, Ben Orkow, Tom Buckingham, Paul Perez, Earl Snell, Fred Niblo, Jr., Elynore Dolkart, and three British writers, John Balderston, R.C. Sheriff, and Benn W. Levy. They all made significant contributions to the stage and screen.

Show Boat *was the last motion picture at Universal Pictures directed by James Whale and produced by Carl Laemmle Jr., which reaped a golden harvest for the new Universal management. Photo from the author's collection.*

Magnificent Obsession became one of the studios biggest properties namely for its director John M. Stahl during a time in which the studio was going through the transition of new ownership. Stahl barred Junior Laemmle from any involvement for fear of over budget expenses. Photo from the author's collection.

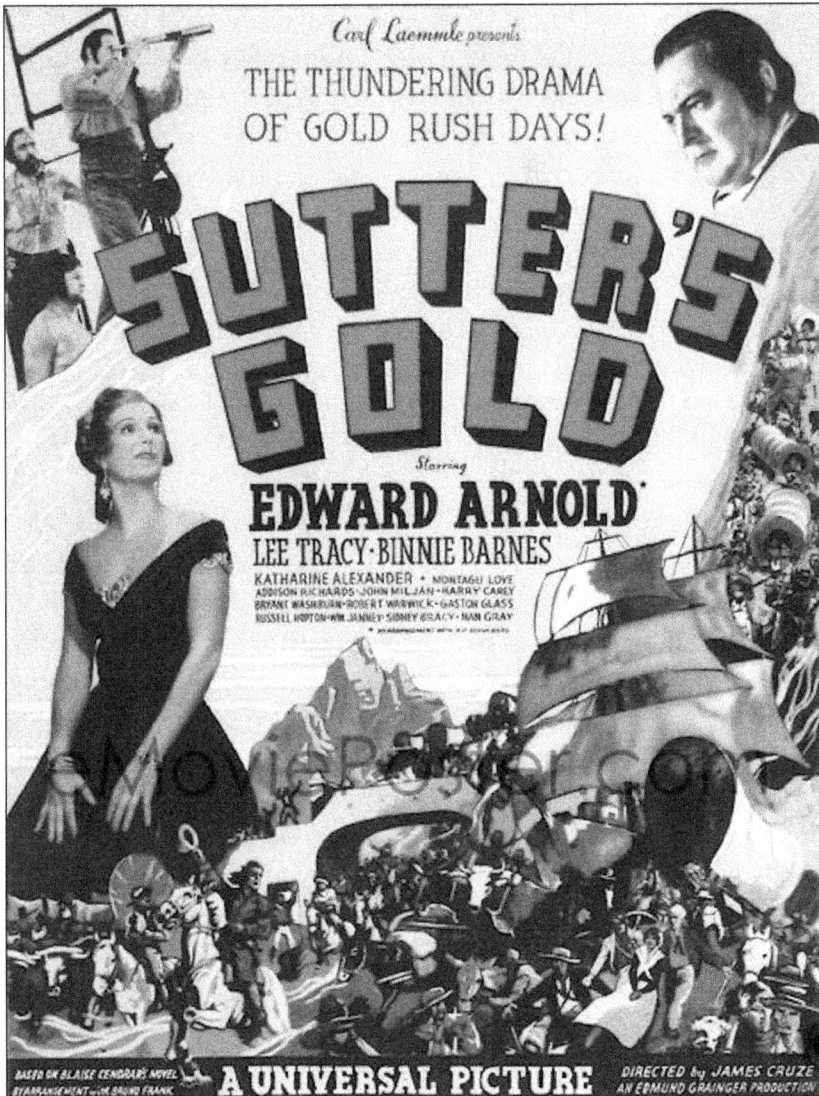

Sutter's Gold was originally to be directed by Howard Hawks. After Hawks left the picture James Cruze took over direction. The production continually had setbacks and ran over budget with changes made to the original story. Junior had worked on the production, but Edmund Grainger took over with little or no momentum. Photo from the author's collection.

Rumors were circulating throughout Hollywood that "Uncle Carl" Laemmle might sell the Universal establishment. It was reported for two years prior to 1935 that Universal might have been short of cash. Carl Laemmle made a plan to operate Universal through associate management with units functioning independently.

Junior, the sensitive young man, who had sworn off marriage, became so absorbed in Universal's survival that he was close to physical and mental exhaustion. Dr. Leland Hawkins, Carl Laemmle's physician, cautioned Junior to slow down.

In a steadfast move to take the workload off his son, Laemmle, Sr., hired Fred S. Meyer, as a temporary general manager. Also on board were the following producers, Stanley Bergerman (Junior's brother-in-law), E.M. Asher, Lou Ostrow, B.F. Zeidman, David Diamond, Jerry Sackheim, John M. Stahl, Henry Henigson, and Edmund Grainger.

Stanley Bergerman was first hired in 1929 as an assistant to Junior Laemmle. He was put in position alongside Frank Mastrole as general manager for the 1934-1935 seasons. Junior was re-assigned to make pictures as a separate unit, but not for long. Stanley Bergerman announced his resignation April 24, 1935 under friendly terms with his father-in-law. Carl Laemmle had other plans for his son-in-law. Junior returned to his post May 1, 1935 working mostly on *Show Boat and overseeing* the other costly productions of the times *Magnificent Obsession* and *Sutter's Gold.*

In November 1935, Carl Laemmle borrowed seven hundred and fifty thousand dollars surely to be paid back within ninety days from Standard Capital Company. Banker J. Cheever Cowdin controlled the group at Standard Capital alongside George Newell Armsby and broker Lawrence W. Fox Jr.

Laemmle borrowed the money as Junior was trying to compete with the top studios to make first-rate pictures with the premise that he most would succeed. In return, Carl Laemmle gave Standard Capital an option on his stock until February 1, 1936. The option was extended for six weeks to no avail or choice by Uncle Carl, he sold his controlling interest in the company; Cowdin bought some 90 percent of Laemmle's common stock for five million and fifty-five thousand dollars. Standard Capital deposited

Carl Laemmle Jr., general manager of Universal Pictures seated at his desk, May 1929. Photo courtesy of Udo Bayer.

one million three hundred thousand dollars in a New York bank on March 16, 1936.

An additional deposit of four million dollars was made before the last day of March 1936 when Universal Pictures Corporation was now in the hands of its new owners. The new management was formed as a holding company that would also control Universal City Studios without the Laemmles. Mr. Laemmle was asked to stay on as the corporation's chairman of the board, but he graciously left it all behind, humbly retiring.

J. Cheever Cowdin was elected chairman of the Universal Pictures Corporation. Robert H. Cochrane, who was Carl Laemmle's vice-president and advertiser for over thirty years, was named the new president. Mr. Cochrane retained the post until the end of December 1937. (13)

It was reported that Junior Laemmle would likely remain at Universal. However, he resigned April 2, 1936 and left Universal City entirely on April 18, 1936. His replacement was Charles R. Rogers, an indepen-

Carl Laemmle Jr. was eager to educate this author about The
Collegians, *the stories of college life during the 1920s, which he wrote
and supervised as "featurettes" produced by Universal Pictures. Photo
from the author's collection.*

dent producer who once served temporarily as head of production at
RKO. He was named Universal's executive vice-president. (14)

Fast forward to Junior Laemmle's bedroom in July 1979. Once
rapport was established, Junior said to this writer. "Let's say we
get on with the interview." Junior started by telling how he got
started at Universal:

> First, I want you to know that I had a thumb on the popu-
> lar movie going public of my time. I was part of the stage
> and movie audiences like many people were. I attended fre-
> quently. I really knew what they wanted. I was seventeen
> when I started writing a series of stories based on college
> life. It became a Universal serial called *The Collegians* with
> many episodes.
>
> [*The Collegians* first episode was released in movie the-
> aters across the country in the fall of 1926. The final forty-
> fourth episode was released in the fall of 1929.]

Graduation Daze *(Universal Pictures, 1929) was released in September 1929, the last of forty-four featurettes starring George (J.) Lewis (as Ed Benson) and Dorothy Gulliver (as June Maxwell), the college sweethearts. Photo courtesy of Philip J. Riley.*

I doubt that you ever heard of it, Atkins. It was a big hit in the silent days. I wrote the stories and became the production supervisor. That meant I could cast the serial too. And I did. Remember it to your notes.

When asked about his first childhood memory seeing moving pictures, Junior said the following.

It was in New York. I was five when my nurse Margaret [Kramer] took me to a private showing of my father's first production *Hiawatha* several years after its first release [in 1909].

The films of Charles Chaplin later captivated young Laemmle. He was taken by Chaplin's multi-talented expertise as a filmmaker, producer, director, writer, and musical director. The latter by which Junior understood as "the mood of a picture." Junior said:

Charles "Charlie" Chaplin, as he appeared in The Gold Rush *(United Artists, 1925). Junior Laemmle idolized the talented actor, director, producer and writer. Photo from author's collection.*

My father discovered that Chaplin was too damned expensive. Chaplin knew what he wanted in business and he usually got it. My father was reluctant about talkies for some years. But Chaplin was terrified by the talkies.

Concluding excerpts from the "Biographical Resume of Carl Laemmle Jr." written by publicity director John LeRoy Johnston at Universal City in spring of 1931 follow.

How well Carl Laemmle Jr. succeeded in the task is indicated by the fact that Universal now occupies a position in the world of entertainment such as it has never held before. It has lately produced some of the most successful screenplays in the history of the motion picture industry. ...

For his first work at Universal City, young Laemmle conceived the idea of producing a series of short subjects known as "The Collegians," preparing the stories and supervising their filming. So successful did these prove that he eventually produced four series -- a total of 44 pictures.

Carl Laemmle and Erich Maria Remarque at Carlsbad discussing plans for the film version of All Quiet on the Western Front *(June 1928). Photo courtesy of Zachary Zito.*

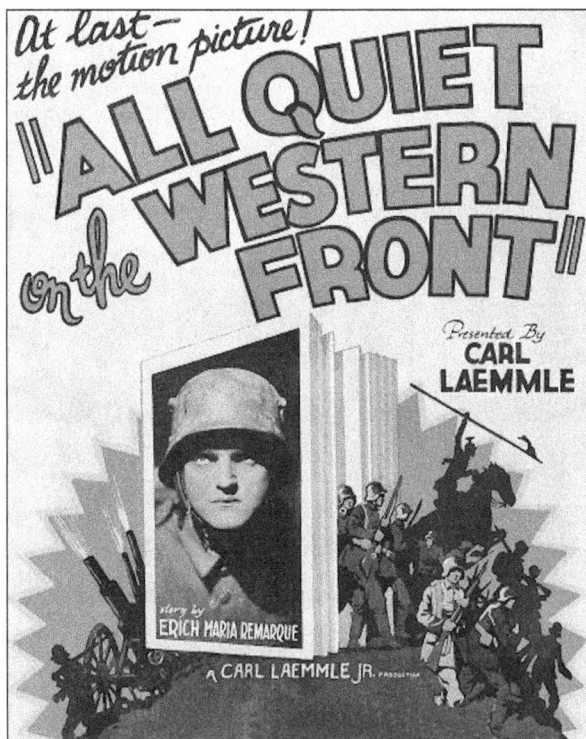

Universal's publicity campaign was huge for All Quiet on the Western Front, *which won Best Picture of 1930. It took two years of preparation at a cost of $1,400,000 for Carl Laemmle Jr. to produce. Photo from the author's collection.*

Universal Pictures reissued All Quiet on the Western Front, *May 15, 1934 in the United States followed by a national and international release of the screen classic. Photo from the author's collection.*

Junior described his tenure to this writer as: "hard work, worry, determination, joy ... and some Laemmle luck." During this period were big challenges to overcome as general manager against the backdrop of a costly transitional period from silent films to talkies. Universal was the last of the Hollywood studios to completely convert to sound pictures. It was the only studio that continued to make silent and sound versions of their films while the other studios did not.

The American film industry as well as American business was encumbered after the Stock Market Crash of 1929, and set off the Great Depression with a rippling effect around the world. It lasted well into the next decade. In the face of adversity, both movie making and stage production became an ultimate juggling act with eagle eyes on the ever-changing box office receipts. This became one of Junior Laemmle's greatest challenges.

In retrospect, movie making during the 1930s proved to be Hollywood's most productive and creative decade. Having been employed through a good part of the decade, most of Junior's pictures were successful. Although he gambled with high stakes in order to make prestige pictures. In the face of more modern adversities, the gamble can be attributed to movie-making today. His first prestigious picture was *All Quiet On the Western Front*. In 1929 Carl Sr., purchased the screen rights from the novelist Erich Maria Remarque in Germany. Junior had previously read the book and was sure that it would make a good film. Lewis Milestone was engaged to direct the picture.

An exceptionally large cast was chosen. *All Quiet on the Western Front* starred Lew Ayres, a young up and coming actor chosen by Junior Laemmle to play one of the soldiers from the German point of view during World War I. For several weeks into production those who doubted its success alluded to the film as "Junior's End," which of course was not accurate.

The picture was eminently successful from both an artistic and a financial angle. This classic depiction of human war drama attracted worldwide attention and became one of Junior's finest achievements winning the Academy Award for Best Picture of 1930. The classic war picture "of all time" was reissued by Uni-

*Junior Laemmle was fascinated by the macabre. One of his early
screen influences at age twelve was The Cabinet of Dr. Caligari (1920),
starring Werner Kraus. Photo from the author's collection.*

versal in 1934, nationally and internationally with a message from
Carl Laemmle with its reissue promotion.

The Academy of Motion Picture Arts and Sciences held the
award ceremonies at the Ambassador Hotel, in Los Angeles, November 5, 1930. Lewis Milestone won (his second of three Academy Awards) for Best Director. Junior said:

> It was Universal's first Best Picture win. It was a proud mo-
> ment for all of us who were involved. My father accepted
> the award. Without him, *All Quiet* as a movie would not
> have been possible. (15)

Carl Laemmle Jr. is best remembered professionally as the trailblazer in a trend of successful horror movies that he produced at
Universal during the early 1930s. Junior said gleefully, "It was my
idea . . . the grand idea." Junior's inspiration was seeded during
his pre-teen years after having seen his first "scary movie," Rob-

Actress Laura LaPlante was a big Universal star and favorite of the Laemmles. The Cat and the Canary was another of Junior's influences because of Paul Leni, the film's director and fantastic film visionary. Photo courtesy of Udo Bayer.

The Last Warning (Universal Pictures, 1929) was Junior Laemmle's
first silent thriller directed by Paul Leni. It was Leni's last film.
Photo courtesy of Udo Bayer.

CARL LAEMMLE PRESENTS

"The CAT CREEPS

WHILE THE CANARY SLEEPS!

with

Helen TWELVETREES
RAYMOND HACKETT · LILYAN TASHMAN
JEAN HERSHOLT · NEIL HAMILTON
MONTAGU LOVE·THEODORE VON ELTZ·LAWRENCE GRANT
ELIZABETH PATTERSON ·BLANCHE FREDERICI

From JOHN WILLARD'S *Great Stage Success*
Directed by RUPERT JULIAN·*Produced by* CARL LAEMMLE,JR.
·A UNIVERSAL PICTURE··

The Cat Creeps *(Universal Pictures, 1930) was Junior's first big attempt with a thriller and sound production. He was obviously disappointed and avoided elaboration with this author about it. Photo from the author's collection.*

ert Wiene's 1919 German production, *The Cabinet of Dr. Caligari.* Junior said:

> I was captivated by all of it. I must have been about eleven years old when I started reading Poe. After that I loved reading as many books as I could get my hands on. I loved the macabre. Leni knew the art of the macabre and I knew that I loved scaring people. (16)

Junior was inspired having worked as a production assistant on *The Cat and the Canary,* the silent thriller from 1927 that was directed by Paul Leni. It starred Laura LaPlante, one of Universal's top movie stars then and a favorite of the Laemmles. Musical scoring after seeing Al Jolson in *The Jazz Singer,* released by Warner Brothers that same year, also influenced Junior. He would later acquire the musical scoring for such future Universal

Dracula (Universal Pictures, 1931). Bela Lugosi starred as Count Dracula. Junior Laemmle chose Tod Browning to direct it. The starring role was intended for Lon Chaney, who passed away several months before. Dracula made Lugosi an overnight sensation. Photo from the author's collection.

productions as *Broadway, King of Jazz, The Invisible Man, Bride of Frankenstein,* and *Show Boat.*

Junior named Paul Leni, James Whale, Edgar G. Ulmer, Charles D. Hall, Charles Stumar, his brother John Stumar, Kurt Neumann, and Jean Renoir among his early European influences. Junior also remembered his director cousins, William Wyler, Robert Wyler, and Nat Ross, in addition to the Canadian-born movie director, Harry Edwards, and director/producer, Henry MacRae, as men who "inspired" him.

Among his American colleagues, Junior said the same for Harry L. Fraser, Ben Holmes, Wesley Ruggles, John M. Stahl, Henry Henigson and Fred S. Meyer. Junior said of Hal Mohr, Arthur Edeson, Merritt B. Gerstad and Karl Freund "[They were] the best cameramen I ever had the pleasure to know."

During the silent days of motion pictures, Universal was known as "The Big U." With the advent of talkies, Junior Laemmle's responsibility was to incorporate sound production. Adventure serials were a big part of the studio's success. Between 1914 and 1936, Universal released ninety-nine adventure serials. Thirty of them, a few with partial sound were released during Junior's tenure.

Soon after Paul Leni's last film, *The Last Warning*, Junior wanted his first thriller *The Cat Creeps*, to star Laura LaPlante. It was to be a talkie remake of the silent 1927 thriller, *The Cat and the Canary*. Junior had hired the director Rupert Julian, who directed Lon Chaney in the 1925 Universal classic, *The Phantom of the Opera*. Junior said:

> Laura LaPlante was doing Showboat at the time and we were running behind schedule, so I hired Helen Twelvetrees instead ... and that's how it all started.

Junior's overzealousness cost him on his first thriller. *The Cat Creeps* ran "impossibly behind schedule." It remains a lost film to this day. Hence, Junior staked his claim on the motion picture properties, *Dracula* and *Frankenstein*, which made overnight stars of the actors, Bela Lugosi and Boris Karloff, respectively. Regarding *Dracula*, Junior said:

> Forget about *The Cat Creeps*, Atkins! It wasn't good enough to me!
>
> After I saw Bela Lugosi play the lead in *Dracula* on stage in New York, we went with him after many other considerations. I wasn't sure if we should be touting the picture a romance or a thriller. We finally decided to hype it as both. I never regretted it. For Dracula, I hired Tod Browning, the director who had worked a lot with Lon Chaney, to direct my next thriller.
>
> I wanted to work with Lon Chaney and Paul Leni, but it never happened. I watched them work separately and admired them both. Unfortunately, they died before I could work with them. (17)

After the success of *Dracula*, a Spanish version had been released. This began in 1930 for Universal's transition to sound and

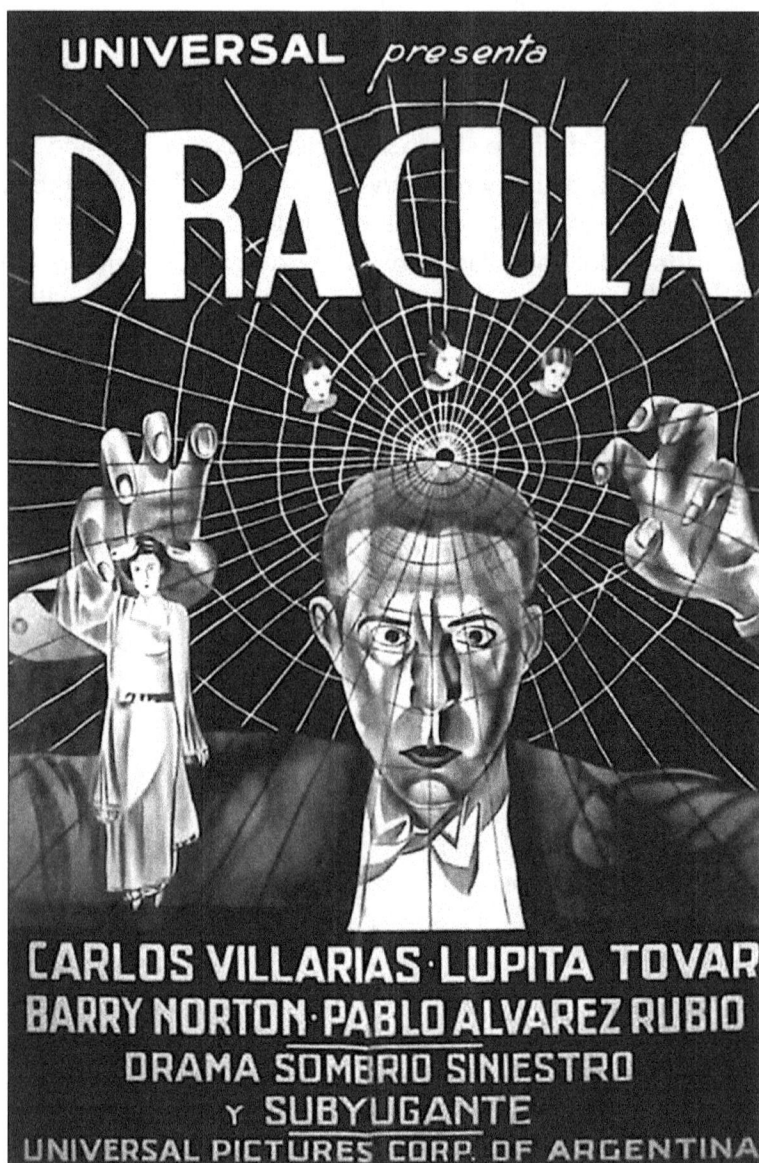

Drácula (Spanish version) (Universal Pictures, 1931). Filmed simultaneous to the Bela Lugosi version at Universal with the same sets, a different cast, director and cameraman; Produced by Carl Laemmle Jr. and Paul Kohner (as associate producer); Carlos Villarias starred as Count Dracula. Spanish versions of Universal Pictures were not uncommon then. This cinematic gem was hidden away for years before it was rediscovered and restored. Photo from the author's collection.

Ernst Laemmle (director) and Paul Kohner pictured here in 1929 returning from Germany. Photo courtesy of Udo Bayer.

was popular with movie audiences in Mexico and the USA. Without the usual dubbing technique, the Spanish version of *Dracula* (*Drácula*) was remade entirely with other actors using the exact Universal sets as the English version. *The Cat Creeps* (*La Voluntad del Muerto*) was another example. At this time, twenty-two-year-old Carl Laemmle Jr., was head of the studio. There was another up-and-coming producer at Universal. He had some history of his own. His name was Paul Kohner. (18)

Twenty-eight-year-old Paul Kohner, with ten years of dues paying at the corporation started as an office boy in New York in

Mary Philbin stars with Conrad Veidt in The Man Who Laughs *(Universal Pictures, 1928). In this publicity photo, Miss Philbin with producer Carl Laemmle, the film's production supervisor Paul Kohner (far left second row) and director Paul Leni (above Laemmle) surrounded by supporting painted players. Photo from the author's collection.*

1920. Irving Thalberg was then general manager at Universal. During this period, Kohner sold Carl Laemmle on his own publicity ideas, promotion and distribution work which introduced the Universal Pictures Foreign Division.

Subsequently, Kohner was placed in charge of the European offices of Universal Pictures in Berlin. During the mid-1920s, Kohner was a casting director at Universal City responsible for introducing the ingénue Barbara Kent, who had recently been named "Miss Hollywood," in a beauty contest at Santa Cruz and was placed under contract with the studio.

In 1927, twenty-five-year-old Kohner was supervising Universal productions such as *The Cat and the Canary* and *The Man Who Laughs,* both directed by Paul Leni, and to the envy of nineteen-year-old Junior Laemmle before he was at the helm as general man-

The Man Who Laughs (*Universal Pictures, 1928*). *Photo courtesy of Udo Bayer.*

Lupita Tovar Kohner was born July 27, 1910. She appeared in the 1931 Spanish version of Drácula. She was longtime friends with the Laemmle family and the wife of the late Paul Kohner. Her memoir was published in 2011. Photo from the author's collection.

East of Borneo *(Universal Pictures, 1931); Junior Laemmle produced this action adventure starring Charles Bickford, Lupita Tovar and Rose Hobart, two of Universal's newest finds. Photo from the author's collection.*

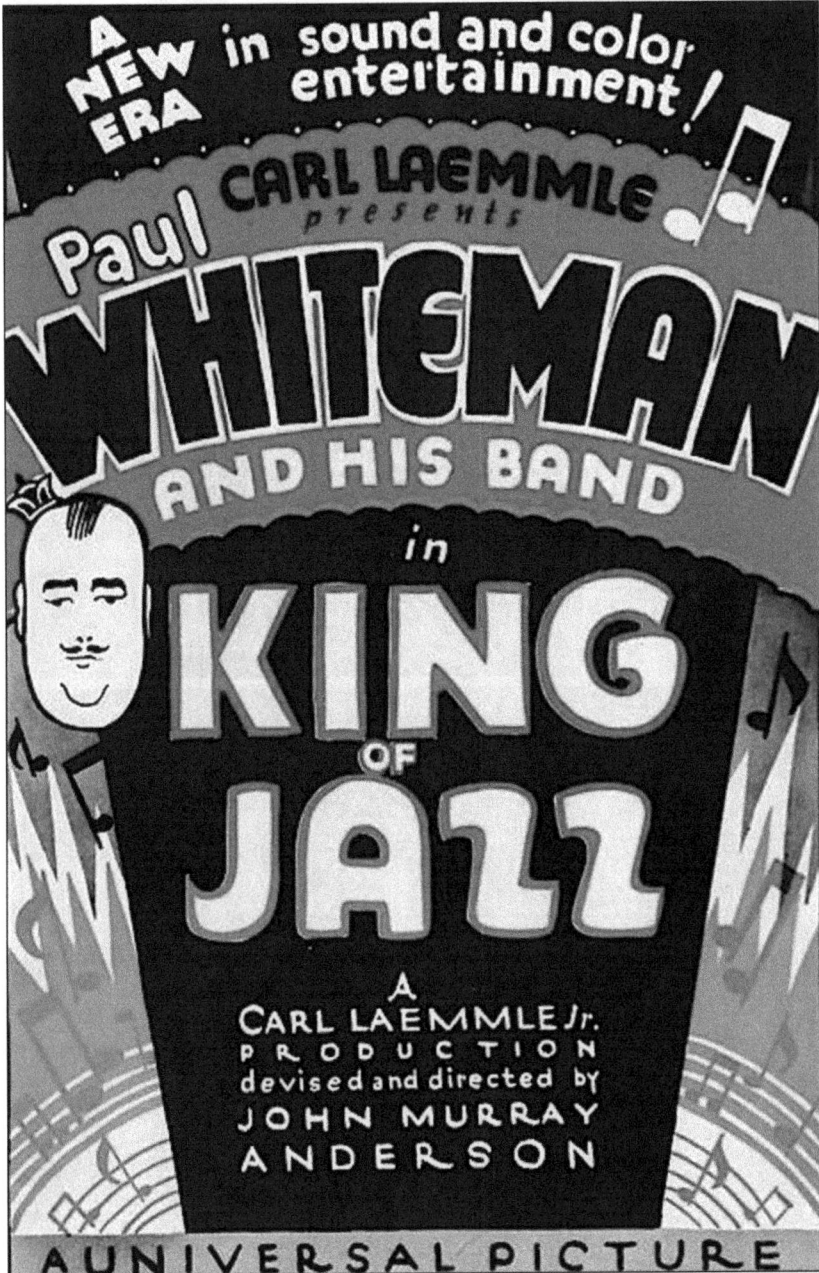

King of Jazz (*Universal Pictures, 1930*) was Paul Whiteman's shining time. It was also the first motion picture to introduce crooner Bing Crosby. Photo courtesy of Neil Lipes.

Paul Whiteman and Carl Laemmle Jr. in a welcoming embrace at Universal City, 1929. Photo courtesy of Zachary Zito.

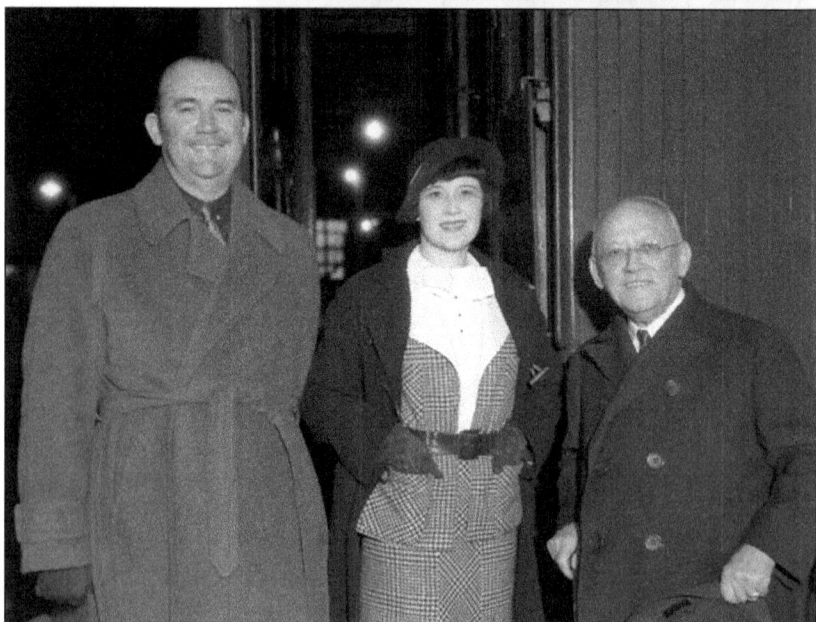

Carl Laemmle with Paul Whiteman and his actress wife Margaret Livingston (1931 photo). Mr. Whiteman, the famed American composer, bandleader, orchestral director and violinist previously starred in King of Jazz *(Universal Pictures, 1930). Photo courtesy of Neil Lipes.*

Beth Laemmle (later known as Carla Laemmle) with the Russell Markert dancers from the Melting Pot sequence in King of Jazz (Universal Pictures, 1930). Two years later, Mr. Markert founded the Rockettes of Radio City Music Hall where he remained their longtime choreographer. Photo courtesy of Zachary Zito.

ager of Universal. Paul Kohner produced the Spanish versions of *The Cat Creeps* and *Dracula*. Lupita Tovar, a Mexican-Irish actress was Kohner's choice for roles in both versions. She also appeared in Universal's *East of Borneo* in 1931. Miss Tovar and Paul Kohner were married in 1932. (19)

Junior Laemmle's niece, Carole Laemmle Bergerman, told this writer that her uncle's envy towards Paul Kohner was true in the beginning. Miss Bergerman said the following.

> My uncle [Junior] told me that he believed my grand-father [Carl Laemmle] would name Paul Kohner the general manager of Universal instead of him, which made him jealous. With years gone by, my uncle said that was one thing he later regretted the most, being selfish and his disappointment with ever producing the English ver-

Little Accident *(Universal Pictures, 1930) was a light-hearted comedy starring Douglas Fairbanks, Jr. and Anita Page that never made it very far. Photo from the author's collection.*

sion of "that cat picture [*The Cat Creeps*]." According to my uncle, my grandfather was concerned about this "scary movie" business. And with that concern, my uncle produced the first all-sound and color musical *King of Jazz* with Paul Whiteman.

My cousin, Carla Laemmle [then known as "Beth Laemmle], was in it showcasing her amazing dancing. I was months

Frankenstein (Universal Pictures, 1931) Directed by James
Whale, produced by Carl Laemmle Jr. and starring Boris Karloff
in his towering immortal character brought another classic
movie monster to life. Photo from the author's collection.

George J. Lewis (1903-1995) was a Mexican-born actor, who became popular with film audiences as Ed Benson between 1926 and 1929 in forty-four episodes of Carl Laemmle, Jr's The Collegians. Junior wanted his lead character to resemble himself. Photo from the author's collection.

Jane Wyatt (1910-2006) got her start at Universal. She and Junior Laemmle remained long-time friends. Jane Wyatt had been to visit Junior Laemmle at his home the day before this author arrived. Photo from the author's collection.

Cesar Romero (1907-1994) was among those who were given opportunity at Universal City. He attended most of the parties given by the Laemmles over the years according to Carole Laemmle Bergerman. Photo from the author's collection.

Rose Hobart (1906-2000) was a stage actress, who signed a contract with Universal Pictures made a blunder by also signing with another studio. She later told this author regarding the majority of actors and execs, "We were all so young and did not know what we were doing. As a result of my temperament with Junior regarding the Universal contract, which I was later held under became a professional thorn in my side, but I weathered through it until it finally terminated." Photo from the author's collection.

Lew Ayres (1908-1996) got his start at Paramount, but soon became a star at Universal after Junior Laemmle cast him in All Quiet on the Western Front *in 1930. According to Junior's niece, Carole Bergerman, Ayres was a frequent visitor during Junior's last years. Photo from the author's collection.*

Genevieve Tobin (1899-1995) Actress of several early Universal films that include, A Lady Surrenders. She remained friends with Carl Laemmle Jr. He cherished one of her artworks especially made for Junior that adorned his bedroom at his Beverly Hills home. Photo from the author's collection.

Waterloo Bridge *(Universal, 1931) starring Douglass Montgomery, Mae Clarke, Bette Davis and E.E. Clive. This was director James Whale's first film for the Laemmles. It was Bette Davis' third film before leaving Universal. Photo from the author's collection.*

from being born, so they've told me. I have seen the film. Carla is amazing! The movie wasn't as successful as they hoped. But it didn't stop my uncle from making other frightful movies, which ended up becoming his trademark.

Before his inception as general manager at Universal, Junior Laemmle wrote the following letter dated February 2, 1929:

Dear Papa,

Soon I will be twenty-one. Mere words lack the power of expression in allowing me to explain how much I appreciate your marvelous guidance in molding me from boy to man . . .

My greatest ambition and aim in this world is to make your task easier by giving forth my life to further and carry on the monument, which you have built through a life's work.

Early publicity photo of Bette Davis. Photo from the author's collection.

Therefore, I pledge myself to follow your slogan "It Can Be Done." As the years roll on my wish is that people say there is a semblance of Carl Sr. in Carl Jr. in honor, ethics and ability. Your grateful and Loving Son, Junior.

After the success of *King of Jazz*, Junior Laemmle had already produced a variety of motion pictures and further embarked on producing a number of romantic comedies, which included *Little Accident*, a Douglas Fairbanks Jr. vehicle with Anita Page, which left little success at the box office. Junior Laemmle was eager to

Actor Slim Summerville (1930s). Photo from the author's collection.

release his next project. *Frankenstein* would be released in December 1931 and he would soon find his niche.

Junior had originally hired Robert Florey to write the script and direct the movie based on the classic novel by Mary Wollstonecraft Shelley. Bela Lugosi was originally cast to play the Monster, but after a test, was made with the actor in the Monster makeup, Junior said:

> Florey came to me as a good scriptwriter. But hiring him as the director was a mistake. Then after I saw Lugosi in the Monster makeup, I laughed like a hyena! I wasn't happy with any of it and I fired Florey, dismissed Lugosi, and cancelled the project for a while. We got some other fellow [Garrett Fort] to finish the script. I chose James Whale, who had directed a previous drama of ours, Waterloo Bridge, to direct Frankenstein. I made the right choice. Whale's genius brought that picture together and made it a box office success.

When asked who chose Boris Karloff for the role of the Monster, Junior said:

> Whale did ... and I agreed... along with anyone else in the studio commissary that he [Karloff] was the right one.

Junior reassigned Robert Florey to write and direct a vehicle for Bela Lugosi, *Murders in the Rue Morgue*. Junior said,

> Florey wasn't happy, so I gave him a picture that starred Lugosi and Sidney Fox. Florey accepted it, but wanted more. We couldn't afford him.

Junior Laemmle is credited with giving the following performers opportunity at Universal City: ("The Collegians" stars) Dorothy Gulliver, George J. Lewis and Hayden Stevenson. They were followed by Beth Laemmle (later known as Carla Laemmle), Lew Ayres, Cesar Romero, Edward G. Robinson, Sue Carol, Mae Clarke, Richard Cromwell, John Boles, Jane Wyatt, Sidney Fox, Leon Waycoff (later known as Leon Ames); Arlene Francis, Genevieve Tobin, Noah Berry, Jr., Joan Bennett, Walter Brennan, Andy Devine, Mary Carlisle, Rose Hobart, Gloria Stuart, Raymond Massey, June Clayworth, Binnie Barnes, Zita Johann, Lupe Velez, Margaret Sullavan, Margaret Lindsay, and Constance Cummings.

Law and Order *(Universal Pictures, 1932) Junior Laemmle also tried his hand at westerns with some of his father's old favorites. However, he became more absorbed in horror movie projects. Photo from the author's collection.*

Murders in the Rue Morgue (Universal Pictures, 1932) was a full-fledged story of the macabre, which successfully kept Junior Laemmle and Universal on top of the genre. Photo from the author's collection.

As part of his job, Junior Laemmle traveled the United States and Europe. He enjoyed his excursions to New York City, which he considered his home. He attended as many Broadway and Off-Broadway plays as he possibly could in search of creative talent.

Another noteworthy performer was given opportunity at Universal during the early 1930s. Her name was Bette Davis. Junior Laemmle admitted to the now classic remark, "She has about as much sex appeal as Slim Summerville," that he made about Davis after seeing her in the final cut of the 1931 production, *Waterloo Bridge*.

Loaning performers to other studios was commonplace among the Hollywood production chiefs. Amidst the hustle and bustle of shopping, a then-unknown Bette Davis, her option with Universal was eventually dropped. Regarding the actress who later became one of America's finest, a two-time Oscar winning actress and ten-time nominee. Junior said:

> Once we dropped her option that was the end of her at Universal. My cousin, Willy [Wyler], later made Davis a star elsewhere. I never regretted saying what I did about her. We didn't know what to do with her.

In maintaining old Universal standards, Junior Laemmle produced a variety of motion pictures including westerns, his father's favorites. He teamed Bela Lugosi and Boris Karloff in their first movie together, *The Black Cat* (1934), under the direction of Edgar G. Ulmer. Junior said:

> It was my idea to cast them in the same picture. Both proved to be successful separately, so why not team them.
>
> Ulmer became a part of our family in a haphazard way. I liked him. We understood each other and worked together. That is how we were able to make the picture. This is how it is supposed to work. Besides *Murders in the Rue Morgue*, I produced *The Old Dark House, The Mummy* [all released in 1932], *The Invisible Man* [1933], *The Man Who Reclaimed His Head, The Black Cat* [both in 1934], *Bride of Frankenstein, Mystery of Edwin Drood,* and *The Raven* [all in 1935].

The last four Universal horror movies, which fell under the "Carl Laemmle Presents" title was *The Raven, Werewolf of Lon-*

Junior Laemmle boosted the budding career of newcomer June Clyde by producing Radio Patrol starring Robert Armstrong (Universal Pictures, 1932). Photo courtesy of Neil Lipes.

The Old Dark House – *Junior Laemmle and James Whale cast this odd picture that was lost for years, rediscovered and commands cult status to this day. Photo from the author's collection.*

The Man Who Reclaimed His Head (*Universal Pictures, 1932) starred Claude Rains, Joan Bennett (later of television's Dark Shadows fame), and Lionel Atwill. Photo from the author's collection.*

The Mummy *(Universal Pictures, 1932)* Junior Laemmle assigned his *(uncredited) brother-in-law Stanley Bergerman, associate producer on this film. Photo from the author's collection.*

The Black Cat *(Universal Pictures, 1934). Junior Laemmle relied on director Edgar G. Ulmer to make this film about death come to life. It is now among the horror classics. Photo from the author's collection.*

Mystery of Edwin Drood *(Universal Pictures, 1935). Junior Laemmle hired Stuart Walker a Dickens enthusiast, who previously and successfully directed* Great Expectations *bringing this unfinished Dickens novel to life. The cast included David Manners (as Edwin Drood), Claude Rains, Douglass Montgomery, Valerie Hobson, and Heather Angel. Photo courtesy of Philip J. Riley.*

don [both in 1935], *The Invisible Ray* and *Dracula's Daughter* [both in 1936]. Junior said the following.

> We hired all the right people for that one [*The Raven*] and it made a good picture. My brother-in-law [Stanley Bergerman] was associate producer on *Werewolf.* I had something to do with it too, Atkins ... But I had nothing to do with the last two pictures [*The Invisible Ray* or *Dracula's Daughter*].

Universal's 1936 -1937 seasons were advertised in the trades as "The New Power in Your Box Office!" Junior's costly features became part of the new company with *Show Boat* being the most successful. The opening banner credits in *Show Boat* gave a celebratory screen credit to its producer and director in what became the last collaboration between James Whale and the Laemmles at "Old Universal."

Werewolf of London (Universal Pictures, 1935) Junior had a hand in with his brother-in-law Stanley Bergerman, who was credited as associate producer. Photo from the author's collection.

The Raven *(Universal Pictures, 1935). This was the last major casting that Junior Laemmle worked on without being credited as a producer although it was advertised a Carl Laemmle presentation. Photo courtesy of Ian Wolfe.*

Junior Laemmle had other prospects in mind once the transfer was made at Universal. In June 1936 there was a distribution deal considered by United Artists for which Junior would produce pictures independently along with James Whale opting to direct one. The consideration held through October 1936 upon the Laemmles' return to America, but no deal was ever finalized. Father and son Laemmle had already set sail in July 1936 for Europe for about three months.

During the interim, news swept across the country reporting the death of Irving Thalberg, who passed away September 14, 1936 from lobular pneumonia and complications of a cardiac condition at his Santa Monica, California home.

With Carl Laemmle and Junior away in Europe, back at home in Beverly Hills, Rosabelle Laemmle Bergerman's grief remained reclusive. Irving Thalberg was thirty-seven. His wife, actress Norma

The Invisible Ray (Universal Pictures, 1936). This was the first and only science-fiction film starring Bela Lugosi and Boris Karloff at Universal. Junior was not involved with this picture although it was a Laemmle property. Photo from the author's collection.

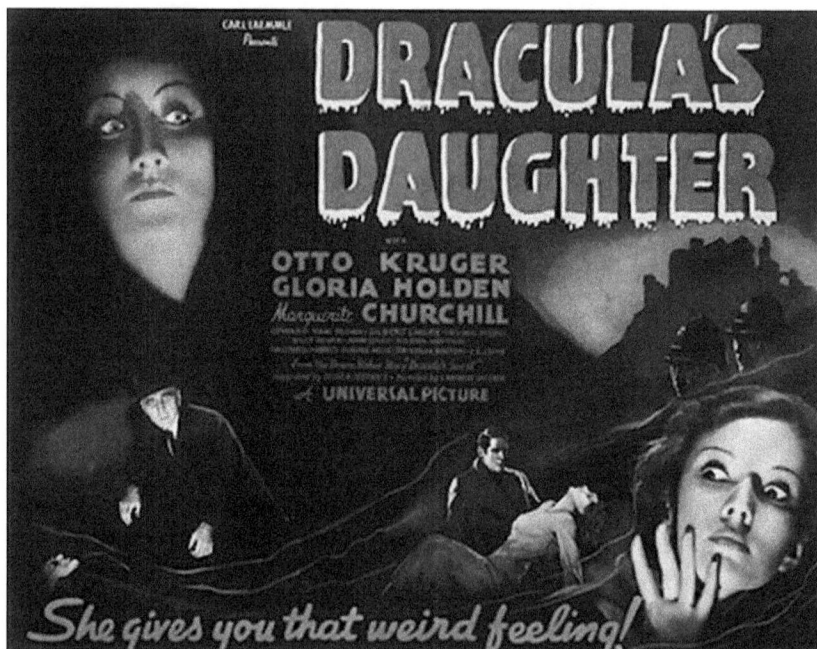

Dracula's Daughter *(Universal Pictures, 1936) was the last of the horror-fantasy films given the "Carl Laemmle presents" prestige. Photo from the author's collection.*

Shearer, and their two young children Irving Thalberg, Jr. (age 6) and Katherine (age 1) survived him.

It was reported on September 29, 1936 from Paris to America via *Variety* that the Laemmles were pessimistic about color movies, predicting "no sensational future." Junior Laemmle's new movie production business was planned to take place at the Pathé movie lot.

Junior purchased the screen rights to *Soul of a Thousand Faces*, an anti-war story by Friges Karinthy and a yarn by George Frazier known as *Nine Officers* that he wanted to produce as a Broadway play. He also bought the rights to the Barré Lyndon play, *The Amazing Dr. Clitterhouse* and sold them to Warner Brothers. Among his other considerations for either stage or motion picture production was: *The Bridge of San Luis Rey, The Cobra Strikes, Yogi, The Captain's Lamp, Wind in the Sails, 17 Days in August, Command Decision, The Apple of His Eye, Song of Niagara,*

The Road Back (Universal Pictures, 1937) was the sequel to All Quiet on the Western Front. Directed by James Whale, and without the Laemmles. Much to Whale's disgust and disinterest with film editors and execs, the film became financial failure. Photo from the author's collection.

and *Unfinished Symphony*. None of these prospects ever came to fruition under Junior's supervision.

Director James Whale stayed on at Universal after his contract was renewed with the new studio management. Following *Show Boat*, he directed *The Road Back*, an Edmund Grainger production based on another Erich Maria Remarque novel. It was a follow-up to the author's classic novel, *All Quiet on the Western Front*. The original cut of *The Road Back* became filled with editing issues. For whatever the reasons, the director did not comply with corrective measures. Thus, Hollywood executives and film editors altered *The Road Back*. Released in June 1937, it became a critical and commercial failure. (20)

Thus, Carl Laemmle Jr and James Whale's final motion picture remained Universal's *Show Boat* released in 1936. Both men had shared a five-year collaboration in ten previous Universal Pictures. Their last screen credits were featured at the beginning of *Show Boat* in celebratory fashion, perhaps with a hint of melancholy. Junior Laemmle remembered his friend and former colleague, James Whale, this way.

Whale was the biggest influence of my professional career. We were friends until the end. I had six palm trees planted in Israel in his honor. (21)

After Junior left Universal, he signed a contract with Louis B. Mayer in 1937 to produce films at Metro-Goldwyn-Mayer. Within a year, Junior asked to be released from the contract. Junior later bought his contract back for twenty-five hundred dollars. While he was at MGM, Junior was briefly reunited with his friend and former associate James Whale. They worked together on the motion picture *Port of Seven Seas*. Junior left while the film was in post-production. When the picture was released in 1938, Junior Laemmle received no screen credit. Regarding his leaving Universal, Junior said the following.

After seven years [as general manager] at Universal, I just wanted out. I actually put in eleven years. And when I got over to MGM, [Preston] Sturges and [Louis B.] Mayer and some other execs, it became too demanding after Thalberg

Public gathering for the funeral service of Carl Laemmle at the B'nai B'rith Temple (later renamed the Wilshire Temple), Los Angeles, California, September 25, 1939. Photo courtesy of Udo Bayer.

died. My father knew him [Thalberg] better than I, but [I noticed] so many changes taking place around me. What I wanted to do was produce motion pictures and plays independently. It never happened. (22)

In July 1939, Rosabelle Laemmle Bergerman relocated her brother, Junior and their ailing father, Carl Laemmle, from the

Inside the Wilshire Temple. Carl Laemmle donated the chandeliers seen here. Photo courtesy of Udo Bayer.

Beverly Hills mansion located at 1051 Benedict Canyon Drive to a one level six-room home located at 1275 Benedict Canyon Drive. This is where Mr. Laemmle passed away Sunday morning September 24, 1939.

Carl Laemmle Jr. and actress Dixie Dunbar in 1938. The two had been dating for about a year before they went their separate ways. Photo from the author's collection.

Carl Laemmle's family, Rosabelle Bergerman (age 38); son, Junior (age 31); son-in-law, Stanley Bergerman; and the two grandchildren, Carole Laemmle Bergerman (age 9); Stanley Bergerman Jr. (age 7); and his two physicians were at his bedside. Survivors included two brothers, Louis Laemmle and Siegfried Laemmle; sister-in-law, Anna Stern Fleckles; brother-in-law, Maurice Fleckles; numerous nieces and nephews and cousins. Mr. Laemmle's body lay in state at the B'nai B'rith Temple on Wilshire Boulevard for two hours before his funeral service began at 12:30 pm Monday, September 25, 1939. Carl Laemmle lived seventy-two years, eight months and one week.

More than two thousand men and women attended Mr. Laemmle's funeral while hundreds of curious onlookers lined the streets outside. The service was officiated by Rabbi Edgar F. Magnin, who delivered the eulogy calling Carl Laemmle, "a little man who was a big man … mourned all over the world." Magnin continue to say:

What makes his life important is not the money he made or the power he wielded –it's what he did with the money and the power. ...Many are mourned after their deaths but few are loved while they are alive.

"Uncle Carl" was kind and sweet –there was nothing of the snob – of arrogance – about him.

He was simple and plain and never forgot he was once a poor boy. He gave generously of his purse and of his heart. He was a fine American. He made American pictures – not only to entertain but also to uplift – one of the men who built the industry to what it is today.

Carl Laemmle was twenty-two when he became a naturalized United States citizen, June 28, 1889. The devoted husband of nearly twenty-one years, loving father and grandfather, who honored and cherished his family, never remarried. He wanted most to be remembered as an American.

Carl Laemmle's body was placed in a vault at Home of Peace Cemetery in Los Angeles, pending the decision of the family on interment in Los Angeles or New York where Mrs. Laemmle was buried. Mr. Laemmle was the first family member to be interred in the Laemmle Family Room at Home of Peace, September 26, 1939 at 12:30 pm.

Carl Laemmle named Rabbi Magnin, the third executor of his estate. Rosabelle and Junior were the other two. Junior once wrote regarding his relationship with the leading Rabbi in Los Angeles:

Magnin has been simply wonderful to me during my illness. I sent him a gift the other day in appreciation and he said that he liked the card that I wrote better than the gift.

I wrote on the card, 'Dear Edgar, thanks for being a second father to me. Love and thanks, Junior.' I told the Rabbi that I had a feeling that my father might have known this. (23)

From his Last Will and Testament, Carl Laemmle left the following "last wish" to his children:

It is my most cherished desire that after my death, the relations between my son and daughter shall be completely harmonious and affectionate, both for sentimental reasons

Evelyn Moriarty during her "Earl Carroll Girl" days (1941 photo). Photo courtesy of Evelyn Moriarty.

Rear side of Dias Dorados. Laemmle's mansion appears to have its own pond when in fact it was a swimming pool. The entire property was razed in the late 1940s. Photo from the author's collection.

and for the practical reason that their financial affairs and property interests will be so bound together that difficulties or misunderstandings between them may react upon them adversely in a purely material way.

Therefore, as my last wish, I enjoin upon my son and my daughter the duty of maintaining towards each other a kindly, sympathetic and understanding attitude so that from time to time as differences of opinion may develop each will have an open mind and for the material welfare of both as well as out of respect to my wishes, mutual concessions will be made and serious differences of opinion and quarrels will be avoided.

In the fall of 1940, Junior remained living in the six-room house at 1275 Benedict Canyon Drive until the 1950s. He also had living quarters in the mansion where his sister and brother-in-law were living since their 1929 marriage. Both Bergerman children, Carole and Stan Jr. were born there. Junior Laemmle was spending more time at the mansion working with his sister and brother-in-

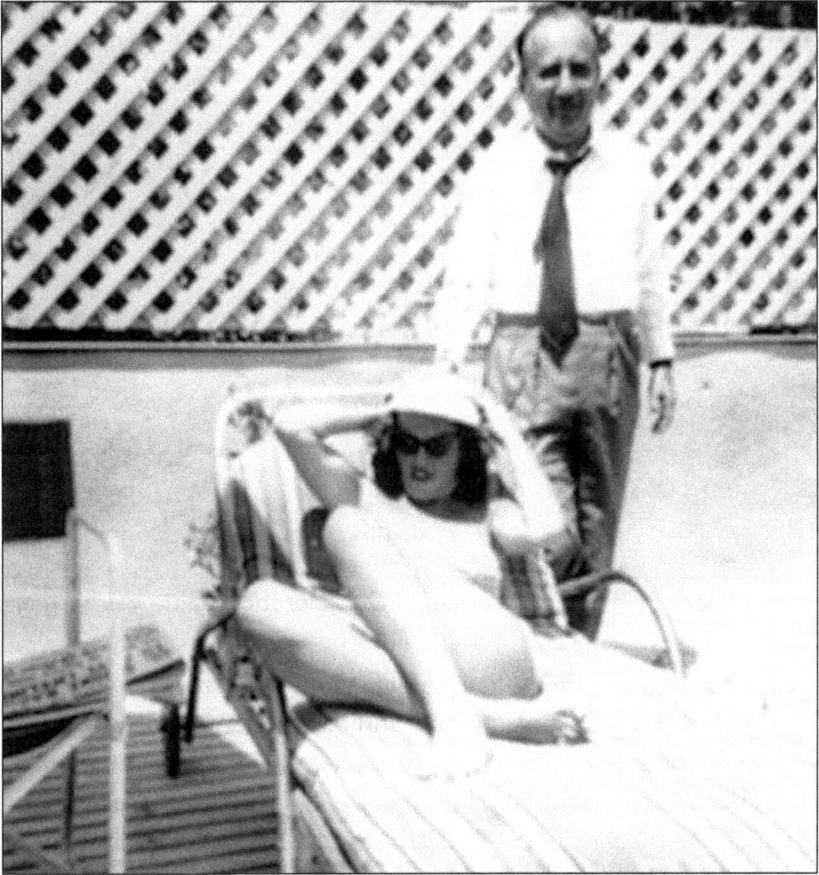

Evelyn Moriarty and Junior Laemmle in more happy times. She loved swimming. Junior had the lattice fence installed for her privacy. Photo courtesy of Evelyn Moriarty.

law on personal matters. His own personal matters were on hold to some degree. After a short romance with actress Dixie Dunbar, Junior would soon meet his best friend.

This exceptional beauty turned many heads. She started out as a part-time model and later became an Earl Carroll Girl. She was a stand-in for Marilyn Monroe on Monroe's last three pictures (then as a stand-in for Ann Margret, Barbara Eden). She was also a movie extra with Paramount Pictures for many years. Her name was Evelyn Moriarty. (24)

In 1997, Evelyn Moriarty told this writer how she and Junior Laemmle met.

Junior Laemmle enjoying the pool at Dias Dorados. Photo courtesy of Evelyn Moriarty.

A gentleman, who was a talent agent and Junior were at the club [Earl Carroll's] when Junior spotted me. It was all very innocent.

There was a respectability that went with Earl Carroll girls much like the girls of George White and Flo Ziegfeld. All three showmen were well respected for their efforts. The Earl Carroll "Vanities" shows were classy and tasteful. The girls were showcased in costumed glamour unlike what you see today. In those days, Burlesque was good entertainment. Nowadays the term is frowned upon. There is no Burlesque today.

Anyhow, Junior and I were formally introduced elsewhere, a few nights later at The Trocadero on Sunset Boulevard. The next day the talent agent had to go through Earl Carroll and escorted me to a big big house. And there coming down this huge staircase was Junior with that big smile. Little did I know that this was where he lived! I remember asking him when he got off work. Junior laughed. He thought that was funny. Well! I had never seen such a big house. I learned later that they called it "The Big House."

Carla Laemmle as she appeared during the time she and Evelyn Moriarty met December 31, 1940. Photo courtesy of Carla Laemmle.

I also learned that Junior had worked for his father at Universal Pictures for many years. His father, as you know founded the studio many years before. Carl Laemmle was deceased by the time Junior and I met. The studio had been sold and Junior was no longer making motion pictures.

I was a young girl and underage. My age was always being protected. Thank God for George White and Earl Carroll. They protected me and Junior later did too. Junior was very

(left) Carla Laemmle, Evelyn Moriarty and the author October 21, 1997, North Hollywood, California. Photo from the author's collection.

good to me and I was very good to him. He loved sports. His two favorite sports figures were also friends of his, Jack Dempsey and Babe Ruth.

Junior was not a smoker or a drinker. I remember he once drank a bottle of scotch to prove to me that he could drink but never drank after that. The bottle was later found under his bed after the incident and after the hangover. Aside from that he did not drink alcohol. He learned that he had an allergy to flowers. Poor Junior.

He would still occasionally send himself flowers. In the earlier days, he loved to take me shopping. Anything I touched was mine. He loved going out. I loved swimming in that humongous pool at the Big House. Sometimes, he joined me. I have pictures that I'll let you copy.

We enjoyed dinner out many Saturday nights. If he didn't pay by check, I would get the change. He didn't want to handle money, which he thought was dirty. I thought he was a poor little rich boy.

Evelyn remained in Junior Laemmle's life for a total of thirty-nine years. However, she told this writer:

Flash Gordon (Universal Pictures 1936) when Carl Laemmle first owned the rights to the comic strip. Photo from the author's collection.

I'll say thirty-eight years because Junior was disappointed after I got married. He asked me if he was lying in the street alongside my husband, and you had to help only one, which one would I help off the street? At first, I thought it was trick question and when I couldn't answer him, he didn't talk to me for a year. Under personal circumstances beyond Junior's control, my marriage was annulled.

Junior was known for hosting top-notch parties. The last party given in the mansion was a New Year's Eve party that Junior hosted in a gathering of over seventy people ringing in 1941. Among the guests were Evelyn Moriarty and Carla Laemmle, first known as Beth Laemmle, dancer and actress at Universal during the 1920s and 30s and first cousin to Junior. After being introduced that evening, Carla and Evelyn remained friends for over sixty-five years. (25)

On July 19, 1941 Rosabelle Laemmle Bergerman and her brother, Junior, made arrangements for the remains of their mother, Recha Laemmle, to be removed from a grave at Salem Fields Cemetery in Brooklyn, New York. Her body was relocated to Home of Peace Mausoleum in California where she was re-interred Wednesday July 23, 1941 in the Laemmle Family Room to rest near her husband.

Also in 1941, Junior's brother-in-law Stanley Bergerman established himself as both a literary and talent agent. He became successful at it representing artists in the entertainment field. Among his clients were Rudy Vallee and Alan Ladd.

On February 21, 1942, Junior Laemmle enlisted in the Army at Fort Macarthur, San Pedro California. He was stationed at Camp Davis, North Carolina where he served as a Private in the Army Signal Corps.

Former Olympian and actor Larry "Buster" Crabbe, who was best known for his film role as *Flash Gordon*, the Universal serial of the late 1930s and early 1940s knew Junior Laemmle. In the fall of 1979, Buster Crabbe told this writer the following:

Henry MacRae was a producer, director and writer who had a knack for producing successful serials, both silent and talkies at Old Universal. He was long associated with Carl Laemmle and Universal City Studios.

In 1935, I learned that Henry MacRae was hired to produce *Flash Gordon*. It was MacRae who hired me to star as *Flash Gordon* after I paid an impromptu visit to the set at Old Universal. I followed the newspaper comic strip and was interested to see the actors being tested for the part. After three serials, a total of forty episodes and two feature length movies that were actually compilations from the first two serials, *Flash Gordon* ended filming in early 1940.

It still amazes me how the serial remains popular today with the newer audiences. My personal favorite of the three *Flash Gordon* serials was the first one. It was the first time a full-fledged science-fiction serial was ever filmed and it was hard work.

This is what you will find interesting, young man. A couple of years after *Flash Gordon* ended, I found myself making training movies during WWII, and here was Junior Laemmle with the Signal Corps working with a motion picture unit at the helm of these pictures for the Army.

That is how we became acquainted.

Junior was one hell of a nice guy. We liked talking politics because we shared mutual interests. Junior's father did some great things during his life. He was also a meticulous man who stayed organized. Obviously, Junior followed suit.

I learned a great deal from Junior about staying organized, which helped me later with my personal clerical skills. During this period, Junior told me that it was he who bought the film rights to Flash Gordon from Alex Raymond's newspaper comic strip under the auspices of his father.

Unfortunately, the Laemmles left Universal before the first serial was completed and released to theaters. We have the Laemmles to thank for the film serial *Flash Gordon*.

Some time ago, I learned through a mutual friend that Junior was not well. I did go up to see him not long before you did. We had a good visit, but it was sad to see him incapacitated.

(left) Carol Laemmle Bergerman, Rosabelle Bergerman, (cousin) Arthur Alexander and his bride Muriel, and Junior Laemmle upon the couple's wedding reception in June 1945. Photo courtesy of Burt Alexander.

I think about Junior Laemmle especially after visiting him. We were about the same age. I got to know him only during the army training films in the early 1940s after which our lives took opposite directions.

While I visited with Junior, he realized his accomplishments as an Academy Award winning producer that followed with his cutting edge horror films at Old Universal.

I believe that any of us red-blooded people have considered the thought of what they as human beings can contribute to mankind before leaving this planet. If my work has brought anybody the slightest bit of entertainment, a smile, a laugh, a tear or two then, I accept this as my contribution. I wish there were more I could say. (26)

Junior and Rosabelle agreed to sell the Laemmle estate and the thirty-five acre property known as "Dias Dorados" while Junior was in the service. By the late 1940s, the building was torn down and the property was later subdivided.

In the spring of 1943, Junior began taking leaves from the service to New York. They no longer occupied the family's West End Avenue apartment house. The Savoy Hotel had a room for Junior but he chose The Plaza Hotel to stay. While in New York, Junior met several times for lunch with his old friend, Paul Fejos, who was living in the city. Junior expressed unhappiness to his friend regarding his stay in the service saying that it was making him ill and talked of plans that when the war ended they could work together again. The former movie director insisted that he was through with motion pictures. Fejos later paid his friend a visit in California. (27)

Carl Laemmle Jr. received an Honorable Discharge from the service April 8, 1944. Subsequently, his sister and brother-in-law met with him in New York, May 1944. Junior returned to his Beverly Hills home at 1275 Benedict Canyon Drive in June 1944. Throughout this chapter in various stages of his life, Junior is seen in photographs, namely a rare 1945 photograph with family at the wedding reception of Arthur Alexander, a cousin related through the Stern family.

In the early 1950s, Junior was approached for financial backing on a forthcoming television series. The deal was never solidified. The television series debuted October 3, 1954 becoming the widely popular *Father Knows Best*. The weekly series starred Robert Young and Jane Wyatt (a longtime friend of Junior's). By this time, Junior no longer considered any future investments regarding the entertainment business. (28)

On the evening of April 28, 1958, some two hundred-fifty people gathered for a party at the Beverly Hills Club on Roxbury Drive to celebrate Junior's fiftieth birthday. The evening was filled with "Junior stories" with the loudest laughter coming from Junior himself. Rosabelle and Stanley Bergerman organized it. Subsequently, Junior was feeling quite well during this point in his life. He was attempted to make a comeback as a motion picture producer. Within the next six months his ambitions had taken a sudden turn.

Previously, Junior had sold his home at 1275 Benedict Canyon Drive and rented a home owned by George Cukor on Cordell Drive in Hollywood. Junior's niece, Carole Bergerman, told this writer about an occurrence in September 1958.

I heard from my uncle early that Saturday. Junior said that he would be busy most of the day. He told me that he and his driver would take me to dinner. It was the week of my birthday. He told Elise that she wouldn't have to prepare dinner and gave her the night off. He asked me that day to phone him later. I did and got no answer. He was always punctual. I phoned again a bit later and nothing! I drove over to his house where I had access. I found him lying on the dining room floor. I could see that he apparently hit his head. There was blood on him and the floor. He was unconscious. We had no idea what happened.

I phoned the police and an ambulance was dispatched rushing him to the hospital. When he regained consciousness, he complained about numbness in his legs and arms.

We [the family] thought he had a stroke. He stayed in the hospital for further tests and later completely recuperated.

He was referred to a neurologist, in and out of the hospital for more tests after which, he was diagnosed with multiple sclerosis.

His doctors later explained that he must have suffered what they called "an acute exacerbation" from his then, undiagnosed condition, losing his balance, falling and striking his head. It was sad to see him decline like he did. I don't want to talk about this anymore. You saw him. You know. I know that my uncle must have liked you or he would not have invited you to his house.

I don't think that you know I wrote my thesis about *All Quiet on the Western Front*. At a UCLA party, I was invited to read it. I'd call that *my* fifteen minutes of fame!!

I can see why my uncle was fond of you. You and I have fun together. I can't say that about many people I know. I spend time with them for one reason or another, but I can't say I enjoy everyone's company like I do yours. (29)

In October 1959, Rosabelle secured the purchase of property in Beverly Hills to have her brother's one-level home built on Tower Grove Drive at Benedict Canyon. Construction began in November 1959.

Julius Baruch Laemmle (1820-1892), father of Carl Laemmle. Rebekka Laemmle (1831-1883), mother of Carl Laemmle. Photos courtesy of Carla Laemmle.

Junior was so impressed with the design of the home he had been renting from his friend, George Cukor, on Cordell Drive that he incorporated some of it into his new home structure, down to the swimming pool. Junior moved into his new home in the summer of 1960. Unfortunately, by this time he was confined to a wheelchair. Junior accepted that a show business comeback was no longer a possibility. Instead, he concentrated on real estate investments, entertaining dinner guests and his poker buddies. Junior took great pride working with his secretary, Lillian Borteck, whom he hired in 1958.

By turning the clock back regarding Carl Sr., Junior Laemmle agreed to talk with this writer given that his father's story is to be included with his. Junior prefaced the following to this writer.

The ship could not dock in the icy waters on the thirteenth day. My father's story in America began on Valentine's Day 1884 when he set foot on American soil in New York City. He was seventeen. If you have any questions while you are here, feel free to ask. I will leave the rest up to you, Atkins.

The Brothers Laemmle in 1926 (from left to right and in accordance to age) Joseph (eldest), Siegfried, Carl and Louis ("Louie"). Photo courtesy of Carla Laemmle.

For purposes of record, Carl Laemmle came from the province of Laupheim, Württemberg, Germany, located southwest at the southern tip of the Bavarian Forest. Carl was the ninth of thirteen children to Julius Baruch Laemmle and Rebekka Laemmle on her thirty-sixth birthday, January 17, 1867. (30) Eight of the thirteen Laemmle siblings passed away before the age of seven. Aside from Carl, the surviving Laemmle children were Joseph, Louis, Siegfried and Karoline. Brothers, Louis and Siegfried, later immigrated to America. Their sister, Karoline, remained in Laupheim her whole life. (31)

Within four months after his mother's death and with his father's blessing, Carl Laemmle left his native Laupheim on January 28, 1884 by way of horse and carriage. Five days later, at the port of Bremen, Germany, he boarded the S.S. Neckar, which would make port in the United States at Castle Garden, the southern tip of Manhattan Island, February 13, 1884. However, icy water and weather conditions kept the ship from port until the follow-

Before Ellis Island there was Castle Garden. This rendering of the circular sandstone fort was America's first immigration station. Carl Laemmle was one of the more than eight million people arriving between 1855 and 1890 before it closed. Ellis Island (1892 -1954) was the newer gateway to millions of immigrants entering the United States. Today, Castle Garden (or Castle Clinton) is part of the National Park Service located at the southern tip of Manhattan Island. Photo courtesy of Udo Bayer.

ing day. Thus, the eleven-day journey to "the new world" began for the young man of great promise February 2, 1884. Carl was the second Laemmle sibling to immigrate to America. His eldest brother, Joseph Laemmle, was the first to immigrate in 1871 when Carl was a toddler.

The first nine years of Carl Laemmle's humble American beginnings were spent in a number of unsatisfying jobs. After attempts at steady employment first in New York, Carl's desire was to find his brother, Joseph, who he believed was living in Chicago. Thus, Carl wrote a letter from New York to the German newspaper, the *Illinois Staatszeitung*. The letter found its way to the Vice-President of the German newspaper, which he had his secretary read to him.

The secretary just happened to be Joseph Laemmle. As the story goes, Joseph sent his brother Carl, ten dollars and a train

Long-time friends Carl Laemmle (age 18) (right) and Theodore Regensteiner (age 17) in Chicago, 1885. Photo courtesy of Udo Bayer.

ticket from New York to Chicago. Within several weeks, Carl arrived in Chicago and the brothers were reunited.

During this time, Carl Laemmle befriended Theodore Regensteiner, a fellow German immigrant new to America. The young men set out together in a search of jobs in South Dakota during the summer of 1885. Several weeks later they returned to Chicago where they both struggled in jobs for the next eight years. These were not the fondest memories, but they later served as

The Continental Clothing Company at Oshkosh, Wisconsin abt.1902.
Photo courtesy of Udo Bayer.

formative times to both men. Theodore Regensteiner later became successful with color printing in Chicago.

In late 1893, when Carl was twenty-seven, he was "tipped off" about a bookkeeping position; Carl was already an experienced bookkeeper. The new position would be at the Continental Clothing Company in Chicago. Samuel Stern, the company owner interviewed Laemmle. Stern gave Laemmle a choice to work in Chicago or at the company's Oshkosh, Wisconsin location. (32) Carl felt that a more rural lifestyle would suit him. Laemmle arrived in Wisconsin soon after where he became a resident for the next twelve years.

Carl Laemmle's most memorable day in Oshkosh, second to his arriving in America was in the fall of 1897. It was the American holiday of Thanksgiving celebrated by the Sterns. Carl was invited to the Chicago home of Samuel Stern and his wife Rosa, at 2963 South Prairie Avenue. Carl Laemmle was introduced to Samuel Stern's guests, two of them were sisters Anna Stern (age 20) and Recha Stern (age 22), Mr. and Mrs. Stern's nieces. (33)

According to Laemmle's son-in-law, Stanley Bergerman, Carl boasted regarding Recha, "It was love at first sight." Carl and

Recha shared common interests. First and foremost, they were headstrong individuals interested in their German-Jewish ancestry between their neighboring European towns. (34)

The couple was married August 28, 1898 at the summer home of Samuel Stern, the bride's uncle, in Highland Park, Illinois, a suburb of Chicago. Prominent Chicago Rabbi, Dr. Moses, solemnized the event that was attended by relatives only. Carl immediately returned to Oshkosh with his bride where they rented a home at 186 Church Street. There was no official honeymoon. (35)

Before the couple's first child, Rose (later known as Rosabelle Laemmle) was born in Oshkosh, December 3, 1901; Recha's sister Anna moved in with the Laemmles. They became respected members of the Oshkosh community and well-liked by the townspeople and city officials. Anna Stern remained living with the Laemmles for about six years.

Samuel Stern and Carl Laemmle did not always get along on several fronts. In September 1898, Laemmle being a loyal and devoted employee with steady patience and hard work was promoted to a store manager. Mr. Laemmle was considered an asset to the company. When he later asked for partnership, he was refused.

Mr. Laemmle's tenure with the Continental Clothing Company in Oshkosh was twelve years before he resigned in the winter of 1905. Carl was soon thirty-eight when he made a risky career move by returning to Chicago with his wife, five-year-old daughter, his sister-in-law, and his life savings of three thousand dollars. From his unpublished 1927 autobiographical manuscript Carl Laemmle wrote:

> My wife and I initially had our sights set on the five and ten-cent chain store idea, which would serve as a nucleus for a chain of similar stores all under the ownership of myself.
>
> It was so remunerative to its founders, Butler Brothers and F.W. Woolworth.

After Laemmle read a 1905 *Chicago Tribune* article "by happenstance" regarding the fledgling nickelodeon business spawned Laemmle's curiosity. Carl wrote of his visit to downtown Chicago one Saturday in January 1906:

While leisurely walking up the Palmer House block my eye caught sight of a flaming banner which almost covered the entrance of a store front. Drawn towards it, I discovered that a picture show was in progress in quarters, which had evidently served as a store. I walked on, however, until I reached State and Polk Streets.

There I came across another store transformed into a motion picture emporium called the Nickelodeon, the derivation of which can be easily guessed. Outside, a man was evidently fulfilling the circus spieler's role, as with cupped hand to his mouth, he yelled 'Step Right up ladies and gentlemen, for half a dime see real winter scenes and summer scenes at the same time. The show starts right away.'

Here the same panorama greeted me -- people lined up in front of the cheaply constructed box office, purchasing admission tickets for five cents, and similarly persons emptying into the street.

I watched this for fully fifteen minutes and before I knew it, I joined the throng eager to enter. My turn finally arrived. I paid the admission fee, handed my ticket to the collector and walked in.

What Carl witnessed that day was capital turnover in a short period of time. He stayed until closing time and introduced himself to the friendly proprietor regarding the prospects of his own venture. The proprietor was willing to impart business with Laemmle. By reviewing his own experience of the day, Carl Laemmle wrote, "I became disinclined to contest Mr. Woolworth's supremacy in the field of five and ten cent stores." Carl dropped his original business intentions and chose the northwest side of Chicago as a location to operate a theatre for the simple reason that none was located in that vicinity.

Promotion had been Laemmle's staple "a main priority." Carl's Chicago-based publicist, Robert H. Cochrane met face-to-face in Chicago, February 1906. Cochrane previously worked with Laemmle on promotions during his business days in Oshkosh. The two men were so pleased with each other and sought a location for Laemmle's first nickelodeon. (36) There were eight other nickel-

1987 photo of the Chicago North Milwaukee Avenue location of the former "Laemmle's Five-cent theatre" (The White Front Theatre). It was razed in 2015. Photo by the author.

odeons operating in Chicago at this time. Laemmle rented the Milwaukee storefront building with a five-year lease clause. The exterior of the building had previously been painted a brilliant white to stand out among its dingy neighbors, which inspired Laemmle to name it The White Front.

Carl Laemmle was thirty-nine when he branched out further as a film distributor and opened the Laemmle Film Service, 1906-1911. Photo courtesy of Udo Bayer.

Laemmle was insistent that the interior be a clean environment, which was sure to attract the feminine clientele. Carl Laemmle wrote the following.

I walked and walked, casting my eye here and there until I came to 909 Milwaukee Avenue, a one story building containing a vacant store, which was for rent . . . a satisfactory lease for five years was duly signed and recorded with [Samuel] Stern as the guarantor.

The Laemmle Film Service headquarters was originally located at Dearborn and Monroe Streets in Chicago, 1907. Photo courtesy of Udo Bayer.

I realized that it behooved me to start some sort of advance campaign to inform people what was coming their way. I hired boys to distribute throughout the neighborhood, small cards announcing the opening of the White Front Theatre on Saturday, February 24, 1906, at 3 P.M. (37)

Carl Laemmle opened with an Indian and Calvary picture. Laemmle was originally going to open with a film entitled, *From Newsboy to Judge*, which became a later feature. Laemmle was self-employed for the first time in his life.

On April 24, 1906, Carl Laemmle opened his second business The Family Theatre at 486 South Halstead Street (today spelled Halsted). The admission was discounted for families. It prospered so well in a surprisingly short time that vacant grocery stores and butcher shops were being transformed into movie parlors. Instead of competing with them Laemmle decided to subscribe to "first run" pictures. To his dismay, the confident exhibitor discovered that the competitors were making similar arrangements. Laemmle wrote, "This abuse was actually suicidal amongst ourselves."

Before the end of 1906, Carl Laemmle became a film distributor. He opened The Laemmle Film Service, first at 167 North Dearborn Street. He was the sole proprietor, manager, bookkeeper
and shipping clerk. Later their headquarters took two storefronts
relocated at 196-198 West Lake Street. Laemmle proved to have
a Midas touch.

That same year, the Carl Laemmle family including Anna Stern
rented a two-story house located at 672 North Hoyne Avenue
on Chicago's Near Northwest side. It was in close proximity to
Laemmle's "White Front Theatre." The owner of the Hoyne Avenue building was Nils Arneson, a Norwegian businessman, who
settled in Chicago after immigrated to America in 1861. Mr. Arneson's house was custom built in 1888. His wife was Hilda (Taftner)
Arneson. The Arnesons had a son and a daughter. By the time the
Arnesons rented their upper quarters to the Laemmles in early
1906 the couple had raised their children. Mr. and Mrs. Arneson
inhabited the lower quarters of the home. The women of the
house shared chores and prepared meals in a full kitchen with
dining quarters. All shared good company for two years.

Chicago in 1907 was the forerunning locale for moving picture
studios before New York or California. Carl Laemmle was a stick-
ler, who stayed on top of current events, which became a turning
point in his life.

Laemmle learned about the growing number of moving picture
studios, which caught his attention. Jobs were growing as film
companies employed stage actors, theatre directors, carpenters
and craftsmen. One of Chicago's first was Selig Polyscope Studios, founded in Chicago by William Selig in 1896. Chicago also
became home to Essanay Studios, founded by George K. Spoor
and Gilbert M. Anderson (a.k.a. the actor "Bronco Billy" Anderson), which opened August 10, 1907. Performers such as Charles
Chaplin and Gloria Swanson got their start with Essanay. (38)

Among the other American motion picture companies of the
times were, Vitagraph Film Company, Star Film Company, Kalem
Company, in the mid-west and New York; The Lubin Manufacturing Company, which was founded in 1896 in Philadelphia.

Earlier in the summer of 1907 at Chicago's Humboldt Park was one of Carl's many cherished memories. Stanley Bergerman shared the following story that had been told on occasion by his father-in-law, Carl Laemmle.

Carl and Recha attended a Fourth of July picnic given by friends. Six-year-old Rosabelle and Aunt Anna Stern were also in attendance.

It was a beautiful Thursday spent with perfect weather, pleasant entertainment and social activities. Rosabelle, a very bright girl, who learning German and had recently finished kindergarten delighted in heartily play at the picnic with the other attending children.

After the family returned home, Rosabelle began asking her Aunt Anna, why Mama and Papa didn't have a sister or brother for her to play. Anna told the child to ask Mama and Papa, which Rosabelle did, repeatedly for days.

Mama Recha learned that summer, she was pregnant.

Recha's delayed answer to her daughter came with news of an expectant playmate, to which Rosabelle replied, "I wish for bruder!"

The fall and winter of 1907 in Chicago arrived bearing political changes with widespread unemployment and labor unrest. This unrest began spreading throughout the country. It made civic authorities uneasy.

When local Chicago prohibition in 1907 was forcing saloonkeepers to close in some 47 precincts, Laemmle sent each of them letters urging them to turn their places of business into nickelodeons. More than two hundred of them did and turned to the Laemmle exchange for pictures.

On November 18, 1907 Anna Stern (age 28), married businessman, Maurice Fleckles (age 36), at the Prairie Avenue home of her uncle, Samuel Stern, in Chicago. The brothers-in-law, Mr. Fleckles and Mr. Laemmle remained close business partners for many years in Chicago and California.

It was during this period when the Laemmle son was born. Recha Laemmle was in her fifth month of pregnancy. Amidst numer-

ous business travels during the winter of 1907, Carl Laemmle relocated his family in late January 1908 from Hoyne Avenue to a
larger and newly built apartment house located at 3520 Grand
Boulevard on Chicago's South Side. Recha was also being treated
for abnormal thyroid function. Dr. Ludwig S. Simons, Recha's obstetrician and endocrinologist, lived within close proximity to the
new Laemmle family address.

In her seventh month of pregnancy, Recha was placed with mid-
wife Mary E. Lear, who was also a licensed nurse. She assisted
Mrs. Laemmle through complicated weeks of special care. Recha
Laemmle was in labor for three days before giving birth to a boy
named Julius Laemmle at their Grand Boulevard home, April 28,
1908. No given name was actually written on the birth record,
which was dated May 1st, 1908. Carl Laemmle's occupation listed
on the birth record was that of "merchant." The only identifica-
tion for the child was "male." This was not an uncommon occurrence of the times. The child was named Julius Laemmle after his
paternal grandfather. Dr. Simons took special care of mother and
son paying frequent house calls throughout the first year. (39)

By 1909, The Laemmle Film Service exchanges had grown by
leaps and bounds. Branch operations were extended to the following cities, Evansville, Indiana; New York City; Memphis Ten-
nessee; Minneapolis, Minnesota; Des Moines, Iowa; Omaha, Nebraska; Portland, Oregon; Salt Lake City, Utah; and two Canadian
locations in Montreal, Quebec and Winnipeg, Manitoba.

Carl Laemmle had a love for western stories. Film rentals were
not easily available in the flicker days even with a good price. Running times at most for the infant films were about ten minutes.
Films came to exhibitors intermittently and were frayed with constant usage. In fact, the film exchange business became worse.
Earlier film exchanges were not so accommodating to the exhibitor. This was the very reason that Laemmle, the well-respected
businessman, wanted to make his own films. Julius Laemmle was
thirteen months old when his father entered the world of motion
picture production in May 1909 and first established the Yankee
Moving Picture Company. He opened an office that was located
at 111 East 14th Street in New York City.

Advertisement for Carl Laemmle's first film production his eastern film studio IMP (Independent Moving Picture Company) [Photo courtesy of Udo Bayer.

Simultaneously, Thomas Edison's Motion Picture Patents Company (also referred to as MPPC or "The Trust") was controlling much of the film product. The Motion Picture Patents Company formed the General Film Company in 1909 in an attempt to monopolize general film distribution. The MPPC was forcing exhibitors to use their fraying films and charging them heavily for them,

Thirty-four-year old Recha Laemmle (Mrs. Carl Laemmle) and their children Rosabelle (age seven) with thirteen-month-old Julius (later known as Carl Laemmle Jr.), in Laupheim, Germany. Photo courtesy of Theo Miller, Laupheim.

which included many restrictions on its patented motion picture equipment by which it was viewed.

The General Film Company also attempted to seize the equipment of the independent distribution companies who were not following guidelines as the MPPC significantly tried to force independent distribution companies to sell out or lose their patent licenses. Carl Laemmle received threats from the MPCC to not sell film. In an effort not to jeopardize his other thriving businesses, Laemmle suspended his Yankee Moving Picture Company project temporarily.

In June 1909, Carl Laemmle inaugurated a contest for a name other than the Yankee Film Company. Laemmle's publicist Robert H. Cochrane worked closely with Laemmle in deciding a winner. The prize was shared equally between two men, who had made the same suggestion. The new name of the company was changed to the Independent Moving Picture Company of America (IMP).

Printed advertisements under the trade name of IMP were accompanied by the illustration of a young mischievous spirit. Studios were established at Coytesville and Bayonne near Fort Lee, New Jersey.

In July 1909, Mr. and Mrs. Carl Laemmle, Rosabelle (age 7) and Julius (14 months) set sail for Germany. Also traveling with the family was a nurse, Margaret Kramer, whom the Laemmles hired after Anna Stern was married.

Within three months on this European trip, Mr. Laemmle also visited England and France to make film surveys of those countries. American film producers had not yet established offices in these regions. They preferred to dispose of their foreign rights to the highest bidder.

Upon Laemmle's return to America, October 19, 1909 his first motion picture production was near complete. "Hiawatha," a one-reeler with a running time of twenty minutes was released October 25, 1909 under the IMP title to gallant ovations. The film was based on Henry Wadsworth Longfellow's poem. Successions of audience enthusiasm proved to Laemmle that his films could compete against other members and "the Trust," which served to spur IMP on to greater activity.

Thomas Edison (bottom row, fourth from left) with his Motion Picture Patents Company posse, 1908. Photo courtesy of Udo Bayer.

Carl Laemmle was the first movie producer to launch the "star system" to the American public, as we know it today. Amidst Laemmle's untiring publicity of actress Florence Lawrence, the former "Biograph Girl," whom he hired and hailed as "The IMP Girl," she ultimately became the first major "movie star."

Mary Pickford was another early IMP actress who got her start with Carl Laemmle. Mary eventually left IMP and achieved further stardom as "America's Sweetheart" in the motion picture world. Other popular IMP productions featured the talents of Owen Moore (Mary Pickford's first husband), Thomas Ince (an actor before Laemmle hired him to direct), Jack Pickford (Mary's brother), and King Baggot.

As a result of the Edison monopoly behind the Motion Picture Patents Company, the General Film Company receipts had fallen off with exhibitors as well as with distributors from all over the country. Carl Laemmle, along with other independents grew dissatisfied that the Patents Company was taking unfair advantage.

Train carrying special guests, employees and prominent journalists arrive at Santa Fe Station, Los Angeles, California for the opening of Universal City to the public March 15, 1915. Photo courtesy of Udo Bayer.

By this time Laemmle withdrew himself as a member of Edison's Patents Company and refused to pay nominal dues to them for film production. Laemmle, the confident producer boldly declared himself an independent. In 1910, he helped to form the Motion Picture Distribution and Sales Company.

During this time, Maurice Fleckles was managing the White Front Theatre and later the Laemmle Film Service headquarters in Chicago. Mr. Laemmle's five-year lease on the White Front Theatre property expired in February 1911. Laemmle resigned himself to the fact that nickelodeons were becoming obsolete.

Carl's eldest brother, Joseph Laemmle, trained neighboring dry good grocers, the Peto Brothers in operating the five-cent theatre before their lease expired. The Peto Brothers did just that, in addition to obtaining an extended one-year lease. Carl's younger brother, Louis Laemmle, had returned from Germany

March 15, 1915. Mr. and Mrs. Carl Laemmle lead the inaugural parade at Universal City with Isadore Bernstein (the general manager) at Laemmle's side. Mr. Bernstein was also a screenwriter at the studio. Immediately following the opening of Universal City, Mr. Bernstein, resigned his managerial post but continued to write screenplays, for Universal Pictures and other production studios. Photo courtesy of Carla Laemmle.

with his bride, Frieda Heller. Louis was hired as an assistant manager at the Film Service in 1911. Fleckles and Louis Laemmle remained with the Laemmle Film Service until 1912 when it was dissolved prior to the establishment of the Universal Film Manufacturing Company.

"The Trust" made infringement charges against Carl Laemmle's IMP Company. The situation grew intolerable as Laemmle gained the support of other independent exhibitors who preferred the newer quality product. In the meantime, Laemmle used French Lumière film. Litigation waged on in the courts for years. (40)

Julius Laemmle was a three-year-old when his father moved the family from Chicago to New York in the fall of 1911. The Laemmle children were usually under the supervision of their mother or their Aunt Anna Fleckles. Anna had accompanied the Laemmle family to New York to help the family get settled into their new

The Administration building at Universal City (1915). It existed from 1914 through 1936 and was located on Lankershim Blvd., near where the Black Tower currently stands. Photo courtesy of NBC Universal

residence at 417 Riverside Drive. Meanwhile, Mr. Fleckles was settling business for Carl in Chicago taking several months.

Carl Laemmle and his Independent Moving Pictures Company joined forces with the Anti-Trust consortium and formed the Universal Film Manufacturing Company, April 30, 1912 with offices at Union Square. This formation took place two days following Julius Laemmle's fourth birthday.

During the infancy of moving pictures, weather conditions in the eastern cities and the mid-west were wary. Primitive cameras operated inefficiently without consistent sunlight. Between 1911 and 1912, Laemmle was busy searching new locations for a film studio. He traveled to California where he purchased the Nestor studio at Sunset Boulevard and Gower Street in Hollywood.

Carl Laemmle previously broke ground in New Jersey for a Universal Studio believing that an east coast facility in the area where his IMP Company first succeeded was a good idea. In California, he subsequently leased a site in the Edendale district in Los Angeles (now known as Echo Park, Los Feliz and Silver Lake) where he could shoot films. He first called this area Universal City. Carl

Future look of the Administrative Building at Universal (1930s). Photo courtesy of Udo Bayer.

Laemmle's ultimate goal was to purchase large-scale property in which to build his dream city.

Political tensions between European countries and America made traveling to and from difficult. In September of 1914, Recha Laemmle made a trip to her homeland with her two children Julius (age 6), Rosabelle (age 12), and Mrs. Laemmle's sister, Anna Stern Fleckles. All four became detainees in Flieden. They were released after Maurice Fleckles was sent from Universal to find the party. Maurice Fleckles was well supplied with American gold, a passport signed by the American Secretary of State and Edgar Haniel Von Haimshausen, Charge d'Affaires in Washington, as well as personal letters from Honorable William Jennings Bryan to the American Diplomatic and Consular Officers of the United States and Europe. The party arrived safely in New York on the Holland-American liner, "Rotterdam," on the 24th of October 1914. (41)

It was a Monday, March 15, 1915 when forty-eight-year-old Carl Laemmle traveled by train from his home in New York and opened the gates to the "New Universal City" in California for a public of over ten thousand. It was a gala affair with ceremonies and festivities that lasted for one week. The rest of the family later joined Laemmle in the festivities. Mrs. Laemmle was thirty-nine; Rosabelle was thirteen. Julius was six.

Universal City had the world's largest moving picture stages, having over four and one half acres of stage space. There were four exterior stages ranging from one hundred, twenty-five feet to five hundred feet with huge muslin screens strung overhead to diffuse the California sunlight. There were two interior, electric-lighted studios, each four hundred by one hundred feet. Other departments that adjoined the big stages were designing, carpentering, scene painting, papier-mâché, and statuary departments. The employed one hundred and fifty people devoted to devising new effects, planning exceptional and novel sets.

Everything used in the production of motion pictures at Universal City, with the exception of furniture, is built inside its walls. A lumberyard, which is larger than some of the yards found in our largest cities, supplied the lumber used in the building of the sets. (42)

There were one hundred carpenters employed at Universal City putting up buildings, erecting small villages, streets of dwellings and practically everything in the line of houses, which is seen in Universal pictures. It is a very small task for these men to erect a solid city block in a few hours, only to pull it down a few hours later.

The first feature length film produced under the Universal Film Manufacturing Company title was *Traffic in Souls* filmed at Laemmle's first Universal Studio in Fort Lee, New Jersey. It was released in late 1913. Social problem films were an early rage, which started with *Traffic in Souls,* the top-grossing example of the times. It became the first movie to be booked simultaneously in thirty New York City theatres.

The first picture completed by Universal City in Los Angeles, California was the epic drama of *Damon and Pythias* that was released in late 1914. It starred William Worthington as Damon and Herbert Rawlinson, the city's first major, as Pythias. It was released in late 1914. The wild chariot race set a pattern for future *Ben-Hur* and other flying toga productions.

The former "IMP Girl," Florence Lawrence, followed Laemmle west and became The First Lady of Universal, billed as "Queen of the Screen." She was paid a then regal $1,000 a week. Including Herbert Rawlinson and William Worthington, Universal City attracted an impressive array of talent; Gladys Nicholsen, Mary Fuller, Rosemary Theby, Ella Hall, William Desmond, Eddie Polo, Annette Kellerman, Jim Corbett, Jack Dempsey, Harold Lloyd, Carter De Haven, Harry Carey, Mae Murray, Laura LaPlante, Mary Philbin, Arthur Lake, Carmel Myers, Edith Roberts, Priscilla Dean, Wallace Reid, Anna Pavlova, Barbara Kent, Merna Kennedy, Reginald Denny, Elissa Landi, and Bebe Daniels.

Universal's early roster included J. Warren Kerrigan, Francis Ford and his younger brother John Ford; Lew Cody Jack Holt, Hoot Gibson, Tom Mix (whom Laemmle personally hired as his number one "all talking cowboy"), Ken Maynard, Buck Jones, Johnny Mack Brown, Erich von Stroheim, Rudolf Valentino and Lon Chaney (his amazing portrayals in the classics *The Hunchback of Notre Dame* and *The Phantom of the Opera* became synonymous with the studio).

A natural showman, Carl Laemmle had bleachers erected overlooking the stages for spectators and tourists at 25 cents a head, which included a box lunch. They were invited to come in, watch, cheer and applaud if they felt like it. Films of course then were silent. Mr. Laemmle was credited with building the first electric lighted movie stage, a closed stage, and a stage for trick photography.

A zoo, which Laemmle acquired, ranked among the most expensive privately owned collections with animal trainers who were

Carl Laemmle's last visitors in 1936 included dancer Florence Walton, conductor Leopold Stokowski, and Rudolph Edgar Block (Jewish American journalist, columnist and author, who wrote under the pen name of Bruno Lessing). Photo courtesy of Carla Laemmle.

famous throughout the world. At the height of western and jungle epics, Universal kept thirty lions, ten leopards, several elephants, scores of monkeys, hundreds of horses and more domesticated animals. By the time Universal incorporated talking pictures, animals couldn't be relied on to keep quiet, either and Laemmle had the zoo dismantled. The only organized city in the world devoted exclusively to the manufacture of motion pictures included many amenities; a U.S. Post Office, a water system, an ice plant, phone service, auto service, an express office, telegraph sub-stations connected with every part of the continent, via Western Union and Postal lines; two restaurants, dormitories and dwellings, a fifty thousand dollar wardrobe department, a picture theatre, tailoring establishment, a blacksmith shop, an arsenal, and fire and police departments. Carl Laemmle was also known for inviting impressive guests to Universal City over the years. Carl Laem-

Carl Laemmle (right) with his German boyhood friend and associate
Sigmund Moos (1870-1933), manager of the leasing department at
Universal City from 1915. Photo courtesy of Carla Laemmle.

mle invited many famous visitors to Universal City over the years,
which included Amelia Earhart.

In the fall of 1916, after Universal City Studios had been operating for well over a year, the Laemmles relocated from their
apartment on Riverside Drive to another Manhattan apartment
house at 365 West End Avenue. Carl usually had his right hand

Carl Laemmle Jr. and Max Friedland in 1941. Mr. Friedland was a cousin to Junior Laemmle by marriage. Photo courtesy of Udo Bayer.

man Sigmund Moos keeping an eye on things out west. The family also had a summer home in Edgemere on Long Island where Recha Laemmle had befriended Henrietta Thalberg, the mother of Irving Thalberg.

Recha Laemmle's early death left a profound effect on future generations of Laemmle/Stern family members, all of who would know of her only through others. Carole Laemmle Bergerman told this writer the following.

*Twenty years later, a 1961 at the Beverly Hills home of Carl Laemmle Jr.
(seated) Junior's guests (from left standing) Max Friedland and Junior's
uncle Julius Bernheim. (Seated is Max's daughter) Gertrude "Trudy"
Friedland and her mother (Mrs. Max Friedland) Irma Jette Friedland
(sister of Julius Bernheim) Photo courtesy of Udo Bayer.*

My mother [Rosabelle] told me that my grandmother [Re-
cha Laemmle] in addition to being a supportive loving wife
and mother had a strong financial backbone. She guarded
the investments, and always discussed prospects with my
grandfather [Carl Laemmle]. I wish I had known her. Most
of the Laemmle/Stern cousins were born after my grandmother died.

Carl Laemmle spent the remainder of his life enjoying his grandchildren and planning other ways to sponsor his fellow European
friends and family to safety during years of war. After Laemmle Sr.
retired, he devoted the greater part of his time with the issuing of
more affidavits (some that may have been issued as early as 1929). It
was a complicated and time-consuming process. Carl Laemmle had

his son promise to bring Max Friedland, his wife, Laemmle's niece, Irma Jette (Bernheim) Friedland, and their two daughters Ruth and Trudy safely to the United States. Junior made this happen in 1941.

By virtue of Carl Laemmle's innate humanity, magnanimity and his life-saving affidavits for hundreds of imperiled German Jews and their families were given the chance to escape Nazi domination and seek refuge here in the United States. Mr. Laemmle succeeded in bringing what is more likely figured today as three hundred or more people to the United States. He was in a constant struggle with The State Department and their exacting requirements. The State Department had to have irrefutable proof that Laemmle Sr. was the financial person capable of assuming so large an obligation, also required absolute assurance that immigrants he transported did not become public charges. Carl Laemmle urged many of his fellow businessmen to help continue this plight; among them were Adolph Zukor and Samuel Goldwyn.

Carl Laemmle made every effort to comply with the requirements regarding his extended family and friends in Laupheim and other parts of Europe. Junior Laemmle said:

> My father pledged to bring over as many people to America as he possibly could in protest of Hitler and the Nazi regime. We considered Laupheim our second home. We traveled there until we could no longer. They were difficult times.

March 1915. Advertising manager takes a picture of Carl Laemmle and his daughter Rosabelle (age 14) at Colorado Springs. Photo courtesy of Carla Laemmle.

The Cohens and Kellys, a 1926 silent comedy film became a Carl Laemmle favorite. It was the first in a series of Universal releases based on the characters most of which were produced by his son. Photo from the author's collection.

Two of Carl Laemmle's triumphant productions, which immortalized actor Lon Chaney synonymous with Universal's The Hunchback of Notre Dame *(1923) and* The Phantom of the Opera *(1925). Photos courtesy of Carla Laemmle.*

My father and I, we were best friends. He knew exactly what he wanted to do when he put me in charge at Universal.

From the start, we had an understanding. He believed in me and I followed through. The War Relief took a lot of time and money. My father stayed committed to this cause after he retired.

Soon before my father died, he had my brother-in-law and me pledge along with as many friends as he possibly could to help secure the last affidavit recipients coming to America. This was carried out.

As for Carl Laemmle, the motion picture producer, he mixed a taste for European culture with a completely Americanized acceptance of social problem films and thrillers. Mr. Laemmle's favorite films were westerns and the Cohens and Kellys series (a tradition

One of the highest tributes paid to Carl Laemmle was his sixtieth birthday banquet. It was a gala affair held on his birthday January 17, 1927 at the Biltmore Hotel in Los Angeles attended by 600 people from the film colony. Pictured here are 50 attendees including the guest of honor. (Top row, all left to right) Harry Zehner, Wilfred Rothschild, Henry Henigson, Jean Hersholt, Erle C. Kenton, Walter Stern, Edward Loeb, Jack Ross, Paul Kohner, Wesley Ruggles, Mike Gore, Martin Murphy, Glenn Tryon, Robert Welsh, Nat Ross, and Hugh Hoffman. (Second Row) Victor Nordlinger, Edward Sloman, Ernst Lubitsch, William Beaudine, Robert Klein, B.P. Schulberg, Samuel Van Ronkle, Norman Kerry, Hans Kraly, Conrad Veidt, Svend Gale, Tom Reed, and Charles Puffy. (Third Row) Harry Pollard, Paul Leni, George Sydney, Isadore Bernstein, Henry MacRae, Carl Laemmle Jr., Carl Laemmle, Joseph Laemmle, Abe Stern, Sigmund Moos, Mannie Lowenstein, William A. Seiter, Edward Montague, and Walter Anthony. (Seated) Walter Hiers, Adolph Klinordlinger, Edward Laemmle, Julius Bernheim, Ernst Laemmle, William Wyler, and Abe Gore (kneeling). Photo courtesy of Carla Laemmle.

Proud Papa Laemmle with his daughter Rosabelle Laemmle
Bergerman and her husband Mark Stanley Bergerman on the couple's
wedding day, January 2, 1929, Beverly Hills, California. Photo courtesy
of Udo Bayer.

Carl Laemmle, in 1929, presented this first film version of Edna
Ferber romantic drama novel, Show Boat, first opened as 1927
play. Junior has some training with (in the partial talkie elements).
Believed to be a lost film, it was rediscovered in recent years.
Photo from the author's collection.

Carl Laemmle at his Beverly Hills home with his granddaughter Carol Laemmle Bergerman in 1931. Photo courtesy of Zachary Zito.

Carl Laemmle celebrated for twenty-five years of work in the motion
picture business (February 1931). Back from left: Will Hays, Irving
Thalberg, and Cecil B. DeMille. (Front from left; Carl Laemmle,
Mary Pickford, Will Rogers, and Carl Laemmle Jr., is holding the
commemorative scroll from industry members. Among those in
attendance were Wallace Beery, Charles "Buddy" Rogers, Sidney Fox,
Slim Summerville, Betty Compson, Mary Brian, Gary Cooper, William
Haines, Ernst Laemmle, C. E. Sullivan, E.B. Derr, Victor McLaglen,
Robert Armstrong, Constance Bennett, Fred Beetson, Al Christie, Sol
Wurtzel, Ronald Colman, John Gilbert, Lew Ayres and others. Photo
courtesy of Zachary Zito.

Mr. Laemmle's middle
name "PROMOTE!"
as he awaits the next
Tom Mix western. Photo
courtesy of Udo Bayer.

Carl Laemmle with his friend and biographer John Drinkwater outside Mr. Laemmle's apartment complex in New York City, 1932. Photo from the author's collection.

continued by his son). Carl Laemmle best described as "a little gi-ant" by his son. The following photos illustrate such a life.

As for Carl Laemmle's daughter Rosabelle, she was formerly ed-ucated in Chicago until the fourth grade before the family moved to New York. Once to New York, Rosabelle was enrolled in the Ethical Culture Fieldston School, an independent and private

Carole Laemmle Bergerman (1930-1994) as she appeared in the summer of 1973. Photo courtesy of Stanley Bergerman.

school where she excelled attended grammar school, high school and later preparatory college courses. She was speaking fluent German by the age of ten. Ethical Culture was located on the Upper West Side of Manhattan. Her brother later followed Rosabelle to this school. He completed high school and some college prep courses there. Rosabelle completed her education at the school prior to her brother. Neither children attended formal college.

The exceptionally bright child, born Julius, became an avid reader. He was ten when his mother passed away, which left an irreparable void. He remembered her as a loving mother sharing that special bond between mother and son. He also remembered that he was thirty-one when his father passed away. Julius Laemmle's education began in the fall of 1915 in Brooklyn, New York with elementary courses at the Clark School of Concentration. His favorite studies were American and British literature, popular culture and sports. He told this writer that one of his cherished comforts was his mother's lentil soup and being read to by his mother, his sister, and his Aunt Anna.

Throughout Junior Laemmle's life there was never a time a caring women didn't surround him.

Anna Stern Fleckles, Junior's aunt, who helped raise both Laemmle children (sister of Recha Stern Laemmle), predeceased her husband, Maurice Fleckles, in Los Angeles, April 14, 1945 at the age of sixty-seven.

Margaret Kramer, Junior's childhood nurse, who later became his housekeeper and remained with him well into her eighties, passed away November 11, 1954. She was eighty-eight.

Elise Nisse joined Junior Laemmle's household in 1949 and remained with him for the thirty years. Rosabelle and Junior kept Elise gainfully employed as a cook and housekeeper by referring her to several Hollywood friends. She passed away November 2, 1985 in Long Beach, California at the age of eighty-four.

Evelyn Moriarty, Junior's closest friend told this writer that when Junior was afflicted with multiple sclerosis that he looked to Dr. Jonas Salk for years hoping for a cure. Evelyn passed away May 21, 2008 at the age of eighty-six. She is interred not far from her friend Marilyn Monroe at Pearce Brothers Westwood Village Memorial Park and Mortuary in Los Angeles.

The immediate family members from the Carl and Recha Laemmle family are no longer alive. On the Saturday morning of November 19, 1965, Carole Bergerman found the body of her mother Rosabelle Laemmle Bergerman, in her Westwood home, twelve days before her sixty-fourth birthday. She apparently died of a heart attack.

Rosabelle's survivors included her husband of thirty-six years, Stanley Bergerman (age 62), her brother Carl Laemmle Jr. (age 57), her daughter, Carole Laemmle Bergerman (age 35), her son Stanley Bergerman Jr. (age 33), and five-year-old granddaughter, Laura Lee Bergerman.

Carole Laemmle Bergerman passed away November 28, 1994 at the age of sixty-four. She was the sixth and final family member interred in the Laemmle family room at Home of Peace Mausoleum.

Stanley Bergerman, Junior Laemmle's brother-in-law passed away July 13, 1998 in Los Angeles at the age of ninety-four. He was interred at Hillside Memorial Park in Culver City, California near his second wife Fay Schiller Bergerman. She passed away March 4, 2005.

Stanley Bergerman Jr. was the last surviving direct family member of the Carl and Recha Laemmle family. He was the son of Rosabelle and Stanley Bergerman and brother of Carole Bergerman.

He yielded possession of his resting place in the Laemmle Family Room for his daughter Laura Lee Bergerman. She was tragically killed in an automobile accident at the age of eighteen May 29, 1978. Stanley Bergerman Jr. passed away November 4, 2010. He was interred in another area at the Home of Peace Mausoleum.

Young Julius Laemmle's physical challenges began at birth. The boy's toddler days were difficult. He had an unconventional way of walking; toe-heal instead of heal-toe. His sister Rosabelle was instrumental in helping her brother breakthrough the adversities of his early development by frequently taking him out to play like other children. His keen interest and highly developing intelligence were positive factors that strengthened his capabilities. Once the family moved to California, Junior, who was a sports enthusiast, managed physically well. He became a fine tennis player. He was selective when dating women. He had been a regular attendee of theatre, motion pictures, and the fights. He acquired a penchant for collecting automobiles, but never actually drove. He frequently took friends and his niece, Carole Bergerman, to the movies. She once told this writer:

> My uncle always liked to sit in the back row at a movie theater. I finally asked him why? His answer was different than what I thought. He told me that he had a fear of the mob and his chances were that by sitting in the back row, the possibility of getting shot from behind or having someone sneeze on you from behind was nil.

Junior was an avid fan of horse racing insuring healthy dividends to Hollypark and Santa Anita for many years. His birthday parties were usually combined with the annual Kentucky Derby celebration held as one lavish celebrity party. Junior, the confirmed bachelor, said that he gave up racehorse gambling in 1951 to which one friend quipped, "It's a safe bet that he'll gamble on anything but marriage."

In spite of his physically challenged life, Carl Laemmle Jr. outlived many of his contemporaries, but was the first of his contemporaries to retire from the business at the ripe ol' age of twenty-nine. Although Junior had been referred to as a recluse he would

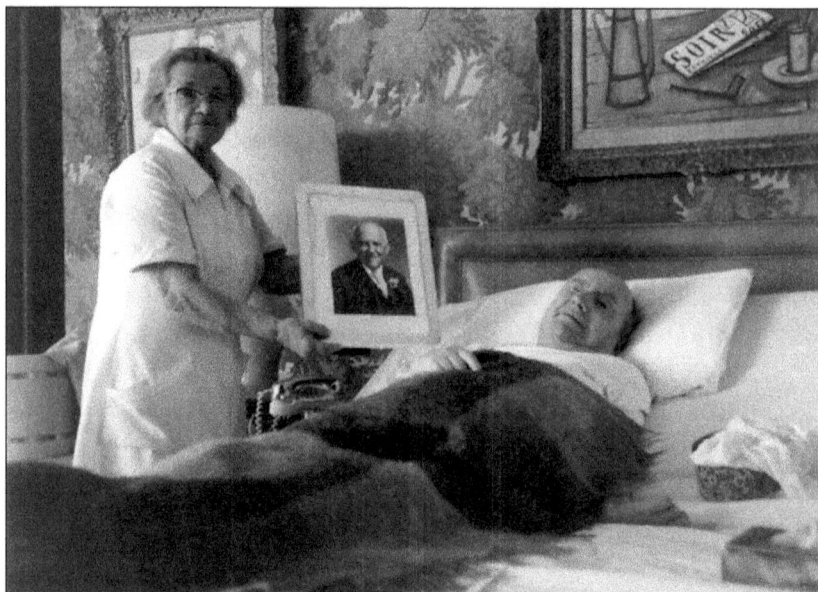

Author's photo of Junior Laemmle with his cook and housekeeper and friend Elise Nisse holding photo of Papa Laemmle (July 6, 1979).

jokingly refer to himself as, "the Hermit of Benedict Canyon." It wasn't until 1958 Junior wasn't able to be outdoors as much. Many who were not then aware of his illness thought of him as a recluse?

From the time Junior was an impressionable youth, remedies for better health constantly intrigued him. He acquired pills for most everything. His pill collection was once fabulous. Damon Runyon used to say that when Schwab's needed a rare medicine, they came to Junior.

One lunch hour at the Brown Derby, Junior along with Mervyn LeRoy and Sydney Skolsky, two other well-known hypochondriacs, were scanning some papers. A curious tourist asked if the trio were discussing scripts. "No," replied the headwaiter, "They're just comparing prescriptions." (43)

The late movie and stage actress, Fay Wray, whose career began at Universal, told this writer in 1979, "Junior Laemmle had pills for most everything! It started with homeopathic remedies that anyone could buy over the counter. With time, he had his own complete medicine collection. It was sad to see how Junior struggled professionally after his father died and pitiful to know

Junior insisted that Elise take a picture of him with this author (July 6, 1979).

about his battle with Multiple Sclerosis. My husband [Dr. Sanford Rothenberg] was his neurologist."

Stanley Bergerman told this writer of Junior's years of patronage at the famed Drucker's Barber Shop (now Gornik and Drucker) in Beverly Hills. Junior single-handedly waged the battle against "The Unfriendly Five"—five barbers who quit Harry Drucker's shop to go on their own. Junior's fight to ask the name customers to remain was the result of many calls being made interrupting film executives to the Dore Scharys, Buddy Adlers, Lew Wassermans, Mervyn LeRoys, etc., with the battle cry: "Don't quit Drucker's!" They didn't. (44)

The afternoon sunset was descending from above Benedict Canyon. This writer asked Junior Laemmle if he wouldn't mind being in a photograph with Elise. Junior said, "I would like to have my father in the picture with us too. I know Elise won't mind. She knew my father."

Elise lifted the framed portrait of Carl Laemmle that sat on a dresser facing Junior's bed. She walked within this writer's camera range holding the picture near Junior. Elise said, "What a handsome man he was." After which Junior said, "Now, take the picture, Atkins," and managed a grin.

Junior began to nod off after this writer thanked him and Elise for their hospitality and patience. This writer whispered to Elise about directions to Pacific Palisades. Junior's voice rang out!

> Take Beverly Glen down to Sunset . . . End of Sunset is the ocean . . . Make a right and follow your signs . . . Atkins. Shouldn't you have a picture of you and me together? Go to the living room and bring my OSCAR here. Elise can take the picture.

This writer told Mr. Laemmle that he is synonymous with early Universal horror movies much like John Wayne was with westerns. Junior responded with emotion:

> Thank you, Atkins. I never doubted the success of many of those pictures. Maybe one, but you already know about that.

The last question to Junior: 'Do you have any regrets and what would you change if you had to?' Looking upward, Carl Laemmle Jr. simply answered, "I wouldn't have changed a thing," after which, he drifted to sleep.

This writer fell short of asking Junior to sign a vintage photograph, which was brought along. It was left with Elise. A letter dated August 7, 1979 followed:

> Dear Mr. Atkins:
>
> It was nice seeing you when you were in California. I am returning herewith your photo and am sorry that I cannot autograph it. I am unable to write anymore, as much as I would like to. When I wrote you last, the stationary had my autograph on the letterhead and perhaps this will suffice for your purpose. I hope so.
>
> I wish you every success with your book and I feel certain it will be very interesting. Happy Birthday to you and many happy returns and when you come to California again, I would like to see you.
>
> Sincerely,
> Carl Laemmle Jr.

Another letter followed. It was dated September 25, 1979.

Dear Mr. Atkins:

Mr. Laemmle, as you know, has not been well for some time. He has enjoyed meeting you and liked your interesting letters. Yesterday, in his sleep, he passed away and the world has lost a great man. I know you will miss him as we all do. It was a privilege knowing him. I have been his secretary for over twenty-one years.

Sincerely yours,

Lillian Borteck

Coincidentally, father and son Laemmle passed away exactly forty years apart, September 24, 1939 and September 24, 1979, respectively. Junior was interred also forty years to the day after his father. Junior's niece, Carole Laemmle Bergerman (age 49), nephew Stanley Bergerman Jr. (age 46), brother-in-law Stanley Bergerman (age 76), and several cousins survived him. Junior's sister, Rosabelle Laemmle Bergerman, predeceased him. Junior was the fifth Laemmle family member interred in Laemmle Family Room at the Home of Peace Mausoleum. The sixth and last was Carole Bergerman.

Funeral services for Carl Laemmle Jr. were held in East Los Angeles at 11am Wednesday, September 26, 1979 at the Home of Peace Memorial Chapel. Rabbi Edgar F. Magnin officiated the only service for Junior that was attended by a small group of people. Evelyn Moriarty, who was among the mourners told this writer the following.

Listen to me carefully. It was a long drive out there. I first drove to Carole's place to meet her. She insisted that I ride with her in the limousine that had arrived. I said, no. I will drive on my own. The service, as you know was given at the Home of Peace Chapel in the Mausoleum. There was no other service. This was the only goodbye. Carole barely said a word to me when we arrived. I thought that she was mad that I wouldn't ride in the limo.

Anyhow, we got there late but early enough before the service. We walked together behind the curtain where the closed casket was to pay our respects. She asked if I wanted to see him. I said no.

Aside from her purse, Carole was carrying a large canvas bag. She asked me to sit and that she'd join me before the service started. She left her purse with me, but took the bag with her. Back behind the curtain she went. I sat and waited for her.

When Carole returned, she had folded the empty canvas bag and used it as a seat cushion. She leaned over to me and whispered, "He's taking it [Academy Award] with him."

I replied to Carole in a louder tone, 'And you say you're taking all of the flowers with you? Carole said, "Yes." And she did. I already knew what she was up to. I loved Junior like a brother. I never tried to vie for Junior's affection either. I didn't know his sister, Rosabelle well at all. I was also acquainted with Stanley Bergerman and his son, Stan Jr. I liked them both, but never butted into their affairs. Junior built Rosabelle up to me as someone I wouldn't like, so I was never interested in getting to know her. When she died, Junior was very sad. I don't care what the family thought of me. There was nothing going on. As for Elise, I saw her as strict and later redundant, but she was always kind to visitors. Junior and I were friends when we met and friends we stayed until the end. (45)

In looking back there was one last proud achievement that Junior Laemmle said, "I formed the Universal Pictures basketball team." Stanley Bergerman later explained to this writer in 1996, "The players were the first to compete in the United States Olympic basketball team in the Summer Games at Berlin, Germany in 1936. They brought home some gold."

"Pauline," a former cook whose mother was also employed by Rosabelle Bergerman at Dias Dorados shared some of her experience in October 1982:

Junior loved smoked smelts and he'd have them flown in from New York every week. I would have to cook them. I never liked them myself. Lordy! And the smell they would make in the kitchen. Rosabelle put a stop to that after a while. I started him liken' other things like my fried okra. He liked bacon too, but he thought he was a bad Jew because of it. I loved Junior. I loved his humor and his laugh. He was a good man.

I looked after Rosabelle's children, little Carole and Stan Jr. for many years. They were all good people and good to my family. God bless them all.

Margot Martin, a nurse whom Rosabelle first hired for herself in early 1960, and later sent her to care for Junior. She became his live-in nurse. Margot remained with Junior until 1966, about a year after Rosabelle died. Margot told this writer of the dreadful November day in 1965.

Junior buzzed for me to come to his room that Saturday when he told me that his brother-in-law had just phoned him with the terrible news that Rosabelle died. I felt so sorry for Junior. I did not know what to say. I think for the next year that I became like a substitute for Rosabelle.

Junior would ask my opinion about things more I believe because he felt so lost without his sister. Rosabelle made mostly all of Junior's decisions. He didn't make a business move without her.

Margot also remembered Junior's poker buddies.

Richard Conte and Lee J. Cobb were regulars. James Coburn and Tony Curtis were occasionally there when the stakes were high. The poker games stopped after Junior lost the use of his hands. There were many people coming and going from the house. During the day, it was mostly family.

I told Junior that we should put a revolving door up in the front with all the traffic that came in and out of there.

Margot fondly remembers how he spinned the ROLODEX and other times she would spin as Junior would say, "Who will we invite over tonight, Margot?"

In late 1966, a male nurse named Jerry was hired soon before Margot left. Margot said, "Junior was pretty immobile and needed someone physically stronger to look after him and be able to literally lift him." Jerry was devoted to Junior and remained with him for thirteen years until he passed.

Evelyn Moriarty knew Carl Laemmle Jr. as nobody else did. She generously contributed much to this writer including the "poodle letters" written to her by Junior in the summer of 1960 while Evelyn was working on location with Marilyn Monroe in Reno, Nevada during the filming of *The Misfits*. Evelyn wrote the following letter of introduction to this writer to the bits of whimsy that follow.

Dear Rick,

Junior was very modest. He usually didn't act very important. I knew he brought in a lot of stars. He once summed up his days at Universal by telling me, "I am yesterday's mashed potatoes."

He always said that I made him laugh. Why? I don't know. Well, he did have a good sense of humor. In all of our years of friendship, it was strictly platonic. The letters show a lighter side to Junior. He poodle sat while "Mother" was away in Reno. He really didn't have any of his own.

Years before this he took great pride in raising Irish Setters. One of my three smaller dogs belonged to Junior, but I had to raise him because Junior was renting a house then. Once Junior moved into his house, he didn't want to break the bond the dogs had together.

Before I left for Reno, I had to learn how to drive. Never had driven before that. I took six lessons. Junior would sit in the front of the car and the chauffeur in the back and I was doing the driving.

Junior also wanted to help me with Patti-Cake (was the son), Dighty (short for Aphrodite, the daughter), and Charcoal (or "Charky") (was their mother). Junior called himself a poodle sitter. One day coming from Cedar's, he would stop and have lunch at the Farmer's Market. They [the chauffeur and Junior] left and as they were driving to the barber discovered that Patti-Cake was missing.

A lady at the Farmer's Market found him. A guard told her that the dog came every day in a white chauffeured driven car.

Luckily, Junior got the dog back. He said that if he didn't find him, he would have to skip town.

Love and kisses,

Evelyn.

July 26, 1960

Dear Mother:

We hope you are well and happy. Thank you very much for sending your love to us in your letter to Mr. Laemmle. We like it here very much. Plenty of places to run around although it has been very hot, but no hotter than at home.

We understand it is very hot in Reno. The food here is excellent. Steak the first night, chicken the second, steak the third. Beef hearts the fourth night. A little dull. We thought we got away from them when we left Larabee, but evidently the big shot millionaire is trying to economize. Poor us.

We sleep right through the night very well. We don't get many catnaps during the day because a parade of strange people come in and out. Everybody makes a fuss over us and is very sweet.

I, Dighty, sleep on Elise's bed. Charcoal and Patti-Cake sleep on one of our old rugs outside of Elise's room. Mr. Laemmle plays the television most of the time at night. Seems to have a dull life. Doesn't he have any girl friends? He's very nice and has been kind to us but you are right—like all big shots, he is a little eccentric.

There's a big hole in the front yard, which we understand will be a swimming pool. He throws a fit every time we get too close to it so we want to stay far away especially as we don't want to displease him as we heard him order lamb on the telephone from the butcher and you know how we love lamb.

Thanks for asking about us when you called the big man the other night. We hope you are well and happy and the picture is going fine.

Give our love to Marilyn and our cousin her little poodle.
With plenty of love to yourself ....
Your caring daughters,
Charcoal & Dighty
And your favorite son, Hurry back home.
Patti-Cake
  P.S. Hi, Evelyn:
Hope you are feeling better and the picture is going well.
Am sure they will get you a doctor if you need it.
  Say hello to John [Huston] for me. The children are fine
and are good company for me. They are having a lot of fun,
but we all miss you.
  Love, Junior

August 11, 1960
Dear Mother:
Thank you for your lovely letter. We love hearing from
you. We are glad the picture is going well. It has to be a
great success with Marilyn, Clark and Monty and with a brilliant director like John Huston. I'm not being a bad boy. I
bit Charcoal by accident. I wouldn't bite my mother for the
world. I love her.
  We were playing as we usually do and my foot slipped on
the cement, my jaws went into her harder than I meant. I felt
very upset about this. We missed Charcoal very much. She
told me that she is very glad to be back. I still love it here.
Plenty of chicken and lamb and steaks. They occasionally
give us beef hearts so as not to forget Larabee and not to
be spoiled. I've been a good boy.
  The only thing that I do that upsets Elise and Mr. Laemmle
is that they put a beautiful plant in the living room. Whoever
heard of a plant being in the living room? And I wee-wee on
the plant. Of course, I'm not going to do this anymore as I
see that they are very upset by this.
  Love,
  Your favorite son,
  Patti-Cake.

P.S. The parade of people still goes on. A gentleman the other day said Patti-Cake is a sissy name. I should be called Pat. So how about it, Ma?

Dear Mother:

Patti is telling the truth. He didn't mean to bite me. I was in the hospital for a week but feel fine again. The wound is all healed. Glad to be back as the food is so much better. They have been giving us plenty of chicken and steak. Very extravagant! But then you know I never liked kennel food.

[The doctor] was here today and says Mr. Laemmle is getting better. He is always very nice to us. He loves poodles. The place is a madhouse. Seems like there are dozens of Mexicans putting in the planting. The place is run over with them. The plants look beautiful. Should be a Shangri-La before it is finished.

Hope you received the bottles of Restoril. I know they are sending you lollipops tomorrow. Hope you are having some fun besides all the work. I felt very unhappy about the bird passing away. Evidently his heart gave out. He got wonderful care. It was one of the acts of God that it happened.

Stay well and come back soon.

Charky. Dear Mother:

Nice to hear from you. We are all well and happy. Elise's bed is very soft—just as soft as yours. She's been a doll to all of us. Charky still sits on Mr. Laemmle's lap and occasionally I do the honors to the great man. Patti-Cake doesn't want to be a sissy so he doesn't sit on the man's lap. The swimming pool is nearly finished. Do you think we might dare venture? Come back soon.

Lots of love,

Dighty

Dear Evelyn:

The kids were over to the dog groomer. He did a fine job. Charcoal didn't go because she was in the hospital. Regards to everybody. Take care of yourself. No other news. Love,

Junior

Alan Napier's best-remembered role as Alfred the butler from the Batman *television series of the late 1960s. Photo from the author's collection.*

(left) Burt Ward (Dick Grayson), Adam West (Bruce Wayne) and Alan Napier (Alfred) in a scene from Batman *(1967). Photo from the author's collection.*

Promotional 1960s photo of the caped crusaders Batman and Robin (Adam West and Burt Ward). Photo from the author's collection.

Chapter 3
Alan Napier: The Classic Gentleman

It was through the medium of American television by which the talented character player Alan Napier is best remembered. His role as Alfred, trusted butler to billionaire Bruce Wayne, his ward Dick Grayson and Harriett Cooper (maternal aunt to Grayson), won over a generation of young audiences and families who tuned in to the *BATMAN* television series. Television reruns of the series continued airing nationally and internationally for some forty-plus years after its original run, January 12, 1966 until March 14, 1968. (1) This author was a third grader then marveled by "Alfred the butler," who protected the true identities of "the caped crusaders" Batman and Robin. Alan Napier appeared in all but nine of the one hundred and twenty episodes filmed. He was sixty-three when the show premiered.

In the winter of 1975, this author learned that Alan Napier was alive and well and living in California with an address listed for him! A letter of introduction was quickly mailed along with a Christmas card. His Christmas Eve reply follows.

> Dear Rick Atkins,
> Thank you for your Christmas card and good wishes.
> Sure - give me a call when you come to California. I'm home most of the time and will be pleased to have a chat with you.
> Sincerely,
> Alan Napier

The following story is written in its entirety for the first time. There is yet a roving question often asked of this author. Was Alan Napier and Alfred the butler one in the same? The reader may decide.

Junior Laemmle's driving directions to Pacific Palisades were precise. The weather changed from partly sunny to overcast late Friday afternoon, July 6, 1979. After turning from Sunset Boulevard onto the Pacific Coast Highway, it began drizzling. The ocean sight was enchanting.

Porto Marina Way was the street where Alan Napier's Oceanside home was located wasn't but a short drive ahead. The street began as a winding and rather steep incline. It was one of several neighboring ocean cliffs. By following the addresses stenciled on the curbs at each driveway in California fashion, Mr. Napier's home was about a third of the way. The dwelling was a two-level Mediterranean style structure. His garage sat below what appeared to be a porch landing. There was little room for parking. This author parked alongside the closed garage door and stepped out of the car. Suddenly, a familiar voice was heard from the porch landing above. There was Mr. Napier peering his head over and speaking clearly, "Ah! Mr. Atkins. Welcome! You will not be able to park there. I will be right down." Mr. Napier made his way down the white cement tiers of stairway and greeted this author with a warm courteous smile and a firm handshake. His large hands and long fingers were cool to the touch. Formalities were exchanged after which this author asked his first question, 'Exactly how tall are you, Mr. Napier?' He replied without hesitation, "Do call me Alan. Today, Rick, at seventy-six, I am six-feet-four-inches tall. I'm afraid I have shrunk an inch!" Alan continued talking, "It is best I direct you alongside the embankment rail to park. Your automobile will be safer there. The rain up here creates a nuisance for the neighbors. Once parked, we will go inside and have some tea and a nibble. You must be famished?"

Once the car was parked safely, Alan and I walked the steep concrete steps and entered his living room through the rustic looking front door. The abode was charming and comfortable. Alan's beloved Cairn terrier, Libby, was lying inconspicuously among a few throw pillows on a sectional sofa. A huge picture window faced out from the living room to a spectacular view of the Pacific Ocean below. Alan said:

> To your left, on a clear day you can see Catalina Island. I do not entertain half as much as I did, Rick. Loving memories were made here with family and friends. If there are any ghosts in this house, I assure you they are quite friendly.
>
> I bought this home for just over six thousand dollars in 1942. It has recently been appraised at worth of three quarters of a million dollars. I feel my Gyp's [his nickname for second wife Aileen] presence here. It has been difficult since her death. (2) With love we survivors strive to make new memories. Do make yourself comfortable, Rick. I must get to the tea. Set up anything that you may need before we continue.

Alan's kitchen wasn't far from the living room. After hearing the whistle of the teakettle, Alan returned to the living room carrying a tray with hot tea and warm scones with butter. He said, "I apologize for not having more to offer you. It is nothing fancy, but it shall get us through." At that moment, the enthusiast voice in back of this author's head was saying, 'WOW! The teatime living room scene is set! How cool! Hello fellow third graders! Get a load of this! ... Alfred the butler is serving Ricky tea! We both enjoyed the refreshments. As the afternoon moved on, learning more about Alan and his accomplished career was fascinating.

Alan was aware of the previous commitment this author had in Beverly Hills. While sipping our tea, Alan said, "What a wonderful thing for you to have had this connection with old Carl Laemmle, one of the greatest figures of the motion picture world and meeting his son. It is something you'll remember – a link with the past – all your life." Alan asked, "How is Junior [Laemmle]?"A reciprocal answer to Alan's question was not quick. The emotions of the day had taken their toll with this author. A spontaneous swelling of the throat triggered immediate tears. Alan's baritone voice soothed, "I'm so sorry, Rick. I'm sure you'll welcome a glass of sherry about now and we can talk about it?" While sharing libation, Alan asked, "If you enjoy tobacco, you may want to join me in a smoke? I smoke as the Englishman I am, moderate!"

It was that pivotal moment, which changed our perception of each other from that day forward. We smoked like two refined Englishmen while Alan's question was being answered. From an open window played the music of the ocean with its relaxing surf accompanied by the sounds of the seagulls. We engaged each other in conversation for nearly two hours. After a couple of weeks, this author received the following note from Alan.

Dear Rick,

I hope you got to San Diego without any trouble that night? The San Diego Freeway is now the best route. (Last time I made the trip the San Diego Freeway hadn't been completed and one used the Santa Anna Freeway.) However, that's ancient history by now.

Sherry? Oh, nothing special — Christian Brothers cocktail sherry, I think. And good luck with your book. (3)

Sincerely,

Alan Napier

He was born Alan William Napier-Clavering, January 7, 1903 in Kings Norton, Worcestershire, Birmingham, England. The "stage-struck" young man with the baritone voice grew up in England.

English playwright, composer, director, actor and singer, Noel Coward (1899-1973) was responsible for the successful operetta (in three acts), Bitter Sweet *boosting Alan Napier's career as part of the cast during its near two year run (1929-1931) in London. Photo from the author's collection.*

A graduate of Clifton College, Mr. Napier began to study acting as his profession. He appeared successfully in numerous stage productions and nine motion pictures, all in the UK between 1924 and 1937.

John Houseman (1902-1988) and Alan Napier went back many years as "school chums" in England. They remained friends after being reunited in America. Photo from the author's collection.

Alan Napier left the port at Southampton, England aboard the S.S. Champlain, April 21, 1939. The thirty-six-year-old actor arrived at the port of New York, April 28, 1939 where an advance accommodation was made for him at the Bedford Hotel where he stayed for "a few months." After arriving in California, it wasn't long before he made it his permanent home. The modest actor has appeared in various motion picture performances, appeared on Broadway and other American stage engagements. Over the years, he has also acted in a variety of radio broadcasts and appeared in television over two hundred times.

Mr. Napier made his television debut in March 25, 1949 as super sleuth Sherlock Holmes in "The Adventure of the Speckled Band," a half-hour adaptation on *Your Show Time,* a NBC television series. (4) His last television performance was in *The Monkey Mission,* a made for television movie in 1981. His final television appearance was April 28, 1988 as himself on a Batman reunion broadcast over *Fox's The Late Show.*

Rewind to the relaxing sounds of the ocean from Alan's living room window. Once the tables were turned, this author was more interested in the evolution of Alan Napier. The first question: When, where and how did you get started in show business?

> When? ...That would be 1923. There I was, a desperate young actor with a terrible stammer. I was twenty, the same age you are now, Rick. Where? ... I began training first at The Royal Academy of Dramatic Art in London. (5) How? ... It wasn't but a matter of time before I joined the Oxford players. My public *debut* was at the Oxford Playhouse in 1924. (6) I played a policeman in *Dandy Dick.* I -- never let -- them -- forget -- it [he said in a thundering voice].
>
> I had no ambition to become a star. Fortunately, having received opportunity on the stage where I could be someone else for a time helped to relieve my stammer.

Alan Napier experienced a breakthrough performance as an actor when Noel Coward cast Alan Napier in the long running "smash" play, *Bittersweet.* It ran for two years (1929-1931) at His Majesty's Theatre in London. (7)

> Noel Coward discovered that I had a gift in portraying old men. For me, the more eccentric they were the better. How strange that you should know Zita Johann. I met her when she and John Houseman were married in 1930. They were over in London and came to see me in the original stage production of Noel Coward's *Bitter Sweet,* in which I played the Marquis of Shayne. I was then 27.

American theatrical producer and director Brock Pemberton (1885-1950). He was also the founder of the Tony Awards having named the award after his professional partner Antoinette Perry. Photo from the author's collection.

Houseman was my oldest friend from schooldays back in England. I liked Zita. She was a beautiful and charming young woman. She and Houseman had been divorced for several years after he and I reunited in New York. He later married again as did I – and our spouses had first marriages

Orson Welles (1915-1985), together with John Houseman were responsible for launching Alan Napier's early radio and film careers. Photo from the author's collection.

as well – our second wives shared a stalwart friendship with each other.

There was a playful reunion of sorts when I had an opportunity to appear with Houseman in an episode of his suc-

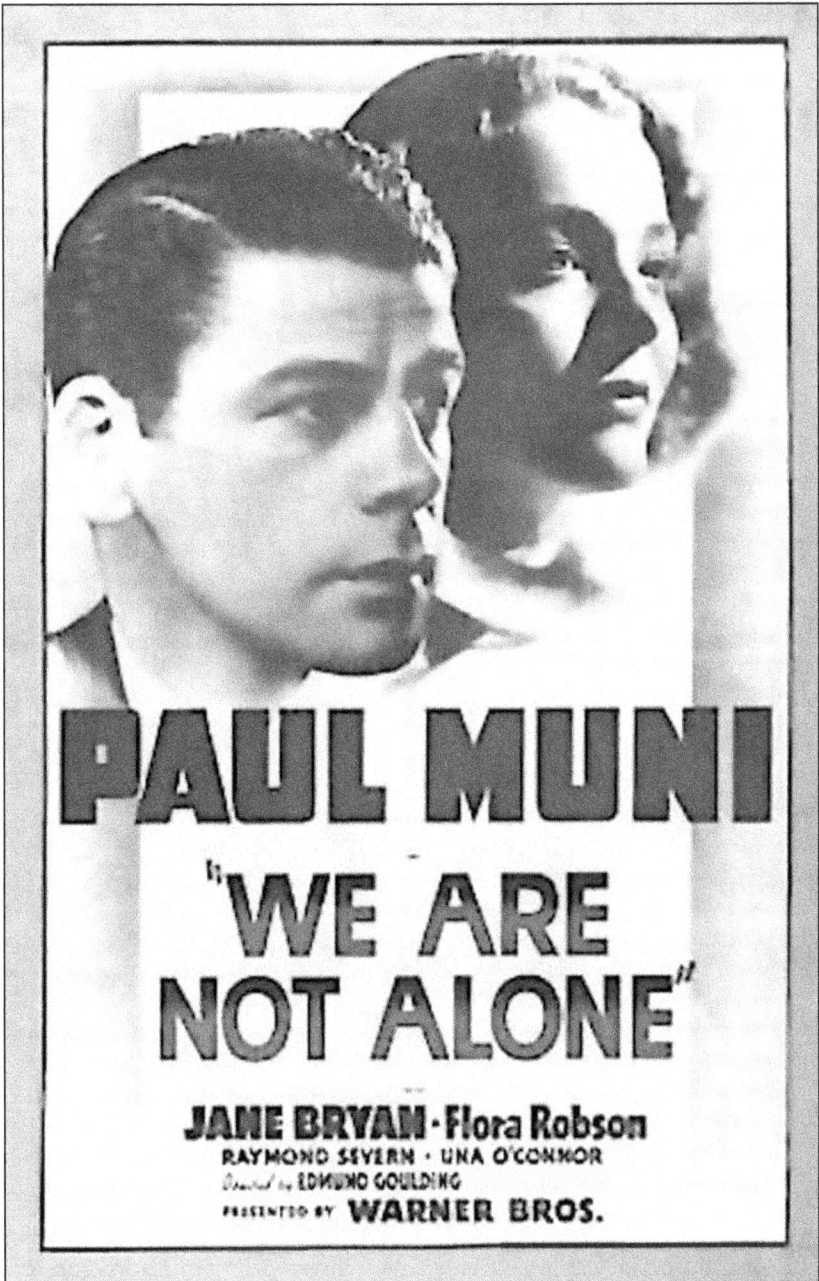

Warner Brothers' We Are Not Alone (1939) starred Paul Muni. This movie marked the American film debut of both Alan Napier and Flora Robson. Photo from the author's collection.

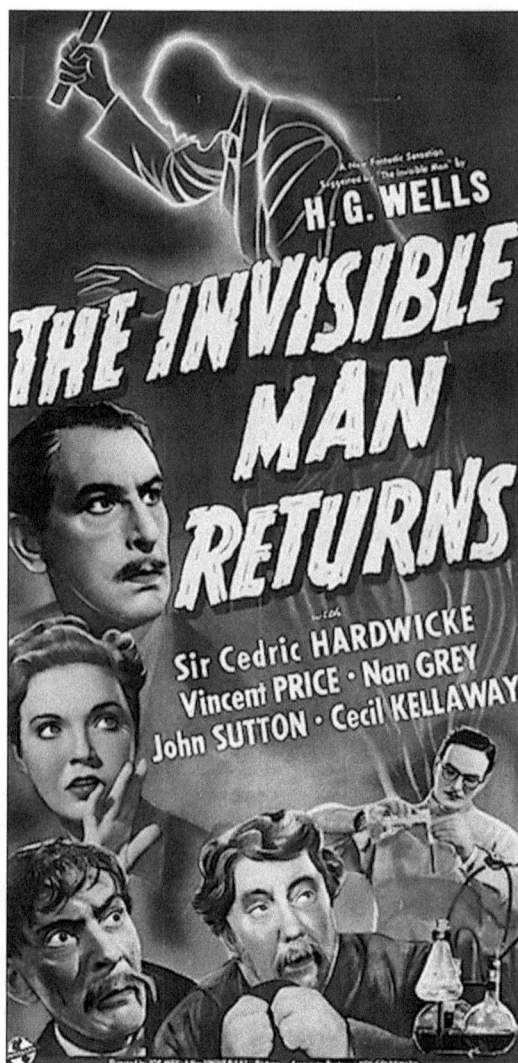

The Invisible Man Returns *was Alan Napier's second motion picture appearance directed by Joe May, released by Universal Pictures in 1940. Photo from the author's collection.*

cessful television series [*The Paper Chase*] playing a colleague from his past. (8)

Alan's first British film was *Caste*, a United Artists UK drama released in 1930. He played Captain Hawtree under the direction of Campbell Gullan. *Caste* was a directorial collaboration for Mr. Gullan and Michael Powell (who later became an acclaimed film director). Mr. Powell is credited for writing the screenplay based on T.W. Robertson's novel, but given no screen credit as a co-director. The last of Alan Napier's nine screen appearances in

England was the General in *For Valour*, directed by and starred the British stage comedian Tom Walls.

Between 1937 and 1939 was a difficult time for England and for Alan Napier. Amidst the onset of WWII, he was dealing with personal struggles in his life determined to find new direction. (9) American theatrical producer, Brock Pemberton was familiar with Mr. Napier's embodiment of aristocratic work on stage and offered Alan opportunity in America. (10) It would be another year before Alan Napier was introduced to the Broadway stage. Arrangements were made to introduce Alan Napier in Hollywood.

> The move to America not only made it possible for me to leave Blighty, it ultimately allowed further opportunity for my young daughter to be brought safely here by her mother "Nan," my first wife. [Nan later returned to England.] (11)
> I am grateful to Brock Pemberton – and happy to have told him so – remarkable timing! In biding that extra time, I bought an automobile and drove myself to California. I had a wonderful time doing so. After I arrived, John Houseman and Orson Welles were available. We went to work!

First at Warner Brothers, Alan Napier played the Archdeacon in *We Are Not Alone*, starring Paul Muni. British movie director Edmund Goulding directed it. Following the filming of Alan's scenes at Warner Brothers, John Houseman produced a live radiobroadcast of Agatha Christie's *The Murder of Roger Ackroyd*. Orson Welles directed and starred as detective Hercule Poirot. Alan Napier was Roger Ackroyd. It aired live November 12, 1939 from Hollywood over The Campbell Playhouse. (12) The Lux Radio Theatre followed with the November 20, 1939 live radiobroadcast of *Goodbye Mr. Chips*. It starred Lawrence Olivier, Edna Best, Alan Napier and Frederick Worlock. Cecil B. DeMille presented it.

Five days later, November 25, 1939, Warner Brothers released *We Are Not Alone*. The film was well received. It was Alan Napier's first motion picture appearance in America. Alan Napier referring of him to this author, "That *was* good exposure for the ol' boy."

Gladys George and Alan Napier in a scene from Lady in Waiting, *the 1940 stage play produced by Brock Pemberton and staged by Antoinette Perry. Photo from the author's collection.*

On December 16, 1939, John Houseman quit The Mercury Theatre that he co-founded with Orson Welles in 1937. Their association continued periodically before it exhausted after a few short years. Later, both men worked again with Alan Napier, but separately. (13)

Subsequently, Alan Napier remained in California where he was hired by director Joe May in *The Invisible Man Returns*, with Vincent Price. Alan played Willie Spears, an old coal miner who is pursued by the Invisible Man. This was the actor's second American motion picture appearance and his first of several in the science fiction, horror and fantasy film genre. It was a memorable one. Universal Pictures released the movie in early January 1940.

I played a Lancaster coal miner. Now the fact of the matter is that most coal miners are brawny little fellows about five-foot-six. Here am I, six-foot-five! And at thirty-six, I played it as an older character. I didn't know what the director, Joe

Claud Allister (1888-1970) was an English actor with an extensive career. He immigrated to America in 1924 and entered films in 1929 where he spent the next twenty-six years playing pompous or bumbling upper class twits - replete with monocle. Photo from the author's collection.

May, saw in me, but he had me stand in various ways, also on my knees in that film.

You see my height was always a consideration and some-times a handicap, especially in motion pictures, but it wasn't for Joe May [he said with a chuckle]. He allowed me the

Nigel Bruce (1895-1953) is best known for playing Dr. Watson to Basil Rathbone's Sherlock Holmes in a series of movies beginning in 1939. After a 1931 Hollywood comedy Springtime for Henry, Mr. Bruce was typecast as bumbling English aristocrats, military types or drawing room society snobs, all of which he was excellent at playing. Photo from the author's collection.

range to act as I did for his next film, *The House of Seven Gables* [again with Vincent Price]. (14)

After his introduction in Hollywood, Alan Napier returned to New York. Stage and dress rehearsal preparations were in progress. Alan played the affable Sir William Waring in Brock Pemberton's Broadway comedy production, "Lady in Waiting," starring Gladys George. Mr. Pemberton waited three years to assemble his cast and produce the dramatization of the play from Margery Sharp's novel, The Nutmeg Tree. The first dress performance was played at McCarter Theatre at Princeton University (New Jersey), on Saturday night March 16, 1940.

The following Monday, "Lady In Waiting" had a one-week run at the National Theatre in Washington, D.C. The Broadway opening came March 27, 1940 with an eleven-week run at Martin Beck Theatre. It closed June 8, 1940. It later continued as a road show first in Hartford, Connecticut; Boston, Chicago; and Buffalo, New York. Its final week beginning December 23, 1940 was at the Hanna Theatre in Cleveland, Ohio. American theatre critic, Brooks Atkinson took notice to Alan Napier in his first appearance on the American stage as, "a gentleman as well as an actor." (15) The play was obviously a vehicle for Broadway's popular star, Miss George.

One would think that Alan Napier was a shoo-in for the American stages given his successful background in England. Unfortunately, his stage performances were fewer in America. Alan told this writer the following.

> I learned that the higher type aristocracy, which I played in England, differs in the United States where statures and lesser characters types are better known. I hadn't completely realized this until I first appeared on Broadway. I was neither the funny Claud Allister nor the tubby Nigel Bruce type. (16)
>
> After the road show of *Lady In Waiting*, it was back to California for me – playing character parts in motion pictures and later in television. It was feasible work – which kept me in California. Besides, the California lifestyle and weather suits me dandy.

Alan Napier as he appeared in a 1952 stage publicity photo for the Dial M for Murder road show as Inspector Hubbard. Photo from the author's collection.

Among Alan Napier's stage appearances were in a 1948 Eugenie Leontovich production *And So To Bed* originally entitled, *James B. Fagan's Production of His Own Comedy -Based on the Diary of Samuel Pepys* appearing as Charles II, at the Las Palmas Theatre in Los Angeles. Eugenie Leontovich was a theatre producer and actress, who staged a number of productions in other cities that starred herself, Rollo Peters, Emlyn Williams (one of Alan's favor-

One of Alan Napier's favorite actors and dramatists, Emlyn Williams (1905-1987). Photo from the author's collection.

ite actors), Katherine Wick Kelly, Yvonne Arnaud, Walter Meade, Alan Napier, Walter Kingsford, Claude Rains, and Mary Robson.

In 1952, after appearing mostly in Hollywood motion pictures, Alan Napier was again offered opportunity on the stage. Alan said of the experience, "It was a worthy diversion after all."

First was the 1952 premiere of the popular British comedy *Gertie*, which starred Glynis Johns, in her Broadway debut. It was produced and staged by Herman Shumlin. It opened at the Plymouth Theatre January 30, and closed February 2, after a mere five performances. Alan remembered, "What a dear and talented lady Glynis Johns is! I've worked with her since and much later delighted us all appearing on *Batman*. She and I had the opportunity to laugh it all off about that disastrous play and agreed we all had our share of total b-o-m-b-s!" (17)

Before Hollywood movie director Alfred Hitchcock filmed Ray Milland and his stellar cast in the 1954 release of *Dial M for Murder*. Frederick Knott originally wrote it as a play for the London stages. (18) It debuted at the Westminster Theatre in Victoria, London June 19, 1952 starring Emrys Jones. The play ran four hundred and twenty-five performances.

The successful long-running Broadway version of *Dial M for Murder* opened October 29, 1952 starring Maurice Evans with five hundred and fifty-two performances beginning at New York's Plymouth Theatre and later at the Booth Theatre where it ended February 27, 1954.

Simultaneously, a duplicate road show of the hit Broadway play was spawned at Boston's Wilbur Theatre, December 26, 1952 starring Richard Greene. Alan's friend and fellow actor Frederick Worlock was originally cast in the role of the Inspector, but withdrew for personal reasons. Thus, Alan Napier replaced him as Inspector Hubbard of the Maida Vale police. (19)

> I have been in your fine city, Chicago, on occasion quite a number of years ago. I have no doubt that you were yet born. [Alan said with a quick grin as he continued to speak...] My agent rang me with details of a *kick off* for a stage road show of *Dial M for Murder*. First it played in Boston and then to Chicago. Despite the cold weather, the experience was gratifying for my wife and myself. It was one of my better memories professionally.
>
> Personally, it was gratifying having had the opportunity to take in an evening of our friend Emlyn Williams' remarkable portrayal of Charles Dickens concurrent to our stay in Chicago.

Dial M for Murder opened in Chicago, January 25, 1953 at the Selwyn Theatre (and soon moved to the neighboring Harris Theatre) starring Richard Greene. Alan Napier remained with the

Alan Napier from the 1956 Broadway play Too Late for the Phalarope.
Photo from the author's collection.

long running play until May 17, 1953 when actor J. Pat O'Malley
replaced him concluding its sixteen-week run. (20)

Prior to his stage run, Alan worked on two Hollywood films that
were to be released after his return from Chicago in 1953. First,
Young Bess, which starred Jean Simmons as Queen Elizabeth I.
Second, John Houseman's production of *Julius Caesar*, directed

Alan Napier was the voice of Sir Pellinore in Walt Disney's animated full-length motion picture The Sword in the Stone *(Buena Vista Pictures, 1964). Photo from the author's collection.*

by Joseph L. Mankiewicz, starring Louis Calhern and Marlon Brando. The gripe of this film was its large cast in which bigger names had lesser roles. In November 1952 between the two film productions, Alan and Aileen Napier became naturalized United States citizens.

By December 1953, John Houseman was producing another play, the rarely performed Shakespeare tragedy of *Coriolanus*. This was a difficult production for Houseman from production design to its large cast of forty-two, which included Alan Napier, Mildred Natwick and Robert Ryan as Caius Martius Coriolanus.

Coriolanus opened off-Broadway January 19, 1954 at the Phoenix Theatre. It closed February 28, 1954 after forty-eight performances. Alan returned to Hollywood where played the part of Despereaux in the motion picture, *Désirée* (starring Jean Simmons and Marlon Brando), released in the fall of 1954.

By 1955, television dramas, comedies, variety shows and anthology television became the new wonder. Producer and screenwriter, Joan Harrison, hired Alan Napier for a television episode

Alan Napier, Tippi Hedren and Diane Baker in a scene from Alfred Hitchcock's Marnie *(Universal Pictures, 1964). Photo from the author's collection.*

of *Alfred Hitchcock Presents*, which led the actor to act in several other Hitchcock episodes. Chilling anthology television became contagious with audiences. There were many of them. Over time, Alan Napier appeared in Boris Karloff's *Thriller*, Rod Serling's *Twilight Zone* and Serling's later series *Night Gallery*. (21)

As I continued working with the *Hitchcock series*, my agent rang to offer yet another play on Broadway. I was fortunate to be gainfully employed for a number of reasons, and I accepted it. What I found most appealing about it all was reuniting with friendly fellow actors.

Too Late for the Phalarope, opened on Broadway at the Belasco Theatre October 11, 1956. It was directed by John Stix and written by Robert Yale Libott; Based on the novel by Alan Paton. It was a three-act drama that took place in the southeast Transvaal, Union of South Africa in present time. Alan Napier was among

Batman the Movie *(Twentieth Century Fox, 1966). Photo from the author's collection.*

over thirty cast members. The play closed November 10, 1956 after thirty-six performances. (22) This was Alan Napier's final stage performance. (23)

Among other notable motion pictures was an offer from Walt Disney for his animated motion picture, *The Sword in the Stone* (released in 1963). Alan Napier's baritone voice was used for the animated character of Sir Pellinore. The following year, Alan's voice only was used in areas "a hound and a reporter" in Walt Disney's *Mary Poppins* (1964), the live action/animated motion picture starring Julie Andrews, which won her an Academy Award for Best Actress.

Mr. Hitchcock wanted me for his motion picture, *Marnie* [1964] with Tippi Hedren and Sean Connery. I played Sean Connery's father, but I felt that I was being used more for scenery than anything else. No real acting involved. Nevertheless, I carried on politely.

You see, Mr. Hitchcock once offered a part to me in one of his films that I turned down. He [Hitchcock] and I never re-

The Batmobile, the Dynamic Duo's popular crime fighting vehicle, a creation of the late George Barris (1925-2015). Photo from the author's collection.

ally hit it off. It happens to all of us at times. Not your cup of tea, so to speak. We may as well start wrapping this up. You say that you have to be in San Diego tonight, my dear boy.

According to this fairly accurate list in front of us, I appear in four films after *My Fair Lady*. *Batman* [1966], the movie is listed fourth and last here.

After the *Batman* movie, I didn't act in another film that was sold as a theatrical release. It [*Batman*] was the kiss of death for much of the cast. Nobody's worked since!"

Alan Napier was an exception. After *Batman* was cancelled, he continued to land "suitable work" in a number of television shows and motion pictures made for television through 1981.

I will, however, finish by telling you that the director George Cukor for *My Fair Lady* summoned me. That was a rather tragic and awkward situation for everyone involved. Henry Daniell was a longtime actor in Hollywood, and a damn good one. He was part of Cukor's film – the tragedy remains that Henry Daniell died while working on the set of *My Fair Lady*. Mr. Cukor used me to fill in. You may see a bit of me on film with lovely Audrey Hepburn. The ensemble is my great joy. To me, acting is about what I can offer my colleagues. (24)

English stage and Hollywood film actor Henry Daniell (1894-1963).
Photo from the author's collection.

Alan said, "I'll leave you with one more or anything else will cost you [as he winked]." Alan related the following conversation between him and his agent regarding how his typecast role – as Alfred, the butler came about.

My agent rang me one morning and said, "I think you're going to be Batman's butler."
I said, "What?"

Boris Karloff in a scene from Isle of the Dead *(RKO Radio Pictures, 1945). Photo courtesy of Alan Napier.*

She said, "Don't you read the comics?"

I said, "No. What is a Batman?"

She said, "You even get to drive the Batmobile."

I said, "I don't want to drive the Batmobile. I've never heard of such rubbish. How do I know I want to be Batman's butler? What are you getting me into?"

Alan Napier entertaining the author with scrapbooks from the actor's career. (April 15, 1983). Photo from the author's collection.

She said, "Alan, if all goes well, it could be worth a hundred thousand dollars."

And I said, "Oh … of course I'm going be Batman's butler!"

There was a renaissance in television over motion pictures then. And as you may guess … I played *Alfred the butler* on television for two years. I had never played a butler before and I found that this one had no relationship to the real thing. The only prop they gave me that they thought was butlerish was a feather duster.

I said, "No, that's a housemaid."

They said, "Well, you can dust the Bat machinery."

It earned a good living and got me recognized by the youngsters. I am happy that I did it. And they still to this day rerun them on television. Can you imagine?

The following questions and answers between this author and Alan Napier is mostly related to his appearances in science fiction, horror, and fantasy films following *the Invisible Man Returns* (1940) et al.

RA: Would you like to act in another horror movie or fantastic film?

AN: Yes. But it seems that there isn't any good material for one anymore ... they're running out of ideas. It would be nice to possibly do *The Uninvited* again. It was a huge success. *The Exorcist* I hear was a recent success in the field.

RA: *The Exorcist* was released over five years ago. In my opinion, I call it shock rather than horror. Would you agree that most of these types of movies are not as entertaining as they once were?

AN: Yes. I'll agree with you. That is an interesting point, and very well-articulated. I've not given it much thought, until now, but listening to that I do agree.

The approach to this sort of film is handled in a wrong manner. As I said before, they're running out of ideas. I know that if Boris [Karloff] were still alive, he would be laughing at all of this.

RA: What sort of man was he?

AN: Truly charming, and a real pussycat, surprisingly enough! He was a classic example of true creativity as an actor in horror movies. I'll never forget doing *Isle of the Dead* with him.

There was a scene when Karloff flung open the door and said (as only Karloff could have said it), "Where are the *b-o-dies?*" That was strictly Karloff. I've never forgotten seeing that happen. Boris [Karloff] spent many an evening right here in this very house, this very room where we would have dinner on occasion. We had some wonderful conversations.

RA: You also appeared in a number of things including *The Strange Door* (1951) with Karloff and Charles Laughton. What do you remember of Laughton?

AN: He really got in deep with the character of practically every role he played over the years and, as I understand, this made him very difficult to live with, according to his wife, Elsa Lanchester. Remember the scrapbook that we looked at earlier from my early stage years? My fondest memory was working with Elsa in England in her *title* role as *Little Lord Fauntleroy*. Yes. These are the fond memories!

Charles Laughton was a real perfectionist. I didn't know him well ... only as an actor. I worked in a few American films with him [*The Blue Veil* (1951), *The Strange Door* (1951) and *Young Bess*

Lewis Allen's The Uninvited (Paramount Pictures, 1944). Photo from the author's collection.

Laird Cregar, Alan Napier and Faye Marlowe in a scene from Hangover Square *(Twentieth Century Fox, 1945). Photo from the author's collection.*

(1953)]. I didn't work much with Elsa in America [*Lassie Come Home* (1943)]. She wasn't from our camp, so to speak. Some were in the Oxford Players from England. Of the friendly names there was Robert Morley, James Whale, (Dame) Flora Robson, and (Sir) John Gielgud.

RA: You did appear in *The Uninvited*. What do you remember of it?

AN: During the shooting at Paramount for *The Uninvited*, the whole cast was scared. Some of those tremendous effects, such as doors slamming and windows opening just sent chills through my whole body. It made my hair practically stand on end and not the hair on my head either ... both really [laughing]!

Even though we all (on set) knew it wasn't for real, there was still that feeling of evil presence about us. And the film ... it came over just as strongly.

RA: Was *The Uninvited* one of your favorite horror movies?

AN: Yes... personally as well as professionally. It resonated well.

English film and television actor, singer-songwriter, music composer and author George Sanders (1906-1972). His brother was the English film, television and radio actor Tom Conway (1904-1967). Photos from the author's collection.

RA: You appeared in *Hangover Square* with Laird Cregar and George Sanders. What sort of man was Laird Cregar aside from his career?

AN: Laird Cregar was a talented and well-educated gentleman, who unfortunately died tragically young. Incidentally, he died before the film [*Hangover Square*] was released. I didn't know him well, but I understand that George Sanders did. (25)

RA: What was George Sanders like to work with?

AN: Very difficult, as everyone knew even then about him. And he didn't take crap from anyone. I met George Sanders and his brother, Tom Conway, soon after I came to California. George and I shared a number of films. Tom and I shared one film, *Cat People*. Tom Conway and his wife became good friends with we, Napiers, as we were the Housemans and the Millands. George Sanders was more the renegade. When he wasn't working, he was womanizing, boozing and traveling the country. He was not ashamed. That is how we knew George best. (26)

RA: You appeared in *House of Horrors* with actors Robert Lowery and Rondo Hatton. What do you remember that film?

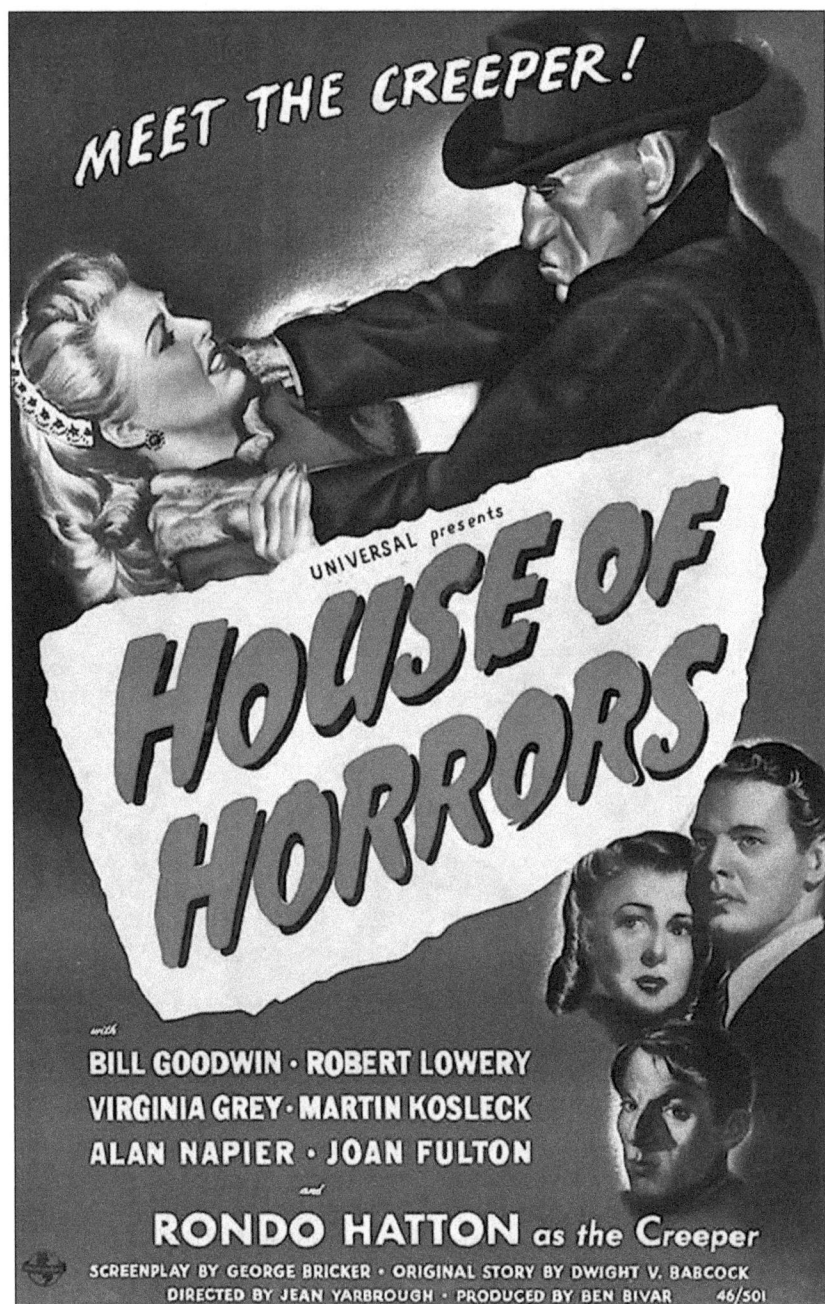

Jean Yarbrough's House of Horrors (Universal Pictures, 1946) starring Rondo "the Creeper" Hatton. Photo from the author's collection.

Alan Napier as Landale in Forever Amber *(Twentieth Century Fox, 1947), from the novel by Kathleen Winsor (1919-2003). Mr. and Mrs. Alan Napier were credited as "dialect directors." Photo from the author's collection.*

AN: Yes. I do remember something about it. Robert Lowery, of course I remember. He was a very nice man and unfortunately, an underrated actor. He looked too much like Clark Gable, which made it difficult for him to get good leading roles. And who was the other actor that you mentioned?

RA: Rondo Hatton. I hear that he required very little makeup.

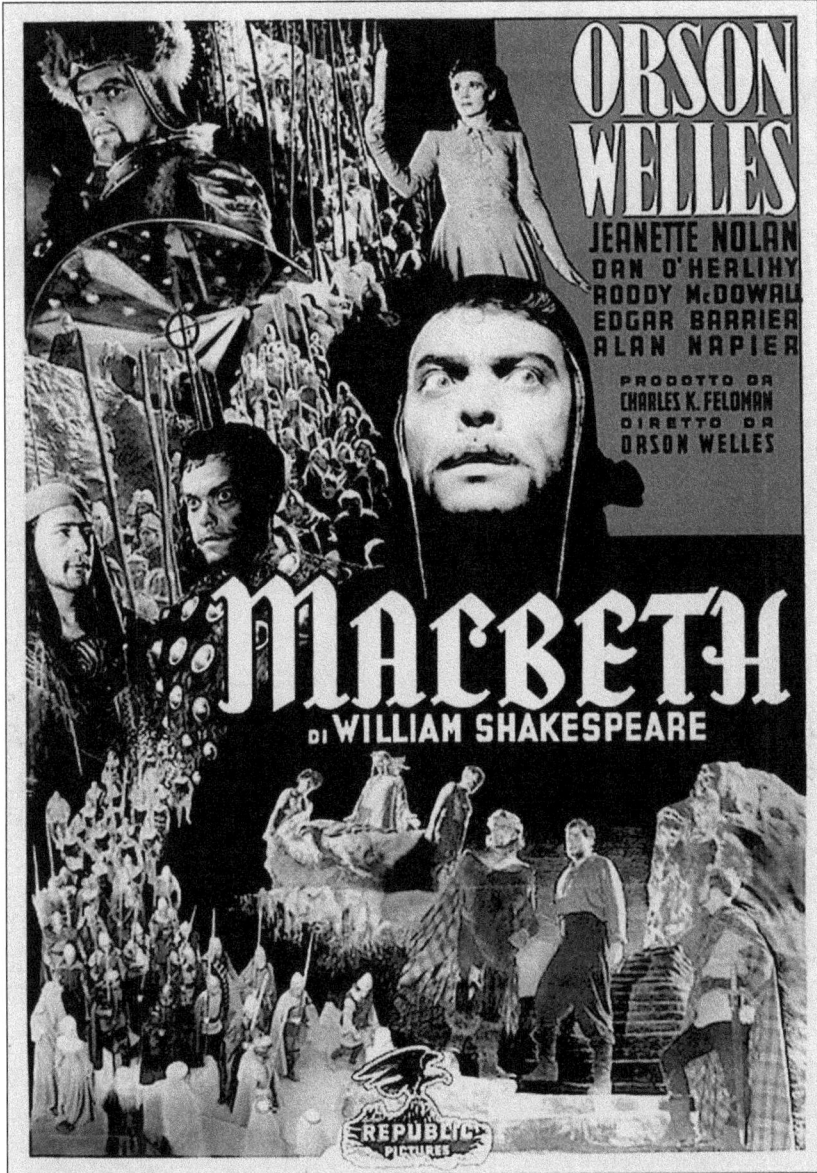

Actor, director, producer and writer Orson Welles' (adaptation of William Shakespeare's) as Macbeth (Republic Pictures, 1948). Photo from the author's collection.

Master Minds (Monogram, 1949) featuring the Bowery Boys. Directed by Jean Yarbrough, Alan Napier appeared as Dr. Druzik in the film. Behind the scenes electrical wizardry by Kenneth Strickfaden left Alan amazed. Photo from the author's collection.

AN: Little or no makeup as I understand. He had the biggest head and hands of any human being I had ever seen in my life. And the unusual fact about him was that he wasn't a very tall man. The studios built him as quite the opposite on the screen to sell tickets. Audiences were made to believe that he was a huge man, but he wasn't.

RA: Wasn't he only about five-feet-six?

AN: Somewhere in that area.

RA: What do you remember about the movie itself?

AN: Not much, except the director was having great difficulties in getting a black cat that was in a scene to do just what he wanted it to. I never seemed to have much luck in movies where I appear with animals.

RA: What can you tell me about the (1947) film *Lured*?

AN: I previously worked for the director [Douglas Sirk] in a couple of films. Sir Cedric [Hardwicke], Boris [Karloff] and the delightful Richard Coote were in the film.

RA: Do you remember Lucille Ball from the film?

AN: Yes. I remember Lucille Ball. What a lovely and smart lady she is – and *look* at how far *she* has come in show business. She has become - what is referred to as- "*an institution*." How many other films do you have listed, Rick?

RA: Five.

AN: Do you mind if we do a run-through?

RA: That's fine with me.

AN: Hence, more memorable films I worked was *Forever Amber* [1947], from which I became an actor and a dialogue coach, along with wife and they gave her a part as well. I appeared in Orson Welles' *Macbeth*. Then I found myself working in a low budget Bowery Boys film, *Master Minds*. Jean Yarborough, the director, was a good man. I worked for him once prior. What I remember most fascinating about working in that film was a gentleman who made a lucrative living supplying electrical gadgetry in films and brought in. It was rather spectacular. Nice chap. His name escapes me.

The Mole People (*Universal-International Pictures, 1956*).
Photo from the author's collection.

Alan Napier as the High Priest Elinu in a scene from The Mole People *(Universal-International Pictures, 1956). Alan thought his character in the film was "rather unique." Photo from the author's collection.*

RA: His name is Kenneth Strickfaden. He furnished his services for many fantastic films over the years, and more recently in Mel Brooks' *Young Frankenstein.*

AN: Are you acquainted with him?

RA: Yes, but only through correspondence so far. We will be meeting in Santa Monica for the first time next week.

AN: Splendid! What are the chances that we'd be talking about someone I brought up who you are meeting next week? What fascinated me about this man was that he manufactured this machinery himself and was incredibly versed about running electrical current. He was evidently a scientist. Rick, you are indeed fortunate to be meeting these clever people with your research.

RA: Thank you, Alan. I appreciate what you said. I consider you one of those people. With four films left in our run-through, I have a quick question before we continue; did you know Ian Wolfe at all? I know you were in a number of films together. I spent a couple of days with him and his wife this week.

Alan Napier (Dr. Gideon Gault) and his longtime friend Ray Milland (Guy Carrell) in a scene from Premature Burial (American-International Pictures, 1962), directed by Roger Corman. Photo from the author's collection.

AN: First, you're very kind. Thank you just the same, Rick. Ah! Good ol' Ian Wolfe! What a fine actor he is. I know him professionally. When you're on set, you don't always have the same scenes together. I found Mr. Wolfe to be a well-mannered and jovial man. (27)

RA: Ian told me that he liked you as an actor too. He also remembered that when he would see you on sets over the years, you'd always have a small dog with you.

AN: This is true. I always preferred smaller dogs so I can carry them. I always found them to be great companions. I'm glad to have a good report from Mr. Wolfe [Alan said with a low chuckle]. Very well, let us continue with the run-through.

The Mole People was a different film. I won't expound on it. There were many people who found me unrecognizable in that unusual makeup [as the High Priest Elinu]. I rather enjoyed the experience.

Val Lewton (1904-1951), the Russian-American film producer and screenwriter. Alan Napier appeared in four of his friend's film productions between 1942 and 1949 Photo from the author's collection.

Island of Lost Women was for monetary reasons. The most important aspect is that I was working. I say this *not* to disappoint.

Journey to the Center of the Earth was another small part in a big film.

The Premature Burial was interesting because I was able to act again [in our third and final film] with my good friend, Ray Milland.

(28) I remember that the director, [Roger] Corman, was quite the [Edgar Allan] Poe enthusiast. He made a good name for himself in that genre.

RA: You asked me earlier to remind you of your late friend Val Lewton. [Alan appeared in four Val Lewton film productions, *Cat People* (1942), *Mademoiselle Fifi* (1944) *Isle of the Dead* (1945), and *My Own True Love* (1949).]

AN: Yes I did. Thank you for reminding me. Half of Val's movies that I appeared in were not horror per se - but horror was the type of film that fascinated Val - which he drew much of his creativity and inspiration. Val was very good at it. He should have been a director. That was a very small part I had in *Cat People*. But as a film, I think it was a well-directed film [by Jacques Tourneur]. I worked again with Val Lewton, Boris Karloff, and the director Mark Robson in *Isle of the Dead*.

RA: I say that Val Lewton was a producer extraordinaire.

AN: James Agee, the great film critic and poet referred to Val as one of the three greatest filmmakers of Hollywood. The other two were Charlie Chaplin and Walt Disney. I, along with others who worked with him or knew hi, would agree. I spoke the eulogy at Val's funeral. I have somehow misplaced it. When I find it, I will send you a copy. You may want to use it. What I would suggest for a complete and very amusing portrait of Val, you should go to pages 182 and 183 of my friend, John Houseman's new book, Front and Center (in which you will also find colorless references to me). He has an established position in the American world of entertainment as "Mr. Culture." Because my friendship with Val was more domestic - our two families became very close - I see him as more relaxed and genial than in Houseman's picture, but that picture is essentially true;

> His unit had become a small, independent kingdom in which he reigned as a benevolent despot whose retinue included some of the brightest young people in the business - writers, musicians, designers, and directors.
>
> Here, as long as he kept within his niggardly budgets, he was free to indulge the romantic fantasies that made him a prolific, short-lived, third-rate novelist in his early twenties.

His unit (known on the lot as the Snake Pit) was a laboratory where – unlike Frankenstein, who labored to make one
single monster – Lewton used his literary erudition and his
own lurid imagination to create a whole gang of vampires,
werewolves, grave robbers and walking dead.

All this was done in an atmosphere of hard work and high
spirits, which was rare in the anxious, high-pressure world of
Hollywood filmmaking. The penury in which his films were
made created its own climate of energy and ingenuity.

I recall the shooting of a climactic scene for what came to
be known as *Isle of the Dead.*

The ingredients were a plain rough wooden coffin set on
a trestle against a black velvet backdrop, a couple of lamps
with gobos (screens used to create shadows), a silent camera and a few hundred feet of film.

Later, music and a sound track would be added: a hollow
knocking that seemed to come from inside the box – soft
and slow at first with the first stirring of the restless corpse,
then louder and faster and more insistent as the spectator's
imagination carried him inside the coffin where the vam-
pire's body strained against its wooden prison in its frantic
struggle to get out and go about its evil business.

Finally, when the suspense was almost unbearable, the
knocking was replaced on the sound track by a horrible
splintering and tearing of nails as the coffin began to burst
apart. At the cost of a few hundred dollars an effect was
achieved that was far more terrifying than any elaborate
camera-moves, light changes or wide-eyed reaction shots
could have made it. (29)

Return to Alan's living room; twilight fell upon us and the room
began to fill with the ocean's cool evening air. As the ocean's
waves grew stronger, Alan closed the window. We proceeded
outside to the backyard admiring Alan's rose garden where he
gave directions for the best route to San Diego. We said our fare-
wells and a hug.

Six months later, this author received from Alan Napier the following. I enclose a copy of the words I spoke at Val's funeral [St.

Matthews Episcopal Church, Pacific Palisades, California March 18, 1951]. It seems a bit sentimental to me now, but it evidently sounded the right vibe then. . . . "

All of us who knew Val – and loved him for his generosity, his gentleness, his gaiety of spirit – (how can we forget that babbling laugh which so often preceded a witty comment or a wonderful story?) think of him first, perhaps, as a creative artist, whether in the studio or at his carpenter's bench at home. It was his nature always to be making something.

It is in the act of creation, fashioning out of this dull earth a thing of proportion, meaning and beauty, in which the breath of life and truth abides for the delight of mankind, that takes to himself something of a divine and the eternal.

But the sensitive artist must pay for the precious gift, this gift of rising on the wings of his imagination into the divine realm of creation. His wings are delicate and easily bruised.

Val gave us of his best and was often hurt in the giving. He was often tormented because of the restraints and limitations imposed on him by the structure of the motion picture industry. Yet this was the field to which he was called. He loved motion pictures. He had a matchless gift for making motion pictures.

Sometimes he felt that his wings had been so clipped that he would never fly again. But nothing could ever quiet that restless spirit of creation.

To the end, Val was soaring aloft on the wings of his creative imagination – wings that have carried him now beyond our ken to a rarer atmosphere, where they can no more suffer the crippling and the bruising of our clumsy, insensitive world.

Let us say goodbye with thankfulness in our hearts that we have known this gay, delightful, tormented, generous and most dear spirit. Rick, Ten days later at a cocktail party I found myself in conversation with a gossip columnist. Val's name came up and she said to me, "Poor Val! I hear Rabbi Nussbaum spoke a most beautiful eulogy at his funeral." I replied, 'Rabbi Nussbaum my foot! It was an Episcopal service and I spoke the eulogy!' Val always wanted to find me

One of the author's favorite shots of Alan Napier as Captain Kidd in a
scene from Double Crossbones (Universal-International Pictures. 1951).
Photo from the author's collection.

a star part in one of his movies. I had it at his funeral and no
Nussbaum was going to take screen credit!' (30)

The thing I like most about my words on Val is that they
glorify the creative artist. People think that Henry Ford and
A. E. Dupont are the "important" people. Not so. It is the
Shakespeares and Beethovens who nourish the spirits of
truly great men. Abraham Lincoln was nourished on Shakespeare, Winston Churchill on Gibbon (Decline and Fall of
the Roman Empire) and so on.

Without any Captain Kidd photos to sign, Alan Napier graciously signed this photo to the author as General Steele in a pre-Batman television series (1962-63) Don't Call Me Charlie, *which aired weekly over the NBC network. Photo courtesy of Alan Napier.*

I am totally preoccupied writing a novel – Whom the Gods Love. The background of the story is the life that I have here. Into this Garden of Eden I drop a very dramatic situation.

At first I thought of it as a play or movie – but the novel gives more scope to develop what goes on under the surface in the mind. Play or movie can come later. (31)

My agent thought it perfectly delicious and anticipated no great difficulty in finding a publisher. That was a year ago. It has been to all the top houses in N.Y. only to be rejected. They want violence and blood. My book is gentle, ironically amusing and urbane. (32)

Best of good fortune to you,

Alan

Our written correspondence continued before and after July 6, 1979. In the spring of 1983, this author returned to California with his sister, Kathy, to celebrate her birthday with two weeks of festivities. This included her meeting Alan Napier. The following note dated March 26, 1983 reads:

So good to hear from you and even better to see you in early April, eh? God willing. I shall be here. My knees are in poor shape, but my head and heart OK. Love, Alan.

The visit was special to us all. Alan and this author were able to talk about many things. Alan was pleased to entertain us and show a few of his scrapbook albums of his long career. This author agreed with his sister that Alan was a truly valued person.

Kathy and Alan got along wonderfully. We also agreed that he was well read and most eloquent in speech and dialect. He valued life. He referred to acting as his "craft," which he took seriously. Kathy noticed a sex appeal about him that did not show up on the screen.

Another note arrived from Alan after our visit, which included the following.

". . . Give my love to Kathy. She is a beautiful person. And much love to yourself. Alan." It was during that visit when Alan spoke of his befriending George Bernard Shaw while Alan was still living in England.

If you are not familiar with George Bernard Shaw, he wrote plays - many of them! He and I didn't start off on the right foot. Before I knew that he was present for a rehearsal, I rebuked the appearance of a beloved literary character of his. After constructive criticism on his part, we became acquainted. I appeared in his immortal play, "Heartbreak

Alan Napier in the comfort of his home, with his beloved Libby. Photo by the author, July 6, 1979. Alan once signed an enlargement of this photo with the following "With fond greeting to my friend Rick – Alan Napier"

House" once as Captain Shotover ... He came to the re-hearsals. He did not direct, although he may as well have.

In another engagement I was cast in the same play as an-other character and Shaw advised me. I do believe he put in a good word when I left for America. I'm fairly sure of that assumption.

Alan Napier was fully retired when this author caught up him, November 24, 1986. His life at his beach paradise was being spent with his family and close friends. Thus, I found myself walking the beach for the first time and seeing the real beauty of the ocean, as well, watching the gulls flock was great. Experiencing the beau-ty of the world in which Alan Napier lived for over forty years of his life was emotional and this author vowed to keep composure before walking any further.

Walking the distance north on the Pacific Coast Highway and up the hill at Porto Marina Way, rays of light were beaming from

Alan's happy home. The walk up the narrow cement steps to the front porch felt like only yesterday.

Knocking at his front door, a woman graciously invited this author in. Alan introduced her as a Connecticut neighbor of the family. Alan spoke with good cheer, "Ah, Rick! Come in. Sit.

Relax and we will fetch you a refreshment." Alan explained that he was instructed to stay off his feet as much as possible and assured that he was in good health. With the three of us seated, we talked for quite a while before she prepared the refreshments.

Our visit lasted roughly two hours. When it came time to leave, Alan stood. After a hug and a kiss, Alan said, "My dear Rick, you once came to this house in tears. I understood. Are you going to leave with tears? To which this author replied, 'these are happy tears. I am thankful that we've remained friends and we were able to visit again tonight. You have always been *the* classic gentleman, Alan. I love you.' Alan removed his eyeglasses for a moment brushing away a tear. He said, "Thank you for saying that Rick, I love you."

Alan instructed to be cautious walking back down the hill at night, which surely felt longer than the walk up in daylight. Alan said, "If you need light, look to the stars. There will be plenty out tonight. " Alan was right. The trek down the hill was dark, but stars showered the sky as far as the eye could see!

Suddenly out of nowhere, a musical blast was heard! It was the 1980s recording *Heaven Must be Missing An Angel* presumably coming from the beach. Learning quickly, the music was coming from a passing car with headlights off and suddenly on. Car lights were visible on the highway by this time down the hill. Alas, the local Los Angeles bus was waiting on schedule a short distance away. This would be the last time Alan Napier and I saw each other.

In July 1987 this author made another trip to California and to visit friends including Alan Napier. After phoning his home, another person answered and informed me that Alan had suffered a stroke and was told to phone him at the Berkley East Convalescent Home in Santa Monica, California.

This author phoned Alan to ask about a visit. Alan said, "Rick, how nice of you to call. I'd rather you wait until I am home. I am far more comfortable there. I haven't a thing here. I've grown a beard that I don't like. I hope you are well? I am not. The stroke affected my hearing, some speech and my sight too. I trust that you are well and my best to you and your family. Goodbye, Rick."

It was April 1988 while at home in Chicago this author had the television set on. A BATMAN reunion was airing over *Fox's The Late Show*. Anxiously wondering what mention there would be of Alan Napier, a VHS tape was quickly placed in the video recorder. After a commercial break there remarkably was Alan sitting in a chair. It was obvious that he had some paralysis and got along quite well talking to the best of his ability. This was Alan's final public appearance.

The following day this author placed a call to the Berkley East Convalescent Home. This time it was long distance. Regarding the show Alan said, "Thank you for phoning ... I had no knowledge of this until I was summoned from my bed, shaved and dressed. I was rushed into a van and the next thing I knew I was in a television studio. It was great to see members of the ensemble and the Batmobile. And I was happy for that shave. I trust you are in good health and doing well in school. My love to you, Rick." To which this author replied, 'I am well thank you. You're such an inspiration to me. My love to you, Alan.'

Nearly four months later, a morning in school, a classmate said, "I guess there are a lot of sad BATMAN fans." I asked my classmate what she was talking about. She answered, "Oh, you didn't hear? ... Alfred the butler died." This author said, 'What?' She said, "It's in the newspaper from a couple of days ago in the lunchroom. I'll show you." There it was in black and white, which read in part . . . **ALAN NAPIER 85, butler to TV BATMAN** passed away August 8, 1988 in Santa Monica, California from pneumonia. (33)

This author gathered his things including the newspaper and left directly for home where a phone call was placed to the Napier residence. Jennifer Nichols, Alan's biological daughter, answered the phone. Our conversation was brief, but with heartfelt mention about whenever Alan spoke of his family, he did so with great pride and admiration. (34)

I read the eulogy that Alan Napier wrote and recited about his friend, Val Lewton, thirty-seven years before Alan passed away. This author followed the phone call by writing a short note along with a card mailed to the Napier family.

This author revisited the neighborhood on Porto Marina Way in Pacific Palisades; October 21, 2011 only to find portions of what remained of Alan's former home left. It had been demolished. What hadn't changed, however, were the song of the ocean and the wonderful talks that once took place in this beautiful setting. With time, earthy things may change but not the memories of a most well-spoken, kind and accomplished human being.

Canadian-born Rauff Acklom (a.k.a. Michael Dawn) in an early 1920s theatre photo during his time with Basil Sydney's touring company. Photo from the author's collection.

Chapter 4
David Manners: A Beacon of Light

David Manners was born Rauff de Ryther Duan Acklom, to British parents Lilian and George Acklom in Halifax, Nova Scotia April 30, 1900. The family included a daughter. She was two years Rauff's senior. Her name was Dorothea "Cecily" Acklom. In 1907, after George Acklom was offered a job in the United States, the family arrived in Boston, Massachusetts. They moved on to Westchester County, New York; first to Mount Vernon before settling in the village of Hastings-on-Hudson in Greenburgh, New York.

Young Rauff acted in several plays during high school and later attended college at the University of Toronto. He chose to follow his urge for acting. In the spring of 1922, he was offered a job with the Theatre Guild in New York as an understudy in Basil Sydney's touring company, which he did under the stage name, Michael Dawn. (1)

During this time, Rauff befriended actresses Zita Johann and Helen Hayes. Another closer friend was actress Eva Le Gallienne, who founded the Civic Repertory Theatre. (2)

Rauff was a traveling man for a good part of the next few years when he met a young lady. Her name was Suzanne Bushnell. (3) They were married May 23, 1929 in Manhattan, New York. The couple diverted to Los Angeles, California where he accepted a small part in *The Sky Hawk,* a Hollywood motion picture at Fox Studios released in 1929. The couple set up residence in Los Angeles.

Soon after, the handsome actor and his wife traveled to New York. It was upon this visit when his friend Eva Le Gallienne was instrumental in helping Rauff cast off the name Michael Dawn. Others helped him adopt the name David Manners (the surname was his mother's maiden name). A small part in the Fox picture led to

As Michael Dawn in the late 1920s, he appeared in his first major long running Broadway play. The young actor would change his name one last time. Photo from the author's collection.

his meeting film director James Whale, who cast David Manners in his first major motion picture *Journey's End*. (4) David Manners appeared in thirty-nine motion pictures mostly as the leading man alongside such notable actresses as Katharine Hepburn, Loretta Young, Ruth Chatterton, Helen Chandler, Barbara Stanwyck, Kay Francis, Marian Marsh, Constance Bennett, Adrienne Ames,

Publicity shot of David Manners in his first major motion picture with British actor Colin Clive (in his American debut) on set of director James Whale's (his first American made film) war drama Journey's End *(Tiffany-Gainsborough Pictures, Ltd., 1930). Photo courtesy of Gregory William Mank.*

Claudette Colbert, Zita Johann, Gloria Stuart, Mae Clarke, Valarie Hobson, and Elizabeth Allan. Much to the former actor's chagrin, he is chiefly remembered for a small number of horror movies produced by Universal Pictures, now considered classics.

Before the end of 1936, David Manners exited Hollywood never to return. He was thirty-six. David Manners eventually moved near the edge of Mojave Desert at Victorville, California where he had purchased land to build a home during the time he worked in Hollywood. He later opened his home to friends. He told this author that it became a guest ranch complete with swimming pool and tennis court. There he lived life and pursued interests as a writer and painter.

During the 1940s, he became the author of two novels under the name David J. (Joseph) Manners and a naturalized citizen. In the 1950s, he sold his Desert home and relocated to Pacific Palisades, California. He later authored self-discovery books.

It was April 1975 when this author caught up with David Manners in Pacific Palisades for his seventy-fifth birthday by mailing a card to him. David replied soon after with a decorative card in which he simply wrote, "Dear 'dear fan'... Thanks for your card of greeting. Sincerely, David Manners." Little did this sixteen-year-old know at the time that our written correspondence and telephone chats would multiply and follow him through the rest of his life? David relocated from Pacific Palisades to Santa Barbara, California with his life partner, Bill Mercer in 1978. Bill passed away several months after the move. David would relocate two additional times in Santa Barbara; then a third, the Valle Verde Convalescent Home, or as David referenced it, "a home for us oldsters." Ultimately, this is where David Manners and this author met for the first and only time. We shared infinite memories of his ninety-seven years.

David Manners, former actor, author and painter sent this fellow author sixty-four-pages of insightful written passages of self-discovery in his own words. Several of these writings follow with added personal notes and letters David wrote to this author. He has and will always remain a beacon of light and love knowing others may share in his light.

CONTEMPLATIONS

I never could make a saint out of an ego more than you can make a silk purse out of a sow's ear. So I quit all that struggling and turned attention to something, which was not going to die ... it's simply a question of loving enough to come to a stop. _David Manners

12/20/84
DeLa Vina St., Santa Barbara, Ca.
Thank you, Rick for your card—Yes, I remember.
Have an extra fine New Year, too.
David Manners

May 1, 85
Dear Rick,
Very touched by your thoughts expressed as a card for April 30.
Thanks, friend –

David.

July 12, 1987
Dear Rick,
You say some of your closest friends are over 80 – mine are below 35! Two fellows are also in their 20's- so it goes. Age is something of belief and not as read as the world seems to think.

I am also working on an autobiography mostly about the movie
and theatre years, but I am doing it as a fiction, a novel under an
alias—Why? Because it frees me to tell the truth and I enjoy it
more. If and when it comes out: I'll let you in on the secret of the
author's name.

My early novels are out of print. Some copies have been found
in second hand bookstores.

One (the first) is called _Convenient Season_ the other, _Under
Running Laughter_. Both were published by E.P. Dutton & Co. [as
David J. Manners]

I can't promise to be of help in your writing-as the days are so
full-but do keep in touch. Yours, David.

8/28/88
Foothill Rd., Santa Barbara, Ca.
Dear Rick,
I am grateful for the young ones such as you who glimpse the
Truth + are in a position to help heal this drug-eroded-world of
separateness + hate. It is through gentle sweetness +not laws +
shooting + imprisonment that the world will be healed. It is not
by looks or preachers but through Love + understanding + the
example we set.

You have learned a lot. Keep your openness + readiness – there
is so much more for you to discover which you + only you can do
for yourself.

Go well--be well -- you are loved -- greatly. It is always with you.
Keep in touch— David.

AUTUMN 1988
In silence, music is heard which fills the heart with questions.
There is music which has no notes nor any instrument to play it. I
find no words to fit, nor have I any knowledge more than a sure-

ness that there is a something else ever present which never can be limited to written thought.

The purity of an empty page that's never stained by ink tells more. I lay down the pen and listen. The ear hears naught. And yet, there is another kind of hearing which, like music may move the heart, not here nor there and not to rise or fall.

This music moves, but not to go or come. It swirls and yet is still, but what have I learned of that which fills the heart with yearning? Nothing, nothing but the fact of something other than this envisioned universe and which is here, forever being.

Suppose you have just met that special one and there is a kind of silent agreement between you. You have never felt like this before. It is new and overwhelming, but how do you express it? What can you say, "Oh, (name) if I could only tell you --" You receive a squeeze of the hand, which tells more than words, and (name) says, "I know. I know."

Now such is what I am trying to tell about the man who loves without object or desire. He doesn't know words that aren't silly or inadequate, but at the same moment he knows words aren't necessary. How does he know this? He can't tell you, but he is aware of something else which confirms.

When I look at the manuscripts written and the journals all-full of statements and claims of knowledge, I shake the head and wonder. I ask who can be sure of written words or spoken phrases. All that I see here of world and universe may be naught but a limited point of view.

Once I looked beyond the farthest star and said, "Beyond that is God." But how can that be when here is something, vast beyond measure, yet right here?

This morning I looked at a tree which I see every day, but suddenly, I had never seen it before and I was amazed. Then there was the planet and all beyond it, more amazing, but most of all it was, that which beheld the images that is amazing beyond words. From soil, grass, tree and on out and in, all of it is a wonder and I cannot give it name or reason. I see, but I don't know what I see. I revel, but don't know why. I am joyful, but I can find no cause. I love, but I know not what love is. I yearn, but there's nothing to yearn for. Now what sort of mess am I?

Winter 1988-89

Originally this letter was to be sent out early in December as a Christmas greeting, but the wait for new lenses for the eyes sent that plan "all aglee." Now I have the opportunity to say thank you for a galaxy of Christmas cards and the gentle thoughts expressed thereon. Especially, I wish to thank those who enclosed the tangible gift, which keeps these letters coming.

As children we were told that December 21st was the winter solstice and the shortest day of the year, but we discovered as we walked through time that long or short, a day was made either in hell or a heaven according to that on which our attention is focused.

If we were focused upon the wonder of conscious awareness and all life as a fascinating mystery, we were as content as the little child who was still unadulterated by personal sense.

If it were possible to write out a formula for the control of attention, it would long ago have been done. We have endless systems with as many claims of success, but each of us discovers that heaven can only be experienced by a deep love and need for it which is strong enough to keep the attention on it.

How to----?

Not long ago a publisher asked if I would write a book on how to achieve the peace of understanding. The request started much questioning within myself. How to, how to, was there any answer? There were a few things I knew and the mist important was to surrender the idea of ever finding answers within a conditioned, personal mind. At first, I asked, what else is there? There was a pure, unsullied mind of the little child before any conditioning of it had set in. How could I recapture it? Did it have to be recaptured, wasn't it still present as it always has been, this fact of consciousness?

Out of this questioning, it occurred at last that the very fact of existing was the utter simplicity of being the consciousness

I already was. This human mind appeared to be bound to make complications. It was forever standing outside as one searching for answers and asking, how to find it, how to find the peace of understanding.

It was beginning to look as if the phrase, *how to find, was* an anachronism and only possible to the personal, human mind which had been educated into thinking of itself as separate and apart. How to smell a rose? How to walk? How to feel happy or sad?

The obvious answer is, I do it. I walk, I smell the rose and I feel. We don't ask silly, obvious things like that. Isn't existing also evident? Aren't we aware of being here? Isn't this very fact of being aware a wonder? Seeing this wonder we are as the only real, isn't this the utter simplicity of understanding, which we have been overlooking? As we begin to view the fact that we are already the wonder, the activity of a greater power <God> isn't this itself understanding and the joy and peace of it?

Unless one was already open in mind and receptive to the attempts to express the wonder of being, it began to be seen that writing or talking about it would never mean anything to the human mind which was all bound up in its belief that it was separate. One conditioned to the duality of *I am here* and *all else is out there*, will scoff at the concept of oneness.

From experience, I discovered that often what is called "personal" tragedy, loss, disappointment, etc.; will open the sufferer to a glimpse of the wonder of being never seen before. At this point, the life of the sufferer takes a turn and begins to heal.

Many of us didn't have to go this route, but as if a curtain around us suddenly rose to reveal an awesome glimpse of the wonder conscious being is, we stepped into a new dimension of understanding.

We are not these animal bodies we inhabit, nor the personal sense of being separate. We know, deep down, that we are something else. As the poet Roethke says, "beyond becoming or perishing." It is this inexpressible knowing which is the peace and joy open to all of us. How do we find it? Look closer. We already *are* IT.

Spring 1990 - NOTES TO SHARE

I am never completely free of doubt that the marks I make on these papers, the Love I might whisper to you or the song I might try to sing mat be tinted, even stained by conditioning, but I do know that I shall make a point of being honest as is possible. The deep wish is to bring the wonder of which I am aware as close to its loveliness as I am at this point, able.

We are seeing great changes, in ourselves and in the world of man, and in spite of these, the fact of being is changeless. The only proof we have of it is that we exist. Some twenty years ago I wrote some pages [for a book] I called LOOK THROUGH, and now I wonder if I saw even a little glimpse of the immensely of that which the title suggests. Did I then foresee the troubling to the person called David or did I walk away and say, I'm busy now, some other day? Can one really walk away? I doubt it, or did I thus go on struggling to release the hold that conditioned beliefs had o'er me? I wonder.

Perhaps in the flush of early glimpses I may have gabbled loud, proud and bold on wonders barely understood, while now I would not dare incase in words this present

Wonder, but rather stand amazed and silent.

How beautiful these simple words, which say, "This is it, always, ever. Seeing the majesty, the infinite glory of it, how could I ever want again, or plan, or be involved?" Thus, the old shell is pushed aside, forgotten and Life Begins. Worldly miles dissolve before the light of love, and with no regard for age, those who recognize each other come together heart to heart as one. It is the most wonderful love there is, wanting nothing, only being. It is the magic healer, immortal Wonder ever present, the pure and ageless Child of God with eyes ashine.

MORE WORDS

The urge to express is always present. Most of the time it is not done because what is being experienced cannot be confined to words. But there is also a deep need to share, to reach out, and the only available means at this point appears to be to write words. I sigh and ask how? You see I have no learning to impart. This cannot be a preachment or a teachment for I am neither preacher nor teacher. It's simply a matter of love. It's a heart or core or a somewhere inside which is bursting with a glow of energy, a special kind of energy which is neither this nor that, but everything, you included. The arms of it are of infinite reach and embrace, not only the whole planet and the immensity it is appearing to be part of, but more, something else ineffable.

I am here sitting in front of this machine, and you are sitting, standing or lying down where you are, yet you say, "I am here." And I say, "I am here."

Therefore we are both here, being as the same conscious awareness. Now what is it that makes us say, "But I am of such and such background and of such and such sex and special name, and therefore, I am different." Do I hear you say, it is genes and different conditioning?

I know nothing about the genes department, and conditioning is but a teacher who has helped us discover. His work is soon ended and he is to be let go with the flesh, but that which has been taught by pain, anguish, brief pleasures and disappointments we bless and give thanks for.

It has led us back to the wonder and happiness in the heart of the child. In this world of appearances of good and evil many ask for conclusions. Leave the concluder with his or her conclusions. We battle not. There is nothing, nor anyone to defend.

9/19/91
Dear friend Rick,
Your letter tells me that in your grief for your beloved friend you have clouded the light of simple Being + the me of Rick gets in the way of perfect peace + happiness which is present everywhere + I know your friend would want you to be free + aware of the great river of Love which draws us all to the Sea.

No. I can't do it for you, nor can anyone—only you can let go + are what is present + how you are related to it + thus be happy.

I love you + wish you release. David.

10/30/93
Santecito Drive, Santa Barbara, Ca.
Dear Rick,

You don't need to be caught up in the appearance of Death of friends + you don't need to feel loss – What has gone is naught but the shell-or cocoon. That which moved the body and spoke through the mouth--is not lost--can't be. It is the conscious aware-ness we are and the <u>ACTION</u> of the far greater power behind all life appearances.

Yours, David.

January 18, 1996
Dear Rick,
Your manuscript is here, but I can't say when I'll be able to go at it. If you were here you'd understand. Eventually, yes. Don't hang by a toenail while you wait to hear from me.

At 96–7, I take a holiday from writing letters. I send blessings and Love, David.

August 3, 1996
Calle De Los Amigos, Santa Barbara, Ca.
Dear Rick,
As you know, there is purpose behind all experiences. Some things never change and one is friendship.

Yes, dear Rick I wish only the best for you. I'd like to know what the bad months have taught you—They do, you know, if you are aware.

Have I told you that your friend here is 96 years old + living in a home for us oldsters? - a nice place – good people + all is well in that department.

I have discovered one thing which never changes and which is above old- It is Love and I don't mean Romance and Possession- No, true Love- It asks nothing, but gives all- It is a joy forever.

Yes, we have known of each other for a long time-good old friends. Bless you and may all go well with you. Let me know what Life is teaching you. Hope you get to call here before I take my leave. I'd love to meet you. Blessings, + may all go well with you. David.

It was the fourteenth of December 1997, a Sunday morning. The previous day by telephone, David Manners stressed, "You know, I am 97 now... so you had better hurry! I can die tomorrow!" David put me on the phone with a worker at Valle Verde Convalescent Home to give me road directions from Los Angeles.

For a week prior, I was staying in Los Angeles with my friend Carla Laemmle, a special holiday visit. I asked Carla if she would like to come along. She said, "I would love to, but I don't want to spoil your moment. You've been waiting for this a long time. This day is meant for you and David. Do send him my love." Later that day, I returned to Carla's to stay Sunday night before returning Monday to Chicago.

This thirty-nine-year–old author left Los Angeles at 8 a.m. for the highly anticipated drive to Santa Barbara. It was the most beautiful, peaceful and effortless two-hour drive from Los Angeles to Santa Barbara with open road all the way.

Once entering Santa Barbara, the warm air embraced sudden changes to a more refreshing climate, as simultaneous glimpses of a sunny scenic Oceanside peeking through the highway brush were heavenly while driving in. What a greeting! When I arrived at Valle Verde and into the parking area, I suddenly felt some nervous tension while gathering items. I brought the notebook containing our correspondence and black and white photos of him from some of his motion pictures. I also brought him a copy of my first published book. Something told me to leave my camera in the car for fear that David may not be comfortable with me snapping pictures. (5)

Walking through the front doors of the facility, I felt David's presence. When I entered his room, he was not there. As I turned around there he was, facing me! He had just returned in his wheelchair from having had his breakfast. He appeared physically weakened, but was mentally alert.

I had seen only one later in life photograph of David when he was sixty-seven that was later purchased. Thirty-years later, this author was astonished by David's physical appearance, better than I expected. He wore large eyeglasses over his gray-colored eyes. He was still handsome and sporting a favorite sweater over a button shirt with the top button buttoned. The skin on his face was that of a man at least thirty-years his junior. I was surprised to also see a good head of hair on a man of ninety-seven. It was not completely white or gray. It was a shade to that of a Russian blue cat.

David's longtime correspondent from Chicago introduced himself. With his ageless all-too-familiar broad smile David said, "*I found YOU!*" I reciprocated the same comment. In shaking hands, David said, "Rick, dear Rick, sweet Rick, you are nervous. You remind me of a good and dear friend, Bill Mercer. He took his *leave* nearly twenty years *ago*. We shared twenty-plus-ten years together. Rick, sit here in this comfortable chair and hold my hands for a while. Close your eyes and R-e-l-a-x." David began gently messaging my hands speaking softly and instructing me to relax and to meditate. I drifted into a catnap holding onto David's hands for what he said was at least 15 minutes. Upon awakening, David asked, "Do you feel better now, Rick? Better than a drug?" I answered with a smile and nodded.

David congratulated me becoming an author. I mentioned his contribution. He was happy to have contributed "in some small way" to my first book, the subject of which was horror movies.

David told me, "It seems to me that those horror pictures I appeared in are shown quite often. I feel that I gave better performances in other pictures that are not given much if any television airing. I gave up watching television some time ago. I had one in my room and had them take it out. It became an evil eye, especially the evening news, the biggest evil nowadays. Unfortunately, the horror pictures are the ones I will be remembered for. Can you imagine?"

I later asked David if he would like to look through my notebook. He delighted in reading some of his own letters. As he got to the photographs, he thought that one of his best film performances was in Frank Capra's THE MIRACLE WOMAN with Barbara Stanwyck. I had respect for Frank Capra. He was a great guy. Bill and I called Stanwyck, "Babs." She was one of our frequently guests at Rancho Yucca Loma. We loved having her there. She was great fun. We adored her.

In seeing a photo of himself from *Journey's End*, David said, "When James Whale and I met, and he thought I would be ideal in his picture. And as they say in the "*biz,*" it was my big break. For me, the best part of it was the people I met along the way. Most were good and kind, some were not. In life we learn from all."

David told this author that after a tiff with Joan Crawford, "I lost all momentum in pictures and literally walked away from it. I don't like talking about this. It's from that other world. I'll succinct it to say, she [Joan] swam against the current, metaphorically speaking. If that was her forte, so be it. It was not mine. And that, dear Rick, is the end of the story.

We spent the rest of the morning sharing song and no talk at times, only meditation. David hadn't attended church that morning because of my 10 am visit. He sang to me the first song that he remembered from Sunday school as a child. It was actually something that his mother taught him to sing. When I asked him what the song is he simply answered, "Mother's Song." The clarity in his voice was amazing! We were both filled with emotion. David particularly enjoyed my nervous rendition of the 1960s song entitled, *"Elusive Butterfly"* that I learned to sing for him. He said, "That was sweet. You're almost there. How lovely that we have finally met but you know we didn't have to. By God's Grace we have. Yes Rick, By God's Grace we have met."

When I asked David if he would like to go for a ride in his wheelchair, he was quick to answer, "Yes! I have to see a nurse about another [morphine] patch. As we rode through the halls of the modern facility, David said he was pleased to have someone else do the driving for a change. "You are an excellent driver. First a stop, the nurses' station, please!"

There, I proudly showed some of the nurses a couple of photographs of David from the 1930s. One nurse swooned, "Oh, M i s t e r M a n n ers!" David told the nurses in jest referring to me, "This one won't be welcomed back!" He then smiled at me and said, "Let's continue our ride."

When we returned to his room I noticed an office desk nearby. David said, "I was kept pretty well supplied for writing but I've been doing away with things. I want to lie down." David told me that he was no longer able to walk because of hip problems, but could climb himself on to his bed from his wheelchair when positioned properly. David got into his bed. He took me by the hand

and closed his eyes. In a solemn voice, he whispered a plea to God, "Let me go!" I sat beside his bed in silence still holding his hand. A restful smile remained on David's face throughout his nap.

When David awakened, he looked across to me and said, "You know- dear Rick, Many places I've been in my life. This place is very good. And you being here is good. My biggest claim to fame these days without apology is I forget. It's called short-term memory loss, but I forget is easier to say;" followed by his gentle giggle.

Our departure was sweet. As I left David lying in his bed, we kissed gently. This time with broad smiles across both our faces, David said, "Go well, be well, and pray for my leave, dear Rick." We shared I love you.

Following our visit, for Christmas 1997, I wrote for David a playful original story/poem entitled MY BROWN PLAID FLANNEL SHIRT. It was written exclusively for him including a photo of my two beloved dogs and me. To my knowledge, no other copies exist. My brown plaid flannel shirt was worn the day, we met. I cherish it as my favorite. David admired it, feeling the fabric of the sleeve commenting, "It looks nice, better . . . It feels . . . w a r m." Had I another shirt with me to change, I would have given him the brown plaid flannel. Instead, it became a lasting memento of that December day in Santa Barbara. The shirt and the memories remain with me to this day.

David's reply came in February 1998 along with an enclosed photograph of his former desert home area. The following is David's last written message to me. "Rick! Rick! Rick, the Rick of Ricks! Yes, I got the doggie photo. Wish you and the dogs were here. The envelope has been sitting on the desk – oh what a poor correspondent am I!! Cats like it [the shirt too]! Rick, Rick Rick—Forgive—I love you, David."

Having had David Manners' friendship taught me acceptance in many areas of life. His heartfelt writings are still read and shared among friends. He took his leave December 23, 1998. Having phoned two days later to wish him a Merry Christmas, I connected with the Administrator. She told me that he peacefully left this world while sitting among his friends having dinner that evening. A lovely Christmas card followed soon after. It was from the Valle

Verde facility, and signed by the staff. Yes. The shell known as David Joseph Manners is gone, but his actions are eternal. His cremated remains were later scattered at his former home near the Mojave Desert. The following writing from David Manners was one of his last.

Fall and Winter 1989-90
(David prefaces: Because of eye surgery it is necessary to combine two quarters as one. I know you understand.)

THE PLACE WHERE I STOP
What am I to do? Where are the words, which can express that which is in the heart? I am helpless. Inspiration has no outlet. I am used to having an outlet, but where has it gone? The skunk, which passes under this window at night, has a way of expressing. It fills this room with its woodland scent. It is being itself. Why can't I?

I don't wish to smell like a skunk, but I do wish to share something wonderful. All I can do is to ask for help and wait. There is a way out of this emptiness and I must find it.

In the first place, how do we get lost in this maze of mental stagnation? It is like a dark forest, but I know it has a purpose, and if I understand the purpose, I will discover the path, which leads out into Light. The heart yearns for Light. It loves Light. How shall I find that path, Oh Father?

I sat in the darkness and waited. Faintly at first, I heard it. I listened intently. There came a feeling that I already knew the answer. I was sure that as consciousness awareness ....ah, yes, when the term consciousness awareness stops being words of planetary origins, the wonder is experienced and Love is unveiled. Now how do I know this?

It must be the experience of timeless wonder right now. It is as if there were nothing but ocean and I am in it at last. I was always in it, but once I believed I was only the river, which went winding in and out, seeking a way to that ocean. Understanding that the ocean is ever present and the only real presence in the end of negation, worry and fear. It is the place where real living is.

But these words are not telling it. They are but a faint echo of the experience. I must return to that place where terms stopped, for within the place of stopping is the art of turning away from personal sense which is like a backwater in a river and goes nowhere. I must again find the main stream, but metaphors will never do it for me. I must see that no form of words can bring about the experience of ever-present wonder.

I have heard the present wonder termed as "the action of God Good," and I say if this or any term sparks a glimpse, then let go of the term and follow the glimpse. If I stick with terms, I am back in the swamp, going nowhere.

The circuitous river does usually come to the sea where its toil is ended, but I am to be aware that the river I suppose I am is not like a Mojave River which in the rainy season, may come roaring through the desert from the mountains only to end up in a desert lake which evaporates and disappears in the summer heat. So much for metaphors.

Fortunately, metaphors are often the only possible something written will hit a bell with someone and reveal the joy that has no end. That joy is ever present. Experienced or not, it is always with us.

If an old man who suffers the pains of physical age can experience joy and be it, then anyone can. It is simply a matter of loving "the father" enough to come to a stop, that place where personal sense is relinquished, and where the experience of ever present, timeless joy is.

There must have been a light shower in the night. This morning as the sunlight glimmers through the trees, I walk the path through the garden.

Every leaf of the rose bushes has diamond on the tip of it like a tiny world of sparkling light. But wait, the lawn is heavily strewn with these glittering jewels. I am in a dream of shimmering light, and like a dream there is no feeling of solidity beneath my feet, but day dream or night dream, I am still in a world of images, appearances, the quality of which in determined by my personal, conditioned experience.

Whether that dream is a happy one or a frightening one, a delight or a pain and sorrow, there is ever the one reality to turn to. Wherever I am, I stop in my tracks, and behold, the wonder of IT,

Consciousness, a wonder relative to the prime cause ever present. Now, the wet sparkling world of light or the dark miserable world of ugliness vanish, and I-----? Can you tell it? Can I? Not Worded, no, but I experience it, a light far more than sunlight, healing, joyous!

Excerpts from a Letter from Mary
"Dear David,
From your books I sensed you have experienced pure awareness without object or desire. That's what I want also. Can you guide me?" David's reply to Mary's letter followed.

"There is news for you Mary, there is no *also*. Pure awareness is what you really are. Nothing can change this. Under the web of personal sense and all its learning is the pure awareness, which is the little unadulterated child, you are. It is always with you. When everything else has gone into the ground or the furnace, that consciousness lives forever."

THE UNCONDITIONED ONE

I awaken silently singing. The wonder grows. Once seen as a wee glimpse, the immensity of the Wonder begins to come upon me as a shock, amazement and unconfirmed joy. The visual world remains, but it is new. Yes, the unconditioned babe is the Truth. It lives right here as this which we are. To discover it is a joy ineffable. The one who experiences it is the one liberated. _ I love you all, David.

Author's note: The majority of the following photographs were part of this author's notebook, which David Manners peered through that December day in 1997. I know that David wouldn't mind me sharing "that world" in pictures.

Billy Bevan and David Manners in a scene from Journey's End *(1930)*
mostly shot in New York. Photo from author's collection.

Loretta Young and David Manners in a scene Kismet (First National, 1930) the first of five movies they appeared in together. Photo from author's collection.

Helen Chandler, David Manners and Dorothy Peterson in a scene from Mothers Cry (1930, First National Pictures).] Helen Chandler and David Manners appeared in four movies together. Photo from author's collection.

Paramount Studios, Hollywood's newcomer of 1930. David Manners appeared in five Paramount productions. Photo from the author's collection.

Ruth Chatterton and David Manners in a scene from The Right to Love *(Paramount, 1930). This was their only film together. Photo from the author's collection.*

David Manners (as John[athan] Harker) and Helen Chandler in her best remembered role (as Mina [Murray] Harker) in a publicity still from Dracula (Universal Pictures, 1931). Photo from the author's collection.

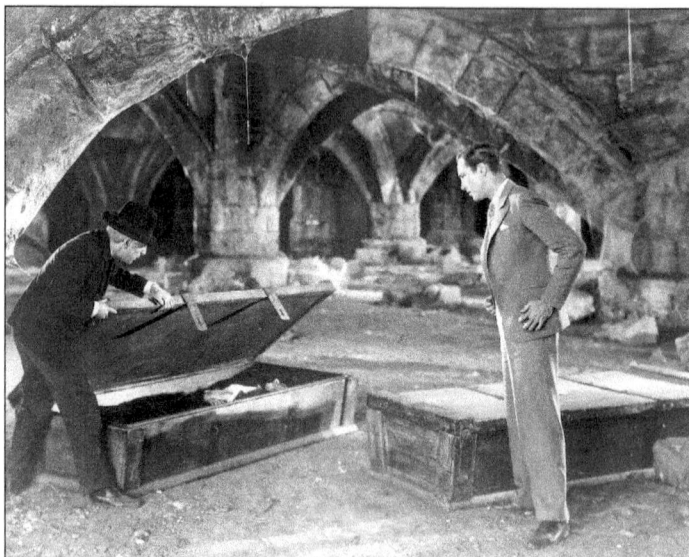

David Manners and Edward Van Sloan (as Dr. [Abraham] Van Helsing) and (an effigy Bela Lugosi stand-in) Count Dracula as he lies in his coffin from a scene in Dracula (Universal Pictures, 1931). Photo from the author's collection.

Barbara Stanwyck, Sam Hardy and David Manners in a scene from The Miracle Woman (Columbia Pictures, 1931). In 1997, David Manners told this author that working with director Frank Capra and Barbara Stanwyck was one of the best experiences of his career. Photo from the author's collection.

Ben Lyon (left), Constance Bennett and David Manners in a scene from the romantic comedy Lady With A Past (RKO Pathé Pictures, 1932). Photo from the author's collection.

David Manners and Kay Francis in a scene from Man Wanted (Warner Bros. Pictures, 1932). Photo from the author's collection.

(from left) Lyle Talbott, Noah Beery [Sr.], Charles "Chic" Sale, and David Manners in a scene from Stranger in Town (Warner Bros., 1932). Photo from the author's collection.

David Manners in a scene from the lead role as Crooner (Warner Bros., 1932), which showcased his talents as a singer in several musical numbers. Photo from the author's collection.

David Manners publicity photo used to promote him in Crooner (Warner Bros., 1932). Photo courtesy of Zachary Zito.

David Manners co-starred with Katharine Hepburn in A Bill of Divorcement. John Barrymore received top billing in Miss Hepburn's motion picture debut directed by George Cukor (RKO Radio Pictures, 1932). Miss Hepburn and David Manners worked for the second and final time together in A Woman Rebels (RKO, 1936). Photo from the author's collection.

Theater lobby card featuring a scene from The Mummy (Universal Pictures, 1932). (From left to right) Edward Van Sloan, Zita Johann, David Manners and Boris Karloff. Zita and David's friendship began prior to this during Basil Sydney's touring theatre company. Photo from the author's collection.

David Manners and Adrienne Ames in From Heaven to Hell (Paramount, 1933). Photos from the author's collection.

David Manners and Claudette Colbert in a publicity photo for Torch
Singer *(Paramount, 1933). This was the last of four David Manners
films that was directed by Alexander Hall. Photo from the author's
collection.*

David Manners and Gloria Stuart in a scene from Roman Scandals. *In 1993, Gloria Stuart said of her co-star; "We were in two motion pictures together. He was a perfect gentleman, very kind and thoughtful during both productions. What I remember the most about David Manners and* Roman Scandals *is that my future husband Arthur [Sheekman], who I met on set, asked David to keep a good eye on me. He did all right!" Photo from the author's collection.*

(left) Boris Karloff, David Manners and Bela Lugosi in a scene from director Edgar G. Ulmer's The Black Cat *(Universal Pictures, 1934). David Manners told this author, "It is the horror pictures that I will be best remembered for. I wouldn't give you two cents for any of those horror pictures. Karloff was a likeable enough fellow. Lugosi was hard to understand on many levels." Photo from the author's collection.*

David Manners in a scene from The Black Cat *(Universal Pictures, 1934). When David Manners looked at this picture, he said, "Who is that handsome fellow? Is it you? Oh! I see. It's me. And you want me to sign this for you? He winked as he said, "Do you think it will ruin the picture if I do sign it?" Photo from the author's collection.*

Camilla Horn, Clifford Mollison, Reginald Purdell, Greta Nissen and David Manners in a scene from the British made romance The Luck of a Sailor (Waldour Films, UK, 1934), shot at the Elstree Studios.

David Manners (Franklin Blake) and Phyllis Barry (Ann Verinder) in a scene from the mystery film, The Moonstone (Monogram Pictures, 1934). Critics were pleased with this rare concise screen adaptation of the Wilkie Collins' first detective novel (published in 1868) in the English language. David Manners told this author, "As an author myself, I was rather pleased with the story." Photo from the author's collection.

Valerie Hobson and David Manners in a scene from Mystery of Edwin Drood *(Universal Pictures, 1935). David told this author; "It was agreed that by my doing that picture would free me from being held to a fifth picture at Universal." Photo courtesy of John Norris.*

David Manners (left), James Dunn and Mae Clarke in a scene from Hearts in Bondage *(Republic Pictures, 1936). Lew Ayres directed the film. Photo from the author's collection.*

Elizabeth Allan and David Manners in the wedding scene of A Woman Rebels (RKO Radio Pictures, 1936). This was David Manners' last film appearance in Hollywood. Katharine Hepburn starred. Photo from the author's collection.

Maxine Doyle, Garland B. Davidson and David Manners in a scene from Lucky Fugitives (Columbia Pictures, 1936). Made in Canada, this became David Manners' final motion picture. Photo from the author's collection.

David Manners as he appeared nearing his sixty-seventh birthday, March 1967. Photo from the author's collection.

David in a scene from The Mummy *(Universal Pictures, 1932). Photo from the author's collection.*

Epilogue by Carla Laemmle

My dear friend, Rick Atkins has honored me significantly. First, by authoring my biography, and then inviting me to write this Epilogue for his long-awaited book, entitled *GUEST PARKING 2*.

I was intrigued by the apt play-on-words title, GUEST PARKING, alluding of course to our very temporal mortal existence here on this Planet Earth. I found the opus thought provoking, moving and meaningful, a warm and inspiring loving tribute to all of his subjects, and to those who helped make it possible. I feel proud to be a part of this book.

As it so happens, I played a part in a chapter about my cousin Carl Laemmle Jr., which Rick labored over for years. Although I did not know Rick when he and Junior met, I am excited with its outcome. And I am sure Junior would be very pleased with it, along with the tribute to my Uncle Carl Laemmle.

Through the author's words, I feel as if I knew the other dear gentlemen featured in this book, Ian Wolfe and Alan Napier. Last, but not least, is David Manners. Despite the fact David Manners and I both appeared in the 1931 movie *Dracula*, at Universal Studios, our scenes were filmed separately. We never met. Now, I wish we had.

To continue along in this vein, I might add the gentlemen in the book were quite aware of their *guest parking* privileges here on Earth. They are an inspiration in striving to live life with honesty, integrity and above all with love. When it runs out, they must leave and move on. I can see why they all liked dear Rick. He's a keeper!

There is only one word that can adequately describe the days of October 20 (my 87th birthday) and 21, 1996 when Rick and I met. It began with our initial meeting: a weird and mystifying drive on the illusive San Vincente trying to get to the Brentwood Country Club. Finally there, we shared our ever so enjoyable double-birthday Sunday brunch celebration with Stanley and Fay Bergerman. This was later followed by our subsequent non-stop-talk-fest back at my house, which we picked up again Monday evening on Rick's 38th birthday. What else but <u>AMAZING</u>!

Rick has become so special to me. I told him that day at the Brentwood Country Club, 'From now on you will be a part of all my future birthdays – until 100, at least. After that you're on your own.' We continue to celebrate together annually, to this day.

As for myself, I am greatly blessed with 102 years of living, learning and experiencing life in this year ending 2011. Among the greatest of these blessings was my extraordinary forty two-year relationship with motion picture writer, director, author, and Baja fisherman, Ray Cannon. He was the love of my life.

Ray taught me what it means to always keep the *child heart* and never lose that sense of *wonder* in the commonplace as in the mysteries of life. An ancient Chinese proverb that Ray sought to live by was, "Make the many happy, expecting no reward." To me, Life is a School whose main subjects taught are: "What to do and what not to do," and following the Tenants: "Harm no one, especially yourself."

Carl Laemmle, of course, was always very good to his brother Joe (my father), my mother, my grandmother and myself. He gave us a wonderful house to live in for sixteen years at Universal. He gave me a contract. Of course, I was thrilled about that and I thought I had it made! But it seemed that nobody wanted to take a chance on me. I'll never know if I would have made it or not ... the bottom line is we cannot change life or people—only our attitude.

I really find it not a little ironic in as much as I used to cast myself in the role of the poor relative "outsider." Here I am now, 80 years later, the one, metaphorically speaking, happily giving new blood transfusions to the Carl Laemmle mystique – and I'm not even Jewish! I'm sure this feeling I had was my own creation. My cousin, Rosabelle Laemmle Bergerman, was always loving and gracious to me. Her brother Junior, however, I never felt comfortable around. He was intimidating to me. After he had been appointed General Manager at Universal, I don't believe he had any faith in my ability as an actress. I think he looked upon me as his first cousin. I was very insecure in those days. After I met Ray

Cannon, he changed the way I thought about myself. He instilled *magic* in me. This brings back some of the fondest memories of a most wondrous time in my life beginning soon after I turned eleven when my family and I relocated from Chicago to Universal City, California as chronicled in my biography. Thank you, Rick!

As I believe, 'our present life here is but one of a continuity of countless previous embodiments in ions past and with countless more to come in the Foreverness of the Eternal Now.' And while on Life's Earthly Plane, we are all on the Path to Greater Good! I know not when my journey here will end or to tell me my allotted time and leave this earthly body. I do not fear it. Possibly, it may so be some other *Guest Parking* arena? My love to all!

Notes

Chapter 1 - Ian Wolfe: The Character Man

1. Ian's appearance as the Minister who had officiated the funeral of Phyllis' husband Lars, and was seen at the reception having a scene with the star Cloris Leachman was the pilot for the series (Season One, Episode One) and aired September 8, 1975 over the CBS television network.

2. Ian Wolfe recalled the following after appearing in *Bedlam*. "The director of *Bedlam* was Mark Robson. He didn't hire me for another job after that. However, the producer, Val Lewton, I worked for a second time in a film called *Please Believe Me*. I remember Robson more than Lewton. It is my understanding that Alan Napier and Val Lewton were good friends."

3. Meryl O'Loughlin (1933-2007); Executive in Charge of Casting at MTM Enterprises, Inc., replied to the author, May 12, 1976.

4. The author's first letter from Ian Wolfe was dated June 5, 1976.

5. The copyright was applied to the Library of Congress on Ian's play "Children of Thunder" (The Brontes of Wuthering Heights), May 26, 1932.

6. Nancy Kelly (1921-1995) was an American actress. A child actress and model, while still in her teens was a repertory cast member of CBS Radio's The March of Time and became a movie-leading lady in the late 1930s. Her greatest success came in the 1955 stage production as the suicidal mother in *The Bad Seed,* for which she won the Tony Award. She reprised that role in the 1955 film adaptation, for which she was nominated for an Academy Award. She was a friend to Beth and Ian Wolfe for many years.

7. Ian Wolfe demonstrated these voices one afternoon in his car while entertaining this author. He also spoke as a three-year old baby, and the Pope. *March of Time* was an American radio news series broadcast from 1931 to 1945 and a companion newsreel series shown in theaters from 1935 to 1951. The series was recognized with an Honorary Academy Award in 1937.

   During the 1940s, Ian continued appearing in such radio programs as, "Pursuit," "The Cavalcade of America," The Hallmark Charlotte Greenwood Show," and numerous episodes of "Suspense;" and several CBS anthology series programs entitled, "Escape." Ian Wolfe was pinned on radio as 'the character man of a thousand voices.' Ian said, "To count the radio programs over the years, I'd have to say that there were at least three dozen, give or take a few."

Radio work ceased for the actor by the summer of 1950. Producers were deluged with talented actors for television, the newer entertainment medium. Ian Wolfe was one actor who made the cut.

8. Hope (Lininger) Lugosi (1919-1997) was Bela Lugosi's fifth and final wife. She lived out her later years in Hawaii. She is interred at Saint Joseph Cemetery at Kamalo, Maui County Hawaii.

9. During a 1982 visit, Ian Wolfe spoke to this author about Jane Wyman. "She always had kind words for me over the years. What a lovely professional actress she turned out to be. I see that just recently she is appearing in a television series that has become very popular. I wish her the best. It was grand that you saw her this afternoon at the studio if only from a distance. It would have been nice to chat with her. But I was napping in full costume."

10. Ian recommended the autobiography of Shelley Winters entitled, "*SHELLEY (Also known as Shirley)*."William Morrow and Company, Inc., 1982, published it.

11. DeForest Kelley (1920-1999), American actor, screenwriter, poet and singer best known for his role as Dr. Leonard "Bones" McCoy in the television and film series *Star Trek*.

12. *Wizards and Warriors* consisted of a pilot along with seven episodes shot. Ian was cast as the Good Wizard Traquil, in four episodes only.

13. After Bill Bixby (1934-1993) shot the footage between Ian and me, the prints were mailed several weeks later. It was a great gift!

14. Euell Gibbons (1911-1975) and outdoorsman and proponent of natural diets during the 1960s. However, his greatest claim to fame in the early 1970s was his commercials endorsing Post Grape-Nuts cereal.

15. The pinecone minus the jellybeans remains an ornamental piece in this author's office.

16. *Somewhere ... Sunrise!* (Poetry and Haiku entries) by Ian Wolfe, Lorraine Babbit and Frances Adams Moore. Ojai Printing and Publishing; Ojai California (*Epitaph of An Actor -- by Ian Wolfe-- Page 38*).

Chapter 2 - Carl Laemmle Jr. . . . It's a Great Big Picture!

1. When revisiting 1641 Tower Grove Drive in October 2011, the grounds appeared smaller. After the property was sold, a brick wall was later added that surrounded the residence. That wall overpowered the beauty that was once remembered. Junior's home was custom built for him. It was a near replica of one of movie director George Cukor's guesthouses where Junior first stayed before renting the Cordell Drive home where he lived while the home on Tower Grove Drive was being built. George Cukor was a longtime friend of the Laemmle family.

2. Elise Nisse, Junior's cook and housekeeper carried interesting history of her own. She immigrated to America from Germany in 1923 when she was twenty-two. The Holthusens of Germany were Elise's connection to the Holthusens of New York. Elise remained employed until 1938 by Lutheran minister Rev. Dr. John Holthusen (1903-1957), who sent her to California to his ailing friend Carl Laemmle, who was in need of a good German cook.

3. The custom-made cigar box that belonged to Carl Laemmle Jr. was given to this writer as a gift from a Laemmle/Stern family relative in 1999. Junior, in spirit, may be happy to know that it now holds assorted playing cards instead of Havana cigars.

4. Junior's weakened voice did not carry over the tape recorder that was brought along. Instead, this writer retrieved to taking notes.

5. The largest addition of land to Laemmle's original 230 acres came in 1950, when Universal purchased one hundred-forty acres of land adjoining the Southern boundary of the studio. The acreage was reduced in 2003, when Vivendi, a former owner of Universal sold the Sheraton and Hilton properties as well as 10 Universal City Plaza. Universal Pictures, Universal Parks & Resorts, NBC News, NBC Entertainment, etc. are all businesses of NBCUniversal. Comcast is the current parent company of NBCUniversal. It presently consists of three hundred-ninety one acres. Tours at Universal Studios were discontinued with the advent of sound. However, modern day tours resumed in 1964. Amusements began operating on the Universal Studios property as early as 1965.

   Over the years, the amusement grounds have grown enormously. Those designated areas are known as the theme park, which have expanded so rapidly the property is known today as Universal Studios Hollywood Theme Park.

6.   Recha and Anna Stern were born in Hintersteinau, Germany. The young ladies immigrated to America from Flieden, Germany (in the district of Fulda, in Hesse, Germany) in 1897. The following year Anna Stern became Carl Laemmle's sister-in-law. Anna was a great deal of support to Recha and Carl Laemmle over the years, beginning in Oshkosh Wisconsin when she moved in with them in 1899. Anna Stern later married Chicago theater exhibitor, Maurice Fleckles. Mr. and Mrs. Fleckles moved from Chicago to New York in 1924 where they took up residence at the West End Avenue apartments where Carl and his family continued residency sporadically until 1932. Mr. and Mrs. Fleckles later moved to California in 1935.

7.   In August 1927, Rosabelle Laemmle met Mark Stanley Bergerman, a May Company merchandising manager at the Coconut Grove. They soon began dating. A few weeks later, Irving Thalberg married movie actress Norma Shearer on the afternoon of September 29, 1927 at a home that the groom was renting on Sunset Boulevard. Miss Shearer converted to Judaism before she married Irving Thalberg and continued to practice the faith for the rest of her life. Stanley Bergerman and Rosabelle Laemmle married on the evening of January 2, 1929 at her father's Beverly Hills home with a gala. Junior Laemmle was the best man.

8.   Paul Fejos became an American citizen in 1930 before he returned to Europe the following year to make films. In the late 1930s, anthropology became his new forte.

     In later years, Fejos became the distinguished Director of Research at the Wenner-Gren Foundation for Anthropological Research, Incorporated in New York. A written correspondence between Junior Laemmle and Paul Fejos ensued for twenty years after they crossed paths in New York in 1943. Paul Fejos passed away April 23, 1963, at the age of sixty-six.

9.   The movie careers of neither Alice Day nor her actress sister, Marceline Day, lasted. Their careers ended in the early 1930s. Alice Day married Jack Cohn, a Laemmle family friend and stockbroker in 1932. The couple divorced in 1939.

     Junior Laemmle lost touch with Alice Day, but never forgot her. She survived him by nearly sixteen years. Junior remembered her with a monetary bequest in his Last Will. Alice Day passed away May 25, 1995 at the age of eighty-nine. Her sister, Marceline Day, was ninety-one when she passed away February 16, 2000. Neither of the sisters would grant but few interviews regarding past movie careers.

10. The WAMPAS Baby Stars was a promotional campaign that began in 1922. Every year the Western Association of Motion Picture Advertisers chose a group of young actresses who were under contract at major studios and believed to be on the threshold of stardom. Awardees were honored at a party called the "Frolic" and were given extensive media coverage.

The awards were not given in 1930 and 1933 due to objections for varied reasons. When the campaign was revived in 1934, freelance actresses along with studio contract players were included as the chosen "Baby Stars." The WAMPAS campaign ended in 1934 when the advertisers disbanded. Several of these actresses had involvement with Junior Laemmle, professionally and others personally. The groups of actresses chosen by year are as follows:

1922: Marion Aye, Helen Ferguson, Lila Lee, Jacqueline Logan, Louise Lorraine, Bessie Love, Kathryn McGuire, Patsy Ruth Miller, Colleen Moore, Mary Philbin, Pauline Starke, Lois Wilson, Claire Windsor.

1923: Eleanor Boardman, Evelyn Brent, Dorothy Devore, Virginia Brown Faire, Betty Francisco, Pauline Garon, Kathleen Key, Laura La Plante, Margaret Leahy, Helen Lynch, Derelys Perdue, Jobyna Ralston, Ethel Shannon

1924: Clara Bow, Elinor Fair, Carmelita Geraghty, Gloria Grey, Ruth Hiatt, Julianne Johnston, Hazel Keener, Dorothy Mackaill, Blanche Mehaffey, Margaret Morris, Marian Nixon, Lucille Ricksen, Alberta Vaughn.

1925: Betty Arlen, Violet La Plante, Olive Borden, Anne Cornwall, Ena Gregory, Madeline Hurlock, Natalie Joyce, June Marlowe, Joan Meredith, Evelyn Peirce, Dorothy Revier, Duane Thompson, Lola Todd.

1926: Mary Astor, Mary Brian, Joyce Compton, Dolores Costello, Joan Crawford, Marceline Day, Dolores del Río, Janet Gaynor, Sally Long, Edna Marion, Sally O'Neil, Vera Reynolds, Fay Wray.

1927: Patricia Avery, Rita Carewe, Helene Costello, Barbara Kent, Natalie Kingston, Frances Lee, Mary McAllister, Gladys McConnell, Sally Phipps, Sally Rand, Martha Sleeper, Iris Stuart, Adamae Vaughn.

1928: Lina Basquette, Flora Bramley, Sue Carol, Ann Christy, June Collyer, Alice Day, Sally Eilers, Audrey Ferris, Dorothy Gulliver, Gwen Lee, Molly O'Day, Ruth Taylor, Lupe Vélez.

1929: Jean Arthur, Sally Blane, Betty Boyd, Ethlyne Clair, Doris Dawson, Josephine Dunn, Helen Foster, Doris Hill, Caryl Lincoln, Anita Page, Mona Rico, Helen Twelvetrees, Loretta Young.

1930: (no event was scheduled)

1931: Joan Blondell, Constance Cummings, Frances Dade, Frances Dee, Sidney Fox, Rochelle Hudson, Anita Louise, Joan Marsh, Marian Marsh, Karen Morley, Marion Shilling, Barbara Weeks, Judith Wood.

1932: Lona Andre, Lilian Bond, Mary Carlisle, Patricia Ellis, Ruth Hall, Eleanor Holm, Evalyn Knapp, Dorothy Layton, Boots Mallory, Toshia Mori, Ginger Rogers, Marian Shockley, Gloria Stuart, Dorothy Wilson, June Clyde.

1933: (no event was scheduled)

1934: There was no "Frolic" party held for this group. However, the following WAMPAS Baby Stars of 1934 appeared in two Hollywood films.

Judith Arlen, Betty Bryson, Jean Carmen, Helen Cohan, Dorothy Drake, Jean Gale, Hazel Hayes, Ann Hovey, Neoma Judge, Lucille Lund, Lu Ann Meredith, Gigi Parrish, Jacqueline Wells, Katherine Williams.

11.   Eleanor Holm, the former 1936 Summer Olympic competitive swimmer, maintained a friendship with Junior after two failed marriages. She married a third time in 1974 to Thomas J. Whelan, a retired oil executive. Mr. Whelan passed away in 1984.

Eleanor Holm never had any children. Her first visit with Junior in many years was in 1960. She stayed with him for a few weeks before moving to Florida. Her last visit with him was in 1978.

On another visit to Los Angeles, Eleanor Holm attended the opening ceremonies of the 1984 Olympics with her friend, Carole Laemmle Bergerman. After eighty-four men emerged onto the stages playing eighty-four Kimball Grand Pianos in spectacular fashion celebrating George Gershwin's "Rhapsody in Blue." The awe-swept women wept fondly remembering that the Gershwin composition was Junior's favorite, introduced to him by his friend Paul Fejos.

Eleanor Holm Jarrett Rose Whalen passed away January 31, 2004 in Miami, Florida. She was ninety.

12.   Claire (Clärle) Einstein was born October 13, 1913. Clara's brother, Siegfried Josef Einstein lived to the age of 63, April 4, 1983.

13. In 1904, Robert H. Cochrane and his brothers, Philip D. Cochrane and Witt K. Cochrane opened the Cochrane Advertising Agency in Chicago. One of their first accounts was the Continental Clothing Store in Oshkosh, Wisconsin where Carl Laemmle was a manager.

In 1906, when Carl Laemmle entered the motion picture business in Chicago, he called on the Cochrane brothers. They helped Mr. Laemmle through his early nickelodeon days, The Laemmle Film Service, Independent Motion Picture Company (IMP) and Universal Pictures where Philip D. Cochrane was the vice-president in charge of advertising. Brother Witt K. Cochrane continued running the advertising business in Illinois. Both Philip D. and Robert H. Cochrane left Universal in 1937.

Robert H. Cochrane passed away July 31, 1973 at the age of ninety-four. A son and a daughter survived him.

14. Charles R. Rogers (1892-1957) and J. Cheever Cowdin (1889-1960) were elected to Universal's Board of Directors April 3, 1936. All of the stock from the new Universal Corporation was placed in a voting trust for ten years. The two men were among seven voting trustees also named.

Mr. Cowdin was a long time financier. He served on the board at Universal Pictures for thirteen years. He resigned in 1949. Remaining employed as a New York City broker, on September 15, 1960, he died in his office of a heart attack. He was seventy-one.

Charles R. Rogers remained with Universal until 1938 after which he returned to independent production, first with Columbia Pictures and later, at United Artists until the early 1950s. In February 1957, he was in a serious car accident in California and died March 29, 1957 from his injuries. He was sixty-four.

It has been written time and again that Junior Laemmle's costly spending was mostly, if not solely to blame for his father's sale of Universal Pictures Corporation over an unpaid $750.000.00 loan. Only in theory, however, could stockholder(s) within the corporation possibly have been involved with other(s) connected to the defunct Motion Picture Patents Company and the Old General Film Company seeking retribution against Uncle Carl? This question was posed over the years and does not necessarily reflect the views or opinion of this author.

15. In the fall of 1929 Carl Laemmle traveled to Berlin, Germany to purchase the rights for the novel, _All Quiet on the Western Front_ from Erich Maria Remarque.

16. Ruth Friedland Regis, a Laemmle cousin told this writer while visiting Laupheim, Germany in 1999: "Junior had a knack for scaring the daylights out of we youngsters, sometimes to tears. His stage in the early 1920s was that old basement at the Laemmle house in Laupheim."

17. Nearly a year apart in death was Paul Leni, September 2, 1929; and Lon Chaney August 26, 1930.

18. Paul Kohner was born in Teplitz-Schoenau, Austria-Hungary in 1902. The region is now known as Telipice, located in the Czechoslovakian Republic. Kohner became a news reporter for his father's weekly Prague based European film magazine. In the spring of 1920, Kohner was eighteen when he met Carl Laemmle in Carlsbad to interview him the family periodical. Mr. Laemmle was so impressed by Kohner that he turned the tables on the young man with questions about his family and his future.

At this period in time, Carl Laemmle had been running Universal City Studios for five years. Consequently, Laemmle had also obtained complete ownership of the Universal Film Manufacturing Company and offered young Kohner work in New York. Kohner accepted Mr. Laemmle's offer and left for America in the fall of 1920. In addition to New York, Paul Kohner has lived in Berlin, Vienna, and Paris. In 1938, he started the Paul Kohner Agency to such legendary stars as Greta Garbo, Marlene Dietrich, and Erich von Stroheim to mention a few. His business represented some of the industry's best-known actors, directors and writers that grew from his early career as a producer at Universal Pictures, later MGM and Columbia. He also helped Carl Laemmle in bringing over European affidavit refugees to the United States during World War II.

19. Paul Kohner and Lupita Tovar's union of marriage produced a daughter and a son; Susan Kohner, and (Paul J.) "Pancho" Kohner.

Susan Kohner was an actress best remembered for her Academy Award nominated role as Sarah Jane in the 1959 remake of Universal's 1934 drama, _Imitation of Life,_ from the novel by Fannie Hurst. Susan left Hollywood acting in 1964 and became Mrs. John Weitz (1923-2002) of New York City. The couple had two sons, (Christopher) "Chris" Weitz and Paul Weitz. The young men have followed a successful Hollywood tradition producing and directing movies such as, *American Pie* and *About a Boy*. Their uncle, Pancho Kohner is a producer of the popular *Madeline* TV series and selected *Madeline* motion pictures. He is also a director and writer. Pancho Kohner married Ellen Picking in 1962. They have two children.

Paul Kohner and his wife Lupita Tovar were married for fifty-six years before he passed away March 16, 1988 in Los Angeles. He was eighty-five. Lupita Tovar celebrated her 105th birthday in July 2015.

20. Before James Whale left Universal in 1939, he reluctantly directed three additional pictures there after *The Road Back*. During the interim, he worked with some flexibility at Warner Brothers, Columbia Pictures, United Artists, which gave him some sense of satisfaction.

By the spring of 1941, James Whale gave up directing motion pictures altogether. Over the next ten years, he took on sporadic other projects before he retired in 1952. After his retirement, he spent a great deal of time oil painting and traveling occasionally.

In 1956, the former movie director began suffering small strokes, which led to incapacitation and depression. On the Wednesday afternoon of May 29, 1957 James Whale's body was found floating at the bottom of his swimming pool. He was sixty-seven. The death was ruled as an accident.

Three decades later, producer David Lewis, Whale's former longtime partner revealed that a suicide note was found. According to author James Curtis, the note was never solely in David Lewis' possession, but later given to him and publicly released shortly before Lewis' death in 1987.

21. Carole Bergerman told this writer that in 1986: "Of the six palm trees that Junior had planted in Israel in Jimmy Whale's memory, one survives."

22. After Junior's favorable departure from MGM in 1937, his contract remained with MGM. In 1944 after Junior Laemmle returned from the army, he purchased his two hundred and fifty thousand dollar contract back from Louis B. Mayer for twenty-five hundred dollars.

23. Rabbi Edgar F. Magnin was a universally admired community leader for nearly 70 years. He was chief rabbi of the reform congregation at the Wilshire Boulevard Temple in Los Angeles, California for over 50 years where the Laemmle family was members. Rabbi Magnin was very active in civic and religious affairs. He was the founding president of the College of Jewish Studies and known to the public through his newspaper column and radio and television messages.

He had close friends in all faiths and in all walks of life including show business. He survived longer than many of the Hollywood actors, producers, directors and writers whom he knew. Rabbi Magnin officiated the funeral services of Carl Laemmle and his two children. He passed July 17, 1984 at his Beverly Hills home. He was ninety-four.

24. She was born Evelyn Margaret Moriarty August 27, 1921 in New York City. At fifteen, she won the attention of theater producer George White, who was like a second father to her. In late 1939, George White brought her to Hollywood where she was placed in his stage production of "Scandals." Evelyn would later be taken under the wing of Earl Carroll. Once she reached the legal age of twenty-one, Evelyn became a full-fledged Earl Carroll Girl. In the meantime, she was given a job as cigarette girl at the Earl Carroll nightclub. Earl Carroll's emblazoned slogan over the doors of his establishments read, "Through These Portals Pass the Most Beautiful Girls in the World."

Evelyn remained employed at Earl Carroll's until after the fifty-five-year-old restaurateur was killed in a tragic plane crash June 17, 1948. Evelyn said of her friend Earl Carroll, "He was a wonderfully smart businessman and an extremely good person. I loved and admired him. And I still miss him."

Evelyn Moriarty had a close friendship with Marilyn Monroe having been her stand-in on Marilyn's last three pictures, *Let's Make Love*, *The Misfits*, (and the unfinished George Cukor movie) *Something's Got to Give*. Two years after Marilyn Monroe died, Evelyn went to work as a stand-in for Ann-Margret and remained with her for eighteen years. Evelyn also worked as a stand-in for Barbara Eden in 138 of the 139 episodes of the "I Dream of Jeannie" between 1965 and 1970.

25. Carla Laemmle (born Rebecca Isabelle Laemmle) was a first cousin to Carl Laemmle Jr. and a niece to Carl Laemmle. She and this writer celebrated her 104th birthday October 20, 2013 at Universal Studios, where she lived with her family between 1921 and 1937. Nearly eight months after that event, Carla Laemmle passed away in her sleep at her home on the evening of June 12, 2014.

26. Buster Crabbe, the former Olympic swimmer won a bronze medal in 1928 and a gold medal in 1932, first for the 1,500 meters freestyle and the 400 meters freestyle. Subsequently, he was placed under contract with Paramount studios. As an actor, he had a variety of film roles, which also meant being loaned out to other studios. His

most memorable film roles where during the early 1930s and 40s, which included *Tarzan, Flash Gordon* and *Buck Rogers.* Adventure serials were a big part of Universal Studio's success. Between 1914 and 1936, Universal released ninety-nine adventure serials. Thirty of them were released during Junior's reign.

Buster Crabbe also starred as Captain Michael Gallant in the NBC television series *Captain Gallant of the Foreign Legion* between 1955 and 1957. His last film appearance was in *The Comeback Trail* in 1982. Buster Crabbe passed away at the age of seventy-five, April 23, 1983. Junior Laemmle passed away eight days after Buster Crabbe and this writer met.

27. There would never be another film collaboration between Junior Laemmle and Paul Fejos. What transpired from their reuniting in 1943 was a continued written correspondence for the next twenty years.

    In March 1961, Paul Fejos and his second wife, Lita Binns Fejos (better known as "Minx"), while traveling the west coast, spent four days with the 52-year-old wheelchair bound Junior ("the kid" [quoting Fejos]) at his new Beverly Hills home on Tower Grove Drive.

28. The television series *Father Knows Best* ran for six seasons with over two hundred episodes winning six Emmy Awards before it officially ended May 23, 1960. Jane Wyatt was a friend of the Laemmle family for many years and visited Junior Laemmle. Wyatt visited Junior the day before this author's visit.

29. Conversations and written correspondence between Carole Laemmle Bergerman and this writer (1979-1994).

30. Rebekka Laemmle passed away October 3, 1883 in Laupheim Germany. She was fifty-two. Her husband Julius Baruch Laemmle passed away July 10, 1892 in Laupheim, Germany. He was seventy-one. Rebekka and Julius Baruch Laemmle were German-Jewish commoners born before the mid-1800s. They and their other eight children are buried in the Laupheim Cemetery along with daughter, Karoline Laemmle Bernheim.

31. Karoline Laemmle Bernheim, who never left Laupheim, Germany passed away there January 20, 1924 at the age of fifty-nine. Carl Laemmle's surviving brothers became American citizens. Carl was three-years-old when eldest brother Joseph immigrated to America. Joseph Laemmle, Louis Laemmle, and Siegfried Laemmle, passed away in the United States, March 22, 1929, February 12, 1956,

and June 11, 1953, respectively. The brothers along with Carl are interred in Los Angeles, California.

32. Samuel Stern had two other store locations besides Chicago and Oshkosh. They were located in Springfield, Illinois and Appleton, Wisconsin.

33. Recha [pronounced Ray-Káh] Stern was born July 8, 1875 in Hinter-steinau, (now called "Steinau an der Straße) Germany. Her parents were (German-Jewish) Malchen (Amalie) and her father Löb Stern, a merchant. Recha and Anna Stern were two of six children. Siblings included a sister, Frieda, a brother, Herman and two other brothers, Abe and Julius, who later worked as producers for Carl Laemmle.

34. Both the Stern and Laemmle families can be traced back hundreds of years in Europe. Their respective locations were Flieden; a municipality located in the district of Fulda in Hesse, Germany in the north roughly three hours south of Laupheim Württemberg Germany, a town that was plagued by threats of wars over many years.

35. The official honeymoon trip can be said to have taken place in 1903 when the couple sailed to Germany for the first time since their marriage along with their daughter

Rosabelle, who was age two years and nine months. A lasting memento from the 1903 "honeymoon journey" was a painting that a New York artist was commissioned to paint of the toddler, Rosabelle, soon before the family's departure.

In 1995, this writer saw the painting of three-year-old Rosabelle proudly displayed in the home of Stanley Bergerman.

36. Robert H. Cochrane and Carl Laemmle would remain in partnership for the next thirty years.

37. Carl Laemmle's brother, Joseph, set up the film equipment and helped with the opening of Carl's first independent business, The White Front, February 26, 1906. The previous renter was an undertaker. They opened with 120 folding chairs. He quickly acquired 70 more. Laemmle maintained that the 190 seats would be sufficient and no more were added. By doing this, his establishment fell under the classification of "Amusement Establishments," subject to an annual tax of twenty-five dollars. Had the establishment contained ten more seats, it would have been termed as a "theatre" and an annual tax of five hundred dollars imposed. The Chicago address directory listed it as "Laemmle's Five-cent Theatre. 909 Milwaukee Avenue."

38. Today, Essanay Studios is home to the main location of St. Augustine College, which was founded in 1980.

39. Dr. Ludwig Simons was born in Washington, Iowa in 1870. He was a graduate of State University of Iowa, 1891, Ph. B.; College of Physicians and Surgeons (Columbia University), New York City, 1894. Two years of special post-graduate work in Munich, Berlin, Prague and Vienna. Practice: obstetrics. He was attending obstetrician at Michael Reese Hospital. Dr. Simons was formerly assistant professor of obstetrics, College of Physicians and Surgeons, Chicago. He was a member of the American Medical Association and American College of Surgeons, also Physicians' Club and City Club.

Much of the surrounding neighborhood near the Michael Reese Hospital Campus and Medical Center was razed. The Chicago apartment house that Carl Laemmle rented at 3520 West Grand Boulevard where Junior Laemmle was born remains standing as the renumbered and renamed street address 3521 King Drive.

40. Laemmle was at the helm of this bitter and legal battle waged against The Trust. He encouraged other distributors and exhibitors to participate. More than 280 lawsuits were filed. After nine years, the pretentious Trust, and all of these cases were abolished by judicial decision. In a final ruling April 9, 1917 by The United States Supreme Court, ordered that the Motion Picture Patents Company and the General Film Company dissolve by the following year. Carl Laemmle rallied to the cause and boldly declared himself an independent filmmaker. The Motion Picture Patents Company was officially dissolved in 1918.

41. Maurice Fleckles, husband of Anna Stern Fleckles passed away June 3, 1946 in Los Angeles, California at the age of seventy-four.

42. Of the more than 50 buildings that were first built at Universal City most of them were reinforced with concrete.

43. Previous two paragraphs excerpted from "Inside Hollywood" by Herb Stein: "Off the Record on CARL LAEMMLE JR." *Daily Racing Form*, Los Angeles, California: April 29, 1958

44. Conversations and written correspondence between Stanley Bergerman and this writer (1995-1998).

45. Conversations and written correspondence between Evelyn Moriarty and this writer (1997-2008).

Chapter 3 - Alan Napier: The Classic Gentleman

1. Batman was introduced in the pages of Detective Comics in May 1939 (No. 27). The characters were depicted later in a matinee series of motion pictures during the 1940s and in the 1960s television series. This exposure ignited comic book sales and retail merchandising of toys, fan magazines and collectibles bearing the Batman name during the late 1960s. In later years, cartoons, video games and blockbuster motion pictures renewed the interest and popularity of the characters employing a newer generation of actors as audiences continue to be entertained.

2. Alan Napier's second wife, Aileen Dickens Bourchier Hawksley Downing Napier, passed away February 12, 1961 in Los Angeles, California. She was the great granddaughter of Charles Dickens.

   Aileen's daughter with actor Terence Downing was actress Jennifer Raine, Alan Napier's stepdaughter. She was born in London in 1932 and passed away January 5, 1993 in West Los Angeles.

3. Letter to author from Alan Napier, July 23, 1979.

4. *The Adventure of the Speckled Band* was originally created as a pilot for a TV series. Alan Napier's friend and former Birmingham, England native was Melville Cooper, who played Dr. Watson. They share the following accomplishments: *Random Harvest* (1942), *The Red Danube* (1949), *Fireside Theatre*—"A Christmas Carol" - (Television 1951), *Moonfleet* (1955), and *Alfred Hitchcock Presents* -"I Killed the Count" Part 1-3, (1957).

   "The Adventure of the Speckled Band" featured beautiful Evelyn Ankers, with whom Alan Napier worked prior in the following motion pictures, *Eagle Squadron* (1942), *The Lone Wolf in London* (1947) and *Tarzan's Magic Fountain* (1949). Alan appeared with her for the last time in TVs "The Empty Room" for *The 20th Century Fox Hour*, which aired in 1956.

5. The Royal Academy of Dramatic Art (RADA) is a drama school in London, England. It is one of the oldest drama schools in the United Kingdom. It was founded in 1904. Herbert Beerbohm Tree established an Academy of Dramatic Art at His Majesty's Theatre in London.

   In 1905 the Academy moved to 62 Gower Street. A managing council was established on which Tree was joined, among others, by Sir Johnston Forbes-Robertson, Sir Arthur Wing Pinero and Sir James Barrie. Within a few years others, including W. S. Gilbert, Irene Vanbrugh and

George Bernard Shaw, augmented them. In 1909 Kenneth Barnes, brother of the Vanbrugh sisters, was appointed principal.

In 1912 George Bernard Shaw donated the royalties from *Pygmalion* to the Academy; it ultimately benefited substantially from the success of the re-titled motion picture version *My Fair Lady*. Pre-First World War graduates of the Academy included Athene Seyler, who became president in 1950. Robert Atkins and Cedric Hardwicke followed. During this period Herbert Beerbohm Tree took some forty academy graduates into his company at His Majesty's.

RADA is an affiliate school of the Conservatoire for Dance and Drama and its higher education awards are validated by King's College London. It is based in the Bloomsbury area of Central London, close to the Senate House complex of the University of London. RADA is based in the Bloomsbury area of Central London. The main RADA building is on Gower Street (with a second entrance on Malet Street), with second premises nearby in Chenies Street. The Goodge Street and Euston Square underground stations are both within walking distance.

The RADA has five theatres (and a cinema). At the Malet Street building, the Jerwood Vanbrugh Theatre is the largest performance space with a capacity of 183, the George Bernard Shaw Theatre is a black box theatre with a capacity of 100, and the John Gielgud Theatre is a black box theatre with a capacity of 70. There is also a 150-seat cinema. In January 2012, RADA acquired the lease to the adjacent Drill Hall venue in Chenies Street and renamed it RADA Studios. This venue has a 200-seat space, the Studio Theatre, and the 50-seat space, Club Theatre.

The RADA library contains nearly 30,000 items. Works include some 10,000 plays; works of or about biography, costume, criticism, film, fine art, poetry, social history, stage design, technical theatre, and theatre history; screenplays; and theatre periodicals. Other facilities at RADA include acting studios, an art workshop, a costume workroom, dance and fight studios, design studios, wood and metal workshops, a sound studio, rehearsal studios, and the RADA Foyer Bar, which includes a fully licensed bar and a box office.

The current director of the academy is Edward Kemp. The president was The Lord Attenborough (until his death in August 2014), the chairman is Sir Stephen Waley-Cohen and the vice-chairman was the late actor Alan Rickman.

Some notable RADA alumni include: Charles Laughton, Vivien Leigh, Sir John Gielgud and Richard Attenborough (both were past presidents of RADA); Sir Alan Bates, Sir Kenneth Branagh, Sir Anthony Hopkins, Sir Ian Holm, Joan Collins, Sir Roger Moore, Glenda Jackson, Sir Tom Courtenay, Clive Owen, Dame Diana Rigg, Peter O'Toole, Jonathan Pryce, Susanna York, John Hurt, and Alan Rickman.

6. The Oxford Playhouse by Oxford UK locals is known as the Playhouse. It is an independent theatre designed by Sir Edward Maufe. It is situated in Beaumont Street, Oxford, opposite the Ashmolean Museum.

The current theatre building on the south side of Beaumont Street was designed by Sir Edward Maufe and was completed in 1938. It is faced with stone, in keeping with other early 19th century Regency buildings in the street.

The Playhouse was originally founded as The Red Barn at 12 Woodstock Road, North Oxford, in 1923 by J. B. (James Bernard) Fagan an Irish-born actor (in Belfast, May 18, 1873), theatre manager, producer and playwright in England, who brought Alan Napier in with the Oxford Players in 1924. He passed away February 17, 1933 at age 59, in Hollywood, California.

A charitable trust owns and runs the Playhouse, through a professional management and direction team, as a theatre for the local community. It was closed for a number of years due to lack of funding, but is now refurbished and thriving. Norman Marshall documents its early history in his 1947 book, The Other Theatre. Don Chapman also provided a comprehensive study of the theatre in his 2008 book, Oxford Playhouse: High and Low Drama in a University City.

Oxford Playhouse has close relations with Oxford University and is the home stage of the Oxford University Dramatic Society. The Playhouse also manages on behalf of the university the nearby Burton Taylor Studio, named in honor of Richard Burton and Elizabeth Taylor.

The Oxford University Dramatic Society (OUDS) was founded in 1885 by Alec MacKinnon and funds many types of show, mostly at the Oxford Playhouse, Burton Taylor Theatre, and the individual college theatres such as the Moser Theatre at Wadham and the O'Reilly Theatre at Keble. All productions put on by Oxford University students can use the society's services, such as the website, the wardrobe, and advice from the committee.

OUDS is the principal funding body and provider of theatrical services to the many independent student productions put on by students in Oxford, England. Not all student productions at Oxford University are awarded funding from the society; however it is rare, for example, for any student production at the Oxford Playhouse not to receive substantial funding from the society.

7. *Bittersweet* is an operetta in three acts, with book, music and lyrics by Noel Coward. The story is set in nineteenth century and early twentieth century England and Austria-Hungary, and centers on a young woman's elopement with her music teacher. The songs from the score include, "The Call of Life," "If You Could Only Come with Me," "I'll See You Again," "Dear Little Café," "If Love Were All," "Ladies of the Town," "Tokay," "Zigeuner," and "Green Carnation". It was written and directed by Noel Coward, opening first July 2, 1929 at the Palace Theatre, Manchester, before the London premiere at His Majesty's Theatre on July18th. It ran in London for 697 performances, at five different theatres, concluding its successful run at the Lyceum.

    Bittersweet also opened on Broadway November 5, 1929 starring Evelyn Laye. Alan Napier was not part of the cast. It would be another ten years before he immigrated to America. The Broadway production ran for 159 performances, closing March 22, 1930. The work has twice been adapted for the cinema, and a complete score was recorded.

    The theatre showcasing the London premiere was known as His Majesty's Theatre from 1901-1952. Since the accession of Elizabeth II in 1952, it was renamed Her Majesty's Theatre. It is located in the West End situated on Haymarket in the City of Westminster, London.

    The present building was designed by Charles J. Phipps and was constructed in 1897 for actor-manager Herbert Beerbohm Tree, who established the Royal Academy of Dramatic Art at the theatre.

    In the early decades of the 20th century, Herbert Beerbohm Tree produced spectacular productions of Shakespeare and other classical works, and the theatre hosted premieres by major playwrights such as George Bernard Shaw, J. M. Synge, Noel Coward and J. B. Priestley.

8. In 1978 Houseman and Napier appeared together in "The Sorcerer's Apprentice" episode of *The Paper Chase*. John Houseman and his longtime friend, Alan Napier, share the following with Houseman as

producer: *Julius Caesar* (1953), *Moonfleet* (1955) and TVs *Playhouse 90-* "The Wings of the Dove (1959)."

9. Living in England during this pre-war time was indeed rough in many ways for its people. Alan Napier, after coming to America made "no great fuss" that he and the British Prime Minister Neville Chamberlain were cousins.

10. Brock Pemberton was a prominent figure in the Broadway arena. Born in Leavenworth, Kansas in 1885, the former newspaper reporter ultimately became associated with Arthur Hopkins. Mr. Pemberton made his initial theatrical venture as producer and director of the successful comedy *Enter Madame* at New York's Garrick Theatre. It ran three hundred and fifty performances between August 16, 1920 and April 1, 1922. He was the founder of the Tony Awards. Brock Pemberton, one of the most successful Broadway producers passed away at his home in New York City March 11, 1950. He was 64.

11. Alan Napier married "Nan" (Emily Nancy Bevill Pethybridge), in England in 1930. Their daughter, Jennifer Mary Napier-Clavering was born in England in 1931. Jennifer Napier married an American actor, Robert Nichols in 1950. He passed away in 2013. Alan Napier did not divorce his first wife "Nan," until he planned to marry his second wife, "Gyp" (Aileen Dickens Bourchier Hawksley) in 1944.

12. The Campbell Playhouse was a continuation of The Mercury Theatre on the Air, which is best known for Orson Welles' controversial and frightening *War of the Worlds* radiobroadcast October 30, 1938.

13. Orson Welles (as writer, performer and director) worked again with Alan Napier in the following: *Radio Almanac* broadcast of June 14, 1944 for the Fifth War Loan Drive. Among the cast was Agnes Moorehead, Keenan Wynn, Franklin Roosevelt and Edgar Barrier; and *This Is My Best* radio series April 10, 1945, The Master of Ballantrae, an adaptation of Robert Louis Stevenson's novel set in Eighteenth Century Scotland. Orson Welles in a cast that included Alan Napier, Agnes Moorehead and Ray Collins.

   Orson Welles directed and appeared in the 1948 motion picture *Macbeth*, by William Shakespeare. Alan Napier was among the large cast. John Houseman produced it.

14. *The House of Seven Gables* (Universal Pictures, 1940) was a screen adaptation of Nathaniel Hawthorne's classic story and Alan Napier's third American motion picture. His character, Fuller the post-

man is worth viewing and memorable watching and listening to him age on film.

15. *Lady In Waiting* (The *New York Times*, theater review, March 28, 1940).

16. Claud Allister was a long-nosed British character actor with large, deep-set eyes and high forehead. He was born in London, England where he began acting on the London stage in 1910. He was later known for film roles in *Bulldog Drummond* (1929), *The Private Life of Henry VIII* (1933) and *The Adventures of Ichabod and Mr. Toad* (1949). He passed away at the age of 81 in Santa Barbara, California in 1970.

   Nigel Bruce was the more popular of the two actors mentioned by Alan Napier to this author in comparison to his own professional persona. Mr. Bruce was born in Ensenada, Mexico. His father Sir William W. Bruce worked as an engineer. His family was part of long-lived English aristocracy. Following his discharge from active service during WWI, Nigel turned to acting in 1919. Ten years later, he achieved a breakthrough in Noel Coward's *This Was a Man* on Broadway. He was a prominent member of the resident English colony in Hollywood along with many friends including Mr. and Mrs. Basil Rathbone.

   Nigel Bruce passed away October 8, 1953 in Santa Monica, California at the age of 58. His ashes are stored in the vault at the Chapel of the Pines Crematory and Columbarium in Los Angeles, the same building Alan Napier's ashes were temporarily kept.

17. Despite the ill-fated Broadway play, *Gertie*, Alan Napier and Glynis Johns later shared the following motion pictures, *The Court Jester* (1955) with Danny Kaye, *Mary Poppins* (1964); and four TV episodes (104-107) of *Batman*. Alan told this author, "I had the opportunity to appear with Glynis' father, the superb actor, Mervyn Johns in the television mini-series *QB VII* ("I saw nothing mini about it.")."

18. Frederick Knott was born in Hankow, China in 1916. He was the son of English missionaries. The English playwright, best known for writing the London-based stage thriller, *Dial M for Murder*, also wrote the 1966 classic *Wait Until Dark*. Both were hits on the stage.

   Mr. Knott also wrote the screenplay for the 1954 Hollywood movie, which Hitchcock filmed for Warner Brothers in 3D, starring Ray Milland and Grace Kelly, with Anthony Dawson and John Williams. Frederick Knott passed away in New York City at the age of 86 in 2002.

19. Alan Napier and London-born actor Frederick Worlock were friends. Alan told this writer in 1982, it was Worlock who suggested Napier as a replacement in the 1950s road engagement for *Dial M for Murder*. The two actors previously shared eleven of the same motion pictures as follows.

    Eagle Squadron (1942), *Random Harvest* (1942), *Appointment in Berlin* (1943), *Madame Curie* (1943), *Hangover Square* (1945), *Forever Amber* (1947), *The Lone Wolf in London* (1947), *Johnny Belinda* (1948), *Joan of Arc* (1948), *Hills of Home* (1948), and *A Connecticut Yankee in King Arthur's Court* (1949). Frederick Worlock passed away at the age of 86, August 1, 1973 in Woodland Hills, California.

20. Pat O'Malley was also a replacement actor for John Williams as the Inspector on Broadway. John Williams originated the part of the Inspector in *Dial M for Murder* on Broadway and won a Tony Award for his performance of Inspector Hubbard. Williams repeated the role for the Alfred Hitchcock film.

    John Williams and Alan Napier appeared in "Deception," an episode of *The 20th Century-Fox Hour* in 1955 and two episodes of *Alfred Hitchcock Presents*, "Whodunit" and the three-part episode "I Killed the Count," 1956 and 1957 respectively. Also known by TV viewers as the second Mr. French from the 1960s TV series *Family Affair*, John Williams passed away at the age of 80, May 5, 1983 in La Jolla, California.

21. Alan Napier's *Alfred Hitchcock Presents* episodes (Joan Harrison, producer: "Into Thin Air" (1955), "Whodunit" (1956), "I Killed the Count" (3 parts-1957), "The Avon Emeralds" (1959); *The Alfred Hitchcock Hour* episodes were: "An Out for Oscar" (1963) and "Thou Still Unravished Bride" (1965).

    Boris Karloff and Alan Napier appeared in four of the same motion pictures, *Isle of the Dead* (1945), *Lured* (1947), *Unconquered* (1947), and *The Strange Door* (1951). Alan Napier later appeared in three of the Boris Karloff *Thriller* episodes: The Purple Room (1960), Hay-Fork and Bill-Hook (1961) and Dark Legacy (1961).

    Alan Napier appeared in one episode of Rod Serling's *Twilight Zone*, "Passage on the Lady Anne" (1963). He later appeared in three episodes of Rod Serling's *Night Gallery*: "House - With Ghost/A Midnight Visit to the Neighborhood Blood Bank/Dr. Stringfellow's Rejuvenator/Hell's Bells" (1971), "The Sins of the Fathers/You Can't Get Help Like That Anymore" (1972), and "Fright Night" (1972).

22. "Source: Internet Broadway Database. Used with permission."

23. Alan Napier had bowed from stage performances altogether and later played an active role with the California Artists Radio Theatre (C.A.R.T.) founded by actress Peggy Webber. She wrote the following e-mail to this author, January 27, 2015.

Dear Rick,

Alan Napier appeared in several stage shows with me. One I produced and did the casting: Brendan Behan's *The Hostage*. Behan wrote to me, when it opened in Los Angeles saying it was the most prestigious cast he had ever had. Alan played The Monsewer, with Bob Denver, Gloria Blondell. Dan O'Herlihy was supposed to play in it but was replaced by Whit Bissell [Alan's son-in-law by his step-daughter Jennifer Raine].

The next was *Heartbreak House* by Shaw, where Alan played Captain Shotover. I produced and directed that in San Luis Obispo County near Hearst's Castle, for a short run for three weeks starring Alan. Shaw himself directed him in the role of Hector in *Heartbreak House* in the first production. The second was with Shaw in London.

I produced and directed my second version of *Heartbreak* with CART in NoHo [North Hollywood]. At the CART Theatre and starred Alan with Leslie Easterbrook as Hesione, Sean Mc Clory as Alfred Mangan, Peggy Rea was Nurse Guiness and Linda Henning was Atiadne, Vance Colvig was the Burglar. Alan was again Capt. Shotover. He was every inch Captain Shotover! And there were other fine players in that version. This last production was with Norman Lloyd playing Shotover and he equaled Alan in his virtuosity and comedy sense of timing and presentation.

In Orson Welles' [1948 film] *Macbeth* was the first time Alan and I worked together. I was Lady Macduff. Orson's version was a babydoll kind of child bride for Lady Macduff. I worked with Alan again many times in radio and was always in awe of him. As I grew to know him, I realized he was very human, a dear and wonderful human being ... And A GREAT ACTOR! He was right up there with Richardson and Olivier and the top English actors. I will never forget his live radio performances. They were smashing and scintillating!!

Best,
Peggy Webber

24. Henry Daniell was born in London, England in 1894. He had a long and prestigious career on the stage in England and America where he was best known for his villainous film roles. On Halloween 1963, in Santa Monica, California, the actor was being filmed on the set of *My Fair Lady,* he suffered a heart attack and passed away a shortly after. He was 69.

   In 1939, Henry Daniell appeared in Alan Napier's first American motion picture, *We Are Not Alone* at Warner Brothers. Twenty years later, they worked together in a *Playhouse 90* episode, "The Wings of the Dove." John Houseman produced it. Alan Napier told this author, "My experience and memory of Henry Daniell is of a consummate actor, a professional in the strictest sense of the word."

25. Laird Cregar passed away December 9, 1944 after he suffered a heart attack a week after undergoing abdominal surgery. He had recently dieted away 100 of his 300 pounds in a short period of time. The Philadelphia-born Cregar began acting while attending school in England with the Stratford-on-Avon players. His reported age at the time of his death was twenty-eight. His mother and five brothers survived him.

26. George Sanders and Alan Napier share the following nine motion pictures and two television appearances: *The House of Seven Gables* (1940), *Appointment in Berlin* (1943), *Action in Arabia* (1944), *Hangover Square* (1945), *A Scandal in Paris* (1946), *The Strange Woman* (1946), *Lured* (1947), *Forever Amber* (1947), and *Moonfleet* (1955). George Sanders played Mr. Freeze in *Batman*, television episodes 7 and 8 "*Instant Freeze*" (1966) and "*Rats Like Cheese*" (1966) respectively.

27. Ian Wolfe and Alan Napier share the following ten motion pictures and one documentary: *Eagle Squadron* (1942), *Random Harvest* (1942), *The Song of Bernadette* (1943), *Three Strangers* (1946), *Johnny Belinda* (1948), *Manhandled* (1949), *The Great Caruso* (1951), *Young Bess* (1953), *Julius Caesar* (1953), and *Moonfleet*. They are mentioned or images used of both actors in the 2008 Feature-Length documentary, "MARTIN SCORSESE PRESENTS VAL LEWTON: THE MAN IN THE SHADOWS."

28. Ray Milland and his close friend, Alan Napier shared the following three motion pictures: *The Uninvited* (1944), *Ministry of Fear* (1944) and *Premature Burial* (1962). Alan Napier said of Ray Milland, "I can tell you that he is a good friend and our friendship is lasting."

29. John Houseman's "portrait" of Val Lewton (pp. 182-183) from his book, "Front and Center" (Simon and Schuster, 1979) was reprinted (from pp. 124-126 of this author's 1997 book, *Let's Scare 'Em!... Grand Interviews and a Filmography of Horrific Proportions, 1930-1961.*)

30. Max Nussbaum was a United States Reform rabbi and Zionist leader. He was born in Suczawa, Bukovina in 1908. His first position in the United States was as rabbi of Temple Beth Ahaba in Muskogee, Oklahoma. He was later appointed in 1942 as rabbi of Temple Israel in Hollywood, California where he remained until his death in 1974.

31. Alan Napier's unpublished biography, *Footsteps in the Sea*, is in the confines of the University of Wyoming's Film Library. He grumbled good- naturedly to this author, "Since I've never committed a major crime and I'm not known to have slept with any famous actresses, it's been very difficult to get published."

32. Letter (with eulogy) to the author from Alan Napier; January 12, 1980.

33. Alan Napier obituary: *Chicago Tribune*, Section 2, Page 11; August 10, 1988.

34. Telephone conversation between this author and Alan's biological daughter, Jennifer Nichols (Friday, August 12, 1988).

Chapter 4 - David Manners: A Beacon of Light

1. Among Michael Dawn's performances as a summer production was *The Devil's Disciple* (1922) with Zita Johann. The two became friends. Ten years later, they appeared together in the now classic horror motion picture, *The Mummy*, starring Boris Karloff. Released by Universal Pictures, the actor was established as David Manners.

    As Michael Dawn his first big appearance following the Theatre Guild introduction on Broadway was in "Dancing Mothers," with Helen Hayes. It opened at Booth Theatre, August 11, 1924. With over 300 performances the successful four-act play ended May 9, 1925.

2. Eva Le Gallienne (1899-1991). She was an English theater actress, producer and director for half a century. She was openly a lesbian, yet she struggled with her lifestyle. Her only known heterosexual affair was with actor Basil Rathbone. She founded the Civic Repertory Theatre in 1926. (*Intimate Circles*, American Women in the Arts: Eva Le Gallienne, online; and Wikipedia.)

3. Suzanne Bushnell was born February 27, 1907 in Springfield, Ohio. She was the granddaughter of Asa Bushnell, the former Governor of Ohio. David Manners was melancholy discussing his marriage to "Suzi" and not so fond in talking about "the celluloid days." He told this author. "After all was said and done; Suzi stayed in New York. I returned to California to finish up the picture [Journey's End]." The marriage was ultimately annulled within a year.

    On May 9, 1931, Miss Bushnell married Wallace Wesley Seymour in Doylestown, Pennsylvania. They made their home in Montclair, New Jersey. And as for the Mecca known as Hollywood, David previously wrote to this author, "I know nothing. I am out of touch with that world."

4. David Manners remembered that his "big movie debut" Journey's End was shot mostly in New York. The film was also the directorial debut for James Whale, who had previously staged the R.C. Sheriff play in England. It had a successful two-year-run.

5. David once wrote a comment at the end of a letter that he wrote after I had sent him a picture of myself. Being reminded of the following convinced me not to bring my camera in. "Thanks for your little [photo] image-but it is not YOU animated."

Selected Bibliography

Anderegg, Michael A., *William Wyler* (Twayne Publishers USA, Boston, 1979).

Atkins, Rick, *Guest Parking: Zita Johann* (Bear Manor Media; Duncan, Oklahoma, 2011).

Atkins, Rick, *Among the Rugged Peaks ... An Intimate Biography of Carla Laemmle* (Midnight Marquee Press, Inc; Baltimore Maryland, 2009).

Atkins, Rick, *Let's Scare 'Em! Grand Interviews and a Filmography of Horrific Proportions, 1930-1961* (McFarland & Company, Inc., Publishers; Jefferson, North Carolina, 1997)

Bansak, Edmund, *Fearing the Dark: The Val Lewton Career* (McFarland & Company, Inc., Publishers; Jefferson, North Carolina, 1995).

Barrow, Kenneth, *Helen Hayes: First Lady of the American Theatre* (DoubleDay & Company, Inc; Garden City, New York, 1985).

Bayer, Udo, *Carl Laemmle: From Laupheim to Hollywood* (Hentrich & Hentrich Verlag Berlin, 2015).

_____, *Laemmle's List: Carl Laemmle's affidavits for Jewish Refugees* (Online: 22 pages. It was also published in *Film History*, April 1998).

Birchard, Robert S., *Images of America: Early Universal City* (Arcadia Publishing; Charleston, SC, Chicago, IL, Portsmouth, NH, San Francisco, CA, 2009).

Chaplin, Charles, *Charles Chaplin: My Autobiography* (Penguin Books by Plume, 1992 reprint of first edition, New York, 1964).

Clarens, Carlos, *An Illustrated History of the Horror Film* (G. P. Putnam's Sons; New York, 1967).

Curtis, James, *James Whale: A New World of Gods and Monsters* (Faber and Faber; Boston-London, 1998).

Dick, Bernard F., *City of Dreams: The Making and Remaking of Universal Pictures* (The University Press of Kentucky; Lexington, Kentucky, 1997).

Drinkwater, John, *The Life and Adventures of Carl Laemmle* (reprinted from a copy in the University of Illinois Library, William Heinemann LTD; London, 1931 by permission of G.P. Putnam's Sons; New York to Arno Press, Inc; 1978).

Eells, George, *Hedda and Louella* (G.P. Putnam's Sons; New York, 1972).

Everson, William K., *Classics of the Horror Film* (Citadel Press, Secaucus, New Jersey, 1974).

_____, *More Classics of the Horror Film* (Citadel Press, Secaucus, New Jersey, 1986).

Finler, Joel W., *The Hollywood Story* (Crown Publishers, Inc; New York, 1988).

Fitzgerald, Michael G., *Universal Pictures* (Arlington House Publishers, Westport, Connecticut, 1977).

Flamini, Roland, *Thalberg: The Last Tycoon and the World of MGM* (Crown Publishers, New York, 1994).

Freulich, Roman and Joan Abramson, *Forty Years in Hollywood: Portraits of a Golden Age* (A. S. Barnes & Company, Inc;/Castle Books-New York, 1971).

Gifford, Denis, *A Pictorial History of Horror Movies* (The Hamlyn Publishing Group Limited, London, New York, Sydney, Toronto, 1973).

Griffith, Richard and Arthur Mayer, *The Movies* (Simon and Schuster, New York, Revised Edition, 1957, 1970).

Hanson, Patricia King (executive editor) and Alan Gevinson (associate editor), *The American Film Institute Catalogue of Motion Pictures (produced in the United States), Feature Films 1931-1940* (University of California Press, Berkeley and Los Angeles, California, 1993).

Herman, Jan, *A Talent for Trouble: The Life of Hollywood's Most Acclaimed Director. William Wyler* (G. P. Putnam's Sons; New York, 1995).

Hirschorn, Clive, *The Universal Story: The Complete History of the Studio and All Its Films* (Crown Publishers, Inc; New York, 1983).

Hobart, Rose, *A Steady Digression to a Fixed Point: The Autobiography of Rose Hobart* (Scarecrow Press, 1994).

Houseman, John, *Front and Center* (Simon and Schuster; New York, 1979).

Kohner, Frederick, *The Magician of Sunset Boulevard: The Improbable Life of Paul Kohner, Hollywood Agent* (Morgan Press, Palos Verdes, CA, 1977).

Laemmle, Carl, *The Business of Motion Pictures* (a unpublished 227-page memoir written by Laemmle and later excerpted for *Film History*, March 1983; courtesy of Udo Bayer).

Lamparski, Richard, *Whatever Became Of...? Eleventh Series* (Crown Publishers, Inc; New York, 1989)

LIFE magazine, *Movie of the Week: Bedlam/Old London's insane asylum is setting for new Karloff thriller* (page 117-122). Also: *Lewton Is B-Film Virtuoso* (p. 123, February 25, 1946).

Mank, Gregory William, *It's Alive! The Classic Cinema Saga of Frankenstein* (A.S. Barnes and Company, Inc; La Jolla, California, 1981).

Manners, David, *Awakening from the Dream of Me* (Non-Stop Books, Minneapolis, Minnesota, 1987).

Manners, David J., *Convenient Season* (E.P. Dutton & Company, Inc; New York, 1941).

_____, *Under Running Laughter* (E.P. Dutton & Company, Inc; New York, 1943).

_____, *Look Through: An Evidence of Self Discovery* (El Cariso Publications, Elsinore, California, 1971).

Marx, Samuel, *Mayer and Thalberg: The Make-Believe Saints* (Warner Books, New York, 1975).

Massey, Raymond, *A Hundred Different Lives: An Autobiography* (Little, Brown and Company, 1979).

McCarthy, Todd and Charles Flynn, *Kings of the Bs: Working Within the Hollywood System/An Anthology of Film History and Criticism* (E.P. Dutton & Company, Inc; New York, 1975).

Milland, Ray, *Wide-Eyed in Babylon/An Autobiography of Ray Milland* (William Morrow & Company, Inc; New York, 1974).

Mordden, Ethan, *The Hollywood Studios/House Style in the Golden Age of the Movies* (Alfred A. Knopf, New York, 1988).

Osborne, Robert, *60 Years of Oscar: The Official History of the Academy Awards* (Abbeville Press, New York, 1989).

Regensteiner, Theodore, *My First Seventy-Five Years* (Reprint by Kessinger Publishing from the original 1943 edition by The Regensteiner Corporation, Chicago).

Russell, Rosalind and Chris Chase, *Life Is a Banquet* (An Ace Book with arrangements by Random House, New York, 1977: First Ace printing, 1979).

Schatz, Thomas (with Preface by Steven Bach), *The Genius of the System/Hollywood Filmmaking in the Studio Era* (Metropolitan Books, Henry Holt and Company, Inc; New York, 1988).

Siegel, Joel, *Val Lewton: The Reality of Terror* (The Viking Press, New York, 1973).

Steinbrunner, Chris and Burt Goldblatt, *Cinema of the Fantastic* (Saturday Review Press, New York, 1972).

Strickland, A.W. and Forrest J Ackerman, *A Reference Guide to American Science Fiction Films* (T.I.S. Publications; Bloomington, Indiana, 1981).

Taylor, John Russell, *Orson Welles: A Celebration* (Applause Books, New York, 1999).

Telotte, J.P., *Dreams of Darkness: Fantasy and the Films of Val Lewton* (University of Illinois Press, Urbana/Chicago, 1985).

Thomas, Bob, *Walt Disney: An American Original* (Hyperion – The Walt Disney Company, New York, 1994).

_____, *Thalberg: Life and Legend* (DoubleDay & Company, Inc; New York, 1969).

Wolfe, Ian, Lorraine Babbitt and Frances Adams Moore, *Somewhere ... Sunrise!* (Poetry and Haiku entries; 50 pages) (Ojai Printing and Publishing Company; Ojai, California, 1978).

Wray, Fay, *On the Other Hand: A Life Story* (St. Martin's Press, New York, 1989).

Zierold, Norman, *The Moguls* (Coward-McCann, Inc; New York, 1969).

APPENDIX
(Listings of subject's accomplishments)

Stage credits for Ian Wolfe
(Legitimate theatre and Broadway-compiled by Ian Wolfe and the author.)
"As a director during the early 1920s in Civic theatres in Santa Barbara, Cali-
  fornia, Tacoma, Washington; and briefly with the New York Theatre Guild
  School ("Not to mention coaching, teaching, etc."). They are the following:"
Right You Are (twice, also as actor - Sig Laudisi, philosopher)
Prunella (twice, also as actor [Grotesque] - Pierrot)
East Come, Easy Go" (also as actor – Elder crook)
Mr. Pim Passes By
Intimate Strangers
Ten Nights in a Bar Room
("And others")
As co-director (early 1920s in Civic Theatres in California):
Liliom (also as actor - Sparrow)
The Green Goddess (also as actor - Cockney butler)
Twelfth Night (also as actor- Fool)
He Who Gets Slapped (also as actor- Count Mancini)
Peer Gynt (Ibsen)
Loyalties
Caesar and Cleopatra (Shaw play)
("And others")
As an actor in legitimate theatre:
Mary the Third (Father)
You Never Can Tell (Father) (Shaw)
Fashions for Men (Old Professor)
Outward Bound (Scrubby)
Beggar on Horseback (Prince, in the pantomime)
The Circle (Clive, the husband)
Fanny's First Play (three parts: Father, "Count" the prologue) (Shaw)
The Hottentot (Farcical butler)
School for Scandal (Joseph)
Wappin Wharf (Pirate Captain)
Loyalties (Host)
Intimate Strangers (Bachelor lover)
Dreamy Kid (Negro) (O'Neill play)
Wedding Bells (Poet in farce)
Rain (Joe Horn, a thin beachcomber)
The Second Man (Mathematician)
The Show Off (Joe, the elder brother)
Broadway and tours:

The Claw
Broadhurst Theatre, New York, NY
Produced and staged by Arthur Hopkins
Written by Henri Bernstein
Star: Lionel Barrymore
Opened: October 17, 1921
Closed: January 1, 1922
Ian Wolfe as Servant
Gods of Lightning
Little Theatre, New York NY (now Helen Hayes Theatre)
Produced by Hamilton MacFadden and Kellogg Gary
Written by Maxwell Anderson and Harold Hickerson
Staged by Hamilton MacFadden
Star: Morris Ankrum
Opened: October 24, 1928
Closed: November 1, 1928
Ian Wolfe as Milkin (the numerologist)
Skyrocket
Lyceum Theatre, New York, NY (has since become a national landmark)
Produced by Gilbert Miller in association with Guthrie McClintic
Written by Mark Reed
Staged by Guthrie McClintic
Star: Dorothie Bigelow
Featuring: Humphrey Bogart (his ninth play on Broadway, before he became
     a Hollywood star)
Opened: January 1, 1929
Closed: January 11, 1929
Ian Wolfe as Frank Greer
At the Bottom
Waldorf Theatre, New York, NY (has since been razed)
Produced by Leo Bulgakov Theatre Associates, Inc.
Written by Maxim Gorky; Book adapted by William L. Lawrence
Staged by Leo Bulgakov
Star: Walter Abel
Opened: January 9, 1930
Closed: March 1, 1930
Featuring: Victor Killian (also: Kilian), would later share eight films with Ian.
Ian Wolfe as Michael Kostilyev (the Innkeeper)
The Seagull
Comedy Theatre, New York NY (a.k.a. Artef Theatre, has since been razed),
     former home of The Mercury Theatre re-opened in 1937 by Orson Welles
     and John Houseman.
Produced by A Cooperative Company
Written by Anton Chekov
Directed by Leo Bulgakov

Star: Walter Abel
Opened: April 9, 1929
Closed: May 1, 1929
Ian M. Wolfe as Medvedenko (the schoolmaster)
Note: This play later opened at the Waldorf Theatre, also staged by Leo Bulgakov. It opened February 25, 1930 and ran 5 performances closing March 1, 1930.
The character Medvedenko was played there also by Ian Wolfe (minus the "M.").
The Age of Innocence (before Broadway road tour)
Opened: in Albany November 8, 1928; also played in Buffalo and Pittsburgh before opening on Broadway, November 27, 1928
Star: Katharine Cornell
Staged by Guthrie McClintic (Katharine Cornell's husband)
Ian Wolfe as Sillerton Jackson
Note: Ian Wolfe met Katharine Cornell in New York, during rehearsals in the fall of 1928 for the road show before the play went to Broadway. The actor William Podmore played the part of Sillerton Jackson in New York.
Cornell promised Ian Wolfe a part in another of her plays, a promise that she kept. Ian Wolfe became devoted to Katharine Cornell through the entire run of both "Lysistrata" and "The Barretts of Wimpole Street."
Lysistrata
44th Street Theatre, New York, NY (has since been razed adding to the New York Times building).
Produced by Philadelphia Theatre Association, Inc.
Written by Aristophanes; Book adapted by Gilbert Seldes
Staged by Norman Bel Geddes
Star: Ernest Truex
Opened: June 5, 1930
Closed: January 1, 1931
Ian Wolfe as Leader of the frenzied Old Man
Note: Included a cast of over sixty-five. Among them were Conrad Cantzen and Sydney Greenstreet in over 250 performances and on the road for an additional 35 weeks.
The Barretts of Wimpole Street
Empire Theatre, New York, NY (has since been razed)
Produced by Katharine Cornell
Written by Rudolf Besier
Directed by Guthrie McClintic
Star: Katharine Cornell
Opened: February 9, 1931
Closing: December 1, 1931
Ian Wolfe as Harry Bevan

Note: Actor John D. Seymour was replaced with Ian Wolfe, at producer Cornell's request. The play ran 370 performances and toured on the road for an additional 55 weeks.

Devil in the Mind

Fulton Theatre, New York, NY (Reopened as Helen Hayes Theatre in 1955 and was razed in 1982. The following year, Little Theatre was renamed Helen Hayes Theatre, located at 240 W. 44th Street, New York City).

Produced by Leo Bulgakov Theatre Associates, Inc.

Written by William L. Laurence from the Russian of Leonid Andreyev

Staged by Leo Bulgakov

Star: Leo Bulgakov

Opened: May 1, 1931

Closed: May 11, 1931

Ian Wolfe as Professor Semyonov

Camille

Morosco Theatre, New York NY (razed in 1982).

Produced by Delos Chappell, Inc.

Written by Alexandre Dumas from the book adapted by Delos Chapopell, Edna Chappell and Robert Edmond Jones

Staged by Robert Edmond Jones

Star: Lillian Gish

Opened: November 1, 1932

Closed: November 12, 1932

Ian Van Wolfe as Count DeGiray/ Gustave

Lone Valley

Plymouth Theatre, New York, NY (renamed Gerald Schoenfeld Theatre)

Produced, Written and Staged by Sophie Treadwell

Star: Oliver Barbour

Opened: March 10, 1933

Closed after three performances.

Ian Wolfe as Lasly

Candide

Booth Theatre, New York, NY

Produced by Michael Meyerberg

Book adapted by Charles Weidman. Based on the novel by Voltaire

Staged by Charles Weidman

Opened: May 15, 1933

Closed: May 23, 1933

Star: Cleo Althenos

Narrative by Ian Wolfe

Men In White

Broadhurst Theatre, New York

Opened: September 26, 1933; Closed: July 1934.

Note: Ian Wolfe told this author, "I was a replacement briefly, maybe a week? I was one of the many doctors in it. That was soon before Irving Thalberg

called me out to California in the spring of 1934. I didn't return to New
York until 1957. It has been back and forth since for live television and some
stage work.

Winesburg, Ohio
National Theatre, New York, NY (renamed Nederlander Theatre in 1980)
Produced by Yvette Schumer, S.L. Adler and The Saba Company
Written by Christopher Sergel
Based on the book by Sherwood Anderson
Directed by Joseph Anthony
Opened: February 5, 1958
Closed: February 15, 1958
Star: Leon Ames
Ian Wolfe as Parcival
The Chalk Garden
Straw Hat tour of New England
Summer of 1960
Ian Wolfe played opposite Helen Hayes
The Deputy
Brooks Atkinson Theatre, New York, NY (formerly known as Mansfield The-
atre)
Produced by Herman Shumlin, Alfred Crown and Zvi Kolitz
Written by Rolf Hochhuth
Book adapted by Jerome Rothenberg
Directed by Herman Shumlin
Opened: February 26, 1964
Closed: November 28, 1964
With a cast of twenty-five including: Jeremy Brett and Emlyn Williams as
Pope Pious XII
Ian Wolfe as Father General
Author's note: The author Rolf Hochhuth's controversial stage production
was nominated at the Eighteenth Annual Tony Awards broadcast May 24,
1964. It won producer/director Herman Shumlin, the "Tony" for the Best
Produced Dramatic Play. "The Deputy" ran 316 performances at the Brooks
Atkinson Theatre and toured for another 16 weeks, in Chicago and Los
Angeles (for The Center Group Theatre; Mark Taper Auditorium).
The Devils
Mark Taper Auditorium, Los Angeles, CA
Produced by the Los Angeles Center Theatre Group
Written by John Whiting
Directed by Gordon Davidson
Premiere season: previews began April 10, 1967
Opened: April 14, 1967
Closed: May 28, 1967
Ian Wolfe as the elderly monk
Murderous Angels

Mark Taper Auditorium, Los Angeles, CA
Produced by the Los Angeles Center Group Theatre
Written by Conor Cruise O'Brien
Directed by Gordon Davidson
World Premiere: previews began January 24, 1970
Opened: February 5, 1970
Closed: March 22, 1970
Ian Wolfe as Lord Tamworth
Note: The west coast run of "Murderous Angels" marked the last stage appearances by Ian Wolfe, and his acquaintance with Gordon Davidson. The play also ran at Playhouse Theatre (renamed Jack Lawrence Theatre) in New York between December 20, 1971 and January 9, 1972, without Ian Wolfe. The actor became more active in television on the west coast at this time. Actor Neil Fitzgerald played the part of Viscount Tamworth through the east coast run.

Carl Laemmle Jr. – Production filmography

(212 credits total)
Junior's first extensive assignment was writing, casting and supervising the production of a successful series of comedy short films about college life. Forty-four silent screen "featurettes" known as *The Collegians* were released by Universal Pictures between 1926 and 1929 under the following titles:

1. *Benson at Calford*
Director - Harry J. Edwards
USA release: November 8, 1926
2. *Fighting to Win*
Director – Harry J. Edwards
USA release: November 22, 1926
3. *Making Good*
Director – Harry J. Edwards
USA release: December 6, 1926
4. *The Last Lap*
Director – Wesley Ruggles
USA release: December 20, 1926
5. *Around the Bases*
Director – Wesley Ruggles
USA release: January 3, 1927
6. *The Fighting Spirit*
Director – Nat Ross
USA release: January 17, 1927
7. *The Relay*
Director – Wesley Ruggles
USA release: January 31, 1927
8. The Cinder Path

Director - Wesley Ruggles
USA release: February 14, 1927
9. *Flashing Oars*
Director - Wesley Ruggles
USA release: February 28, 1927
10. *Breaking Records*
Director - Wesley Ruggles
USA release: March 14, 1927
11. *Crimson Colors*
Director - Nat Ross
USA release: September 12, 1927
12. *The Winning Five*
Director - Nat Ross
USA release: September 26, 1927
13. *The Dazzling Co-Ed*
Director - Nat Ross
USA release: October 10, 1927
14. *A Fighting Finish*
Director - Nat Ross
USA release: October 24, 1927
15. *Samson at Calford*
Director - Nat Ross
USA release: November 7, 1927
16. *The Winning Punch*
Director - Nat Ross
USA release: November 21, 1927
17. *Running Wild*
Director - Nat Ross
USA release: December 5, 1927
18. *Splashing Through*
Director - Nat Ross
USA release: December 19, 1927
19. *The Winning Goal*
Director - Nat Ross
USA release: January 2, 1928
20. *Sliding Home*
Director - Nat Ross
USA release: January 16, 1928
21. *The Junior Year*
Director - Nat Ross
USA release: September 3, 1928
22. *Calford vs. Redskins*
Director - Nat Ross
USA release: September 17, 1928
23. *Kicking Through*

Director – Nat Ross
USA release: October 1, 1928
24. *Calford in the Movies*
Director – Nat Ross
USA release: October 15, 1928
25. *Paddling Co-Eds*
Director – Nat Ross
USA release: October 29, 1928
26. *Fighting for Victory*
Director – Nat Ross
USA release: November 12, 1928
27. *Dear Old Calford*
Director – Nat Ross
USA release: November 26, 1928
28. *Calford on Horseback*
Director – Nat Ross
USA release: December 10, 1928
29. *The Bookworm Hero*
Director – Nat Ross
USA release: December 24, 1928
30. *Speeding Youth*
Director – Nat Ross
USA release: January 7, 1929
31. *The Winning Point*
Director – Nat Ross
USA release: January 21, 1929
32. *Farewell*
Director – Nat Ross
USA release: February 4, 1929
33. *King of the Campus*
Director – Nat Ross
USA release: April 1, 1929
34. *The Rivals*
Director – Nat Ross
USA release: April 15, 1929
35. *On Guard*
Director – Nat Ross
USA release: April 29, 1929
36. *Junior Luck*
Director – Nat Ross
USA release: May 27, 1929
37. *Cross Country Run*
Director – Harry L. Fraser
USA release: June 19, 1929
38. *Sporting Courage*

Director – Nat Ross
USA release: June 24, 1929
39. *The Varsity Drag*
Director – Nat Ross
USA release: July 8, 1929
40. *Flying High*
Director – Ben Holmes
USA release: July 22, 1929
41. *On the Sidelines*
Director – Nat Ross
USA release: August 5, 1929
42. *Use Your Feet*
Director – Nat Ross
USA release: August 19, 1929
43. *Splash Mates*
Director – Ben Holmes
USA release: September 2, 1929
44. *Graduation Daze*
Director – Nat Ross
USA release: September 16, 1929
Additional productions between 1923 and 1936 of which Carl Laemmle Jr. had
involvement are as follows.
1923
1. *The Love Brand* (Junior's very first assignment at age fifteen, as a production assistant on this Universal western.)
Director Stuart Paton
USA release: August 23, 1923
1927
2. *The Dude Desperado* (Western short)
Director – George Hunter
USA release: January 29, 1927
3. *The Rambling Ranger* (feature length Western)
Director – Del Henderson
USA release: April 10, 1927
4. *Running Wild* (W.C. Fields comedy)
Director – Gregory La Cava
USA release: June 11, 1927
5. *A Dog of the Regiment* (a Rin-Tin-Tin adventure)
Director – Ross Lederman
USA release: October 29, 1927
6. *The Irresistible Lover*
Director – William Beaudine
USA release: December 4, 1927
1928
7. *We Americans*

Director – Edward Sloman
USA release: May 6, 1928
1929
8. *The Last Warning*
Director – Paul Leni
USA release: January 6, 1929
9. *Lonesome*
Director – Paul Fejos (Pál Fejös)
USA release: January 20, 1929
10. *The Cohens and Kellys in Atlantic City*
Director – William James Craft
USA release: March 17, 1929
11. *Smilin' Guns* (full-length Hoot Gibson western)
Director – Henry MacRae
USA release: March 31, 1929
12. *The Charlatan*
Director – George Melford
USA release: April 14, 1929
13. *College Love* (same "Collegian" actors playing different roles)
Director – Nat Ross
USA release: July 7, 1929 (full-length sound movie)
14. *Broadway*
Director – Paul Fejos
USA release: September 15, 1929
15. *Barnum was Right*
Director – Del Lord
USA release: September 22, 1929
16. *One Hysterical Night*
Director – William J. Craft
USA release: October 6, 1929
17. *The Last Performance* (alternate title: *Erik the Great*)
Director – Paul Fejos
USA release: October 13, 1929
18. *The Mississippi Gambler*
Director – Reginald Barker
USA release: November 3, 1929
19. *Skinner Steps Out*
Director – William James Craft
USA release: November 24, 1929
1930
20. *Hell's Heroes* (Western)
Director – William Wyler
USA release: January 5, 1930
21. *Night Ride* (aka *Out to Kill* with Edward G. Robinson)
Director – John S. Robertson

USA release: January 12, 1930
22. *Dames Ahoy*
Director - William James Craft
USA release: February 9, 1930
23. *The Cohens and Kellys in Scotland*
Director - William James Craft
USA release: March 17, 1930
24. *Captain of the Guard*
Director - John S. Robertson (replaced Paul Fejos)
USA release March 29, 1930
25. *All Quiet on the Western Front*
Director - Lewis Milestone
USA release: August 24, 1930
German release: December 4, 1930
New York and Washington D.C. revival: April 13, 1934
26. *What Men Want*
Director - Ernst Laemmle
USA release: July 13, 1930
27. *King of Jazz*
Director - John Murray Anderson
USA release: August 17, 1930
28. *Little Accident*
Director - William James Craft
USA release: September 1, 1930
29. *Outside the Law*
Director - Tod Browning
USA release: September 18, 1930
30. *A Lady Surrenders*
Director - John M. Stahl
USA release: October 5, 1930
31. *East is West*
Director - Monta Bell
USA release: October 23, 1930
32. *Oriente es Occidente* (Spanish version of *East is West* with other actors.)
Director: George Melford and Enrique Tovar Ávalos
USA release: October 23, 1930
33. *La voluntad del muerto* (Spanish version of *The Cat Creeps*)
Director - George Melford
USA release: November 5, 1930
34. *The Cat Creeps*
Director - Rupert Julian and John Willard
USA release: November 10, 1930
35. *See America Thirst*
Director - William James Craft
USA release: November 24, 1930

36. *The Boudoir Diplomat*
Director – Malcolm St. Clair
USA release: December 25, 1930
1931
37. *Free Love* (alternate title: *The Modern Wife*)
Director – Hobart Henley
USA release: January 5, 1931
38. *The Cohens and Kellys in Africa*
Director – Vin Moore
USA release: January 19, 1931
39. *Resurrection* (first sound film version from the novel by Leo Tolstoy)
Director – Edwin Carewe
USA release: February 2, 1931
40. *Don Juan diplomático* (Spanish version of *The Boudoir Diplomat*)
Director – George Melford
USA release: 1931
Los Angeles opening: February 13, 1931
41. *Dracula* (from the novel by Bram Stoker)
Director – Tod Browning
USA release: February 14, 1931
42. *Drácula* (Spanish version)
Director – George Melford
Mexico City release: April 4, 1931
USA release: April 24, 1931
43. *Many a Slip* (Comedy)
Director – Vin Moore
USA release: March 2, 1931
44. *Bad Sister* (Bette Davis' film debut)
Director – Hobart Henley
USA release: March 23, 1931
45. *The Virtuous Husband*
Director – Vin Moore
USA release: April 12, 1931
46. *Iron Man*
Director – Tod Browning
USA release: April 30, 1931
47. *Seed*
Director – John M. Stahl
USA release: May 11, 1931
48. *Up for Murder* (a.k.a. *Fires of Youth*)
Director – Monta Bell
USA release: June 15, 1931
49. *Ex-Bad Boy*
Director – Vin Moore
USA release: July 15, 1931

50. *Waterloo Bridge*
Director – James Whale (his directorial debut at Universal Pictures)
USA release: September 1, 1931
51. *East of Borneo*
Director – George Melford
Producers include: George Melford and (associate producer) Paul Kohner
USA release: September 15, 1931
52. *The Homicide Squad*
Director – Edward L. Cahn and George Melford
USA release: September 29, 1931
53. *The Spirit of Notre Dame*
Director – Russell Mack
USA release: October 13, 1931
54. *Reckless Living* (aka: *The Up and Up*)
Director – Cyril Gardner
USA release: October 20, 1931
55. *Lasca of the Rio Grande*
Director – Edward Laemmle
USA release: October 27, 1931
56. *Frankenstein*
Director – James Whale
USA release: November 21, 1931
57. *Nice Women*
Director – Edwin H. Knopf
USA release: November 28, 1931
58. *A House Divided*
Director – William Wyler
USA release: December 5, 1931
59. *Heaven on Earth*
Director – Russell Mack
USA release: December 12, 1931
60. *Strictly Dishonorable*
Director – John M. Stahl
USA release: December 26, 1931
61. *The Last Ride*
Director – Duke Worne
USA release: December 28, 1931
1932
62. *Unexpected Father*
Director – Thornton Freeland
USA release: January 3, 1932
63. *Law and Order*
Director – Edward L. Cahn
USA release: February 7, 1932
64. *Racing Youth*

Director – Vin Moore
USA release: February 14, 1932
65. *Murders in the Rue Morgue*
Director – Robert Florey
USA release: February 21, 1932
66. *The Impatient Maiden*
Director – James Whale
USA release: March 1, 1932
67. *Steady Company*
Director – Edward I. Luddy (a.k.a. Edward Ludwig)
USA release: March 14, 1932
68. *The Cohens and Kellys in Hollywood*
Director: John Frances Dillon
USA release: March 28, 1932
69. *Stowaway*
Director – Phil Whitman
USA release: April 11, 1932
70. *Scandal for Sale*
Director – Russell Mack
USA release: April 17, 1932
71. *Destry Rides Again* (first talkie for screen cowboy Tom Mix)
Director – Ben Stoloff (a.k.a. Benjamin Stoloff)
USA release: April 17, 1932
72. *Night World*
Director – Hobart Henley
USA release: May 5, 1932
73. *Rider of Death Valley*
Director – Albert (S.) Rogell
USA release: May 26, 1932
74. *Radio Patrol*
Director – Edward L. Cahn
USA release: June 2, 1932
75. *Doomed Battalion*
Director – Cyril Gardner and Luis Trenker
(German footage of 1931 directed by Karl Hartl and Luis Trenker.)
USA release: June 16, 1932
76. *Fast Companions*
Director – Kurt Neumann
USA release: June 23, 1932
77. *The Texas Bad Man*
Director – Edward Laemmle
USA release: June 30, 1932
78. *Tom Brown of Culver*
Director – William Wyler
USA release: July 21, 1932

79. *My Pal, the King*
Director – Kurt Neumann
USA release: August 4, 1932
80. *Back Street*
Director – John M. Stahl
USA release: September 1, 1932
81. *Okay, America!*
Director – Tay Garnett
USA release: September 8, 1932
82. *Once in a Lifetime*
Director – Russell Mack
USA release: September 22, 1932
83. *The Fourth Horseman*
Director – Hamilton MacFadden
USA release: September 29, 1932
84. *The All-American*
Director – Russell Mack
USA release: October 13, 1932
85. *The Old Dark House*
Director – James Whale
USA release: October 20, 1932
86. *Air Mail*
Director – John Ford
USA release: November 3, 1932
87. *Hidden Gold*
Director – Arthur Rosson
USA release: November 3, 1932
88. *Merry-Go-Round* (aka: *Afraid to Talk*)
Director – Edward L. Cahn
USA release: November 17, 1932
89. *The Mummy*
Director – Karl Freund (his directorial debut)
USA release: December 22, 1932
90. *Flaming Guns*
Director – Arthur Rosson
USA release: December 22, 1932
1933
91. *They Just Had to Get Married*
Director – Edward Ludwig (a.k.a. Edward I. Luddy)
USA release: January 5, 1933
92. *Nagana*
Director – Ernst L. Frank
USA release: January 9, 1933
93. *Laughter in Hell*
Director – Edward L. Cahn

USA release: January 12, 1933
94. *Terror Trail*
Director – Armand Schaefer
USA release: February 2, 1933
95. *Private Jones*
Director – Russell Mack
USA release: February 16, 1933
96. *The Big Cage*
Director – Kurt Neumann
USA release: March 3, 1933
97. *Rustler's Roundup*
Director – Henry MacRae
USA release: March 16, 1933
98. *Destination Unknown*
Director – Tay Garnett
USA release: March 16, 1933
99. *The Cohens and Kellys in Trouble*
Director – George Stevens
USA release: March 23, 1933
100. *Out All Night*
Director – Sam Taylor
USA release: April 13, 1933
101. *Lucky Dog*
Director – Zion Meyers
USA release: April 20, 1933
102. *The Kiss Before the Mirror*
Director – James Whale
USA release: May 4, 1933
103. *Secret of the Blue Room*
Director – Kurt Neumann
USA release: July 20, 1933
104. *Don't Bet on Love* (a.k.a. *In the Money*)
Director – Murray Roth
USA release: July 29, 1933
105. *Her First Mate* (a.k.a. *Salt Water*)
Director – William Wyler
USA release: August 3, 1933
106. *Ladies Must Love*
Director – Ewald André Dupont (a.k.a. E. A, Dupont)
USA release: September 25, 1933
107. *Saturday's Millions*
Director – Edward Sedgwick
USA release: October 9, 1933
108. *Love, Honor and Oh, Baby!*
Director – Eddie (Edward) Buzzell

USA release: October 16, 1933
109. *S.O.S. Iceberg*
Director – Tay Garnett
Associate producer – Paul Kohner
USA release: October 23, 1933
110. *King for a Night*
Director – Kurt Neumann
USA release: October 30, 1933
111. *Only Yesterday* (movie debut of Margaret Sullavan)
Director – William Wyler
USA release: November 6, 1933
112. *The Invisible Man*
Director – James Whale
USA release: November 13, 1933
113. *Horseplay*
Director – Edward Sedgwick
USA release: November 27, 1933
114. *By Candlelight*
Director – James Whale
USA release: December 18, 1933
115. *Counsellor-at-Law* (stars John Barrymore)
Director – William Wyler
USA release: December 25, 1933
1934
116. *Bombay Mail*
Director – Edwin L. Marin
USA release: January 1, 1934
117. *Madame Spy* (starring Fay Wray)
Director – Karl Freund
Associate producer – (James) Edmund Grainger
USA release: January 8, 1934
118. *Cross Country Cruise* (Musical Comedy)
Director – Edward Buzzell
USA release: January 15, 1934
119. *Beloved*
Director – Victor Schertzinger (former musician)
USA release: January 22, 1934
120. *The Poor Rich*
Director – Edward Sedgwick
USA release: February 28, 1934
121. *The Crosby Case*
Director – Edwin L. Marin
USA release: March 5, 1934
122. *Love Birds* (a/k/a Niagara Falls)
Director – William A. Seiter

USA release: March 12, 1934
123. *Let's Be Ritzy*
Director – Edward Luddy
USA release: March 26, 1934
124. *Glamour*
Director – William Wyler
USA release: April 9, 1934
125. *I'll Tell the World*
Director – Edward Sedgwick
USA release: April 16, 1934
126. *Uncertain Lady*
Director – Karl Freund
USA release: April 23, 1934
127. *Half a Sinner*
Director – Kurt Neumann
USA release: April 30, 1934
128. *The Black Cat*
Director – Edgar G. Ulmer
USA release: May 7, 1934
129. *Little Man, What Now?*
Director – Frank Borzage
USA release: June 4, 1934
130. *Affairs of a Gentleman*
Director – Edwin L. Marin
USA release: May 14, 1934
131. *The Love Captive* (from the play *The Humbug*)
Director – Max Marcin
USA release: May 21, 1934
132. *I Give My Love*
Director – Karl Freund
USA release: June 25, 1934
133. *Embarrassing Moments*
Director – Edward Laemmle
USA release: July 9, 1934
134. *One More River*
Director – James Whale
USA release: August 6, 1934
135. *The Human Side*
Director – Edward Buzzell
USA release: August 27, 1934
136. *Life Returns*
Director – Eugen Frenke
(Premiered September 8 through 19, 1934)
USA re-release: June 10, 1938
137. *There's Always Tomorrow* (aka: *Too Late for Love*)

Director - Edward Sloman
USA release: September 10, 1934
138. *Million Dollar Ransom*
Director - Murray Roth
USA release: September 17, 1934
139. *Gift of Gab*
Director - Karl Freund
USA release: September 24, 1934
140. *Wake Up and Dream*
Director - Kurt Neumann
USA release: October 1, 1934
141. *One Exciting Adventure*
Director - Ernst L. Frank
USA release: October 15, 1934
142. *Great Expectations*
Director - Stuart Walker
USA release: October 22, 1934
143. *Imitation of Life*
Director - John M. Stahl
USA release: November 26, 1934
144. *The Secret of the Chateau*
Director - Richard Thorpe
USA release: December 3, 1934
145. *The Man Who Reclaimed His Head*
Director - Edward Ludwig
USA release: December 24, 1934
1935
146. *A Notorious Gentleman*
Director - Edward Laemmle
USA release: January 21, 1935
147. *Mystery of Edwin Drood*
Director - Stuart Walker
USA release: February 4, 1935
148. *The Good Fairy*
Director - William Wyler
USA release: February 18, 1935
149. *Transient Lady*
Director - Edward Buzzell
USA release: March 4, 1935
150. *Night Life of the Gods*
Director - Lowell Sherman (He passed away nine months after its release.)
USA release: March 11, 1935
151. *Princess O'Hara*
Director - David Burton
USA release: March 25, 1935

152. *Bride of Frankenstein*
Director – James Whale
USA release: April 22, 1935
153. *Mister Dynamite*
Director – Alan Crosland
USA release: April 22, 1935
154. *The Raven*
Director – Lew Landers (a.k.a. Louis (B.) Friedlander
USA release: July 8, 1935
155. *Lady Tubbs*
Director – Alan Crosland
USA release: July 15, 1935
156. *King Solomon of Broadway*
Director – Alan Crosland
USA release: September 21, 1935
157. *Remember Last Night?*
Director – James Whale
USA release: October 28, 1935
1936
Junior Laemmle was determined to produce a full-sound version of Edna
Ferber's *Show Boat* after Universal's widely successful 1933-1934 season.
The Laemmles assigned their remaining properties out to other producers
although he would supervise and hire others working on director John M.
Stahl's *Magnificent Obsession*. *Show Boat* however was Junior's prior-
ity during 1935. *Show Boat* was completed as a musical soon before the
Laemmles left the company. It was the last time its director James Whale
worked with the Laemmles. The motion picture became a hit at the box
office, and profitable for the new management.
My Man Godfrey (starring Carole Lombard and William Powell) and *Three
Smart Girls* (which ultimately made the singing ingénue Deanna Durbin,
a star) were two incomplete Laemmle properties. *Sutter's Gold*, which
was completed and released in early 1936 was supposed to have saved
Universal, which it did not. *My Man Godfrey* and *Three Smart Girls* were
produced by the new studio management and were completed and were
successful. The following titles bore the Laemmle name:
158. *Magnificent Obsession*
Director – John M. Stahl
USA release: January 6, 1936
159. *The Invisible Ray*
Producer – Edmund Grainger and Fred S. Meyer
Director – Lambert Hillyer
USA release: January 20, 1936
160. *Sutter's Gold*
Producer – Edmund Grainger
Director – James Cruze

USA release: March 1, 1936
161. *Dracula's Daughter*
Producer - E.M. Asher
Director - Lambert Hillyer
USA release: May 11. 1936
162. *Werewolf of London*
Executive producer - Stanley Bergerman
Director - Stuart Walker
USA release: May 13, 1936
163. *Show Boat*
Director - James Whale
Produced by Carl Laemmle Jr.
USA release: May 17, 1936

During the 1933 and 1934 season, a number of adventure serials were widely successful, which included such titles as *Clancy of the Mounted, The Phantom of the Air, The Vanishing Shadow, Gordon of Ghost City* and *The Red Rider* (both starring Buck Jones); and *Tailspin Tommy* (first released in 1934). For Universal's 1935 and 1936 season, several long-time talents behind Universal's long-running adventure serials, Henry MacRae & Ray Taylor; Ford Beebe, Clifford Smith and Frederick Stephani joined forces to produce the last three adventure serials for under the Laemmles.

Junior Laemmle was involved long enough to see the following serials to fruition before leaving Universal on April 10, 1936:

164. *Tailspin Tommy in the Great Air Mystery* (12 Chapters)
Director - Ray Taylor
USA release: October 21, 1935
Chapter 1. Wreck of the Dirigible
Chapter 2. Roaring Fire God
Chapter 3. Hurled From the Skies
Chapter 4. Bolt from the Blue
Chapter 5. The Torrent
Chapter 6. Clash in the Clouds
Chapter 7. Flying Death
Chapter 8. Crossed and Double-Crossed
Chapter 9. Wings of Disaster
Chapter 10. Doomed in a Dungeon
Chapter 11. Desperate Chances
Chapter 12. The Last Stand
165. *The Adventures of Frank Merriwell* (12 Chapters)
Director - Ford Beebe and Clifford Smith
USA release: January 13, 1936
Chapter 1. College Hero
Chapter 2. The Death Plunge
Chapter 3. Death at the Crossroads
Chapter 4. Wreck of the Viking

Chapter 5. Capsized in the Cataract
Chapter 6. Descending Doom
Chapter 7. Monster of the Deep
Chapter 8. The Tragic Victory
Chapter 9. Between Savage Foes
Chapter 10. Imprisoned in a Dungeon
Chapter 11. The Crash in the Chasm
Chapter 12. The Winning Play
166. *Flash Gordon* (13 Chapters)
Director – Frederick Stephani
USA release: April 6, 1936
Chapter 1. The Planet of Peril
Chapter 2. The Tunnel of Terror
Chapter 3. Captures by Shark Men
Chapter 4. Battling the Sea Beast
Chapter 5. The Destroying Ray
Chapter 6. Flaming Torture
Chapter 7. Shattering Doom
Chapter 8. Tournament of Death
Chapter 9. Fighting the Dragon
Chapter 10. The Unseen Peril
Chapter 11. In the Claws of Tigron
Chapter 12. Trapped in the Turret
Chapter 13. Rocketing to Earth
 Early in his career, Junior Laemmle was featured as himself in two separate installments of the long-running, in-theatre celebrity film series produced by C.B.C. (Cohn-Brandt-Cohn) Film Sales Company (founded in 1918). The series began as *Hollywood Snapshots* in 1920 and later as *Screen Snapshots*. In 1924, the company was renamed Columbia Pictures and the popular series continued to run until 1958. Each series ran approximately 10 minutes.
167. *Hollywood Snapshots #11* (features Carl Laemmle Jr. and other celebrities)
Producer – Jack Cohn
Host and Narrator: Eddie Lambert
USA release: January 1, 1929
168. *Screen Snapshots, Series 9, No. 11* (features Carl Laemmle Jr. and other celebrities)
Directed by Ralph Staub
USA release: January 1, 1930

Alan Napier Filmography
1. Caste (United Artists Corporation UK, 1930)
Directed by Campbell Gullan and Michael Powell; Produced by Jerome Jackson; Star: Hermione Badley. Alan Napier as Captain Hawtree.
2. *Stamboul* (Paramount British Pictures, 1931)

Directed by Dimitri Buchowetzki; Produced by Walter Morosco; Star: Warwick Ward. Alan Napier as Boucher.
3. *In a Monastery Garden* (Associated Producers & Distributors UK, 1932)
Directed by Maurice Elvey; Produced by Julius Hagen; Star: John Stuart. Alan
Napier as Count Romano.
4. *Bitter Sweet* (United Artists Corporation UK, 1933)
Directed and Produced by Herbert Wilcox. Star: Anna Neagle. Alan Napier
as Marquis of Shayne.
5. *Loyalties* (Associated Talking Pictures UK, 1933)
Directed by Basil Dean and Thorold Dickinson; Produced by Basil Dean; Star:
Basil Rathbone. Alan Napier as General Canynge.
6. *The Wandering Jew* (Gaumont British UK, 1933)
Directed by Maurice Elvey; Produced by Julius Hagen; Star: Conrad Veidt.
Alan Napier as Knight.
7. *Wings Over Africa* (Radio Pictures UK, 1936)
Directed by Ladislao Vajda; Produced by John Stafford; Star: Joan Gardner.
Alan Napier as Redfern.
8. *For Valour* (General Film Distributors UK, 1937)
Directed by Tom Walls; Produced by Max Schach; Star: Tom Walls. Alan
Napier as the General.
9. *The Wife of General Ling* (Radio Pictures UK, 1937)
Directed by Ladislao Vajda; Produced by John Stafford;
Star: Griffith Jones. Alan Napier as Governor.
10. *The Secret Four* (Associated British Film Distributors UK, 1939) aka:
The Four Just Men (Monogram Pictures, 1940)
Directed by Walter Forde; Produced by Michael Balcon and S.C. Balcon;
Star: Hugh Sinclair. Alan Napier as Sir Hamar Ryman M.P.
11. *We Are Not Alone* (Warner Brothers USA, 1939)
Directed by Edmund Goulding; Produced by Henry Blanke and Hal B.
Wallis; Screenwriters: Milton Krims and James Hilton (novel). Star: Paul
Muni. Alan Napier as the Archdeacon.
12. *The Invisible Man Returns* (Universal Pictures, 1940)
Directed by Joe May; Produced by Ken Goldsmith; Screenwriters: H.G. Wells,
Joe May, Curt Siodmak and Lester Cole Star: Cedric Hardwicke. Alan
Napier as Willie Spears.
13. *The House of the Seven Gables* (Universal Pictures, 1940)
Directed by Joe May; Produced by Burt Kelly; Screenwriters: Lester Cole
and Harold Greene. Based on the novel by Nathaniel Hawthorne. Star:
George Sanders. Alan Napier as Fuller.
14. *Confirm or Deny* (Twentieth Century Fox, 1941)
Directed by Archie Mayo and (Fritz Lang-uncredited); Produced by Len Ham-
mond; Screenwriter: Jo Swerling; Story by Henry Wales and Samuel Fuller;
Star: Don Ameche. Alan Napier as Updyke.
15. *We Were Dancing* (Metro-Goldwyn-Mayer, 1942)

Directed by Robert Z. Leonard; Screenwriters: Claudine West, Hans Rameau, George Froeschel, and Lenore Coffee; based partially on the Noel Coward play, *Tonight at 8:30*. Produced by Robert Z. Leonard and Orville O. Dull; Star: Norma Shearer. Alan Napier as Captain Blackstone.

16. *Eagle Squadron* (Universal Pictures, 1942)
Directed by Arthur Lubin; Produced by Walter Wanger; Star: Robert Stack. Alan Napier as Black Watch officer.

17. *Random Harvest* (Metro-Goldwyn-Mayer, 1942)
Directed by Mervyn LeRoy; Produced by Sidney Franklin; Screenwriters: Claudine West, George Froeschel and Arthur Wimperis; based on the novel by James Hilton. Star: Ronald Colman. Alan Napier as Julian.

18. *A Yank at Eton* (Metro-Goldwyn-Mayer, 1942)
Directed by Norman Taurog; Produced by John W. Considine, Jr. Star: Mickey Rooney. Alan Napier as the Restaurateur.

19. *Cat People* (RKO Radio Pictures, 1942)
Directed by Jacques Tourneur; Produced by Val Lewton, Screenwriter: DeWitt Bodeen. Star: Simone Simon. Alan Napier as Doc Carver.

20. *The Song of Bernadette* (Twentieth Century Fox, 1943)
Directed by Henry King; Produced by William Perlberg; Screenwriters: George Seaton and Franz Werfel; Star: Jennifer Jones. Alan Napier as Dr. Debeau.

21. *Lassie Come Home* (Metro-Goldwyn-Mayer, 1943)
Directed by Fred M. Wilcox; Produced by Samuel Marx, Harry Rapf and Dore Schary; Screenwriters: Hugo Butler and Eric Knight. Star: Roddy McDowall. Alan Napier as Jock.

22. *Madame Curie* (Metro-Goldwyn-Mayer, 1943)
Directed by Mervyn LeRoy and Albert Lewin. Produced by Sidney Franklin. Screenwriters: Paul Osborn and Hans Rameau. From the book by Ève Curie (subject's youngest daughter) Star: Greer Garson. Alan Napier as Dr. Bladh.

23. *Assignment in Brittany* (Metro-Goldwyn-Mayer, 1943)
Directed by Jack Conway; Produced by J. Walter Ruben; Star: Jean-Pierre Aumont. Alan Napier as Sam Wells.

24. *Lost Angel* (Metro-Goldwyn-Mayer, 1943)
Directed by Roy Rowland; Produced by Robert Sisk; Star: Margaret O'Brien. Alan Napier as Dr. Woodring.

25. *Appointment in Berlin* (Columbia Pictures, 1943)
Directed by Alfred E. Green; Screenwriters: B.P. Fineman, Michael Hogan and Horace McCoy; Produced by Samuel Bischoff; Star: George Sanders. Alan Napier as Colonel Patterson.

26. *Ministry of Fear* (Paramount Pictures, 1944)
Directed by Fritz Lang; Screenwriter: Seton I. Miller; Based on the novel by Graham Greene. Produced by Seton I. Miller and Buddy G. DeSylva. Star: Ray Milland. Alan Napier as Dr. JM Forrester.

27. *The Uninvited* (Paramount Pictures, 1944)
Directed by Lewis Allen; Screenwriters Dodie Smith and Frank Partos;
Based on Dorothy Macardle's novel "Uneasy Freehold." Produced by
Charles Brackett. Star: Ray Milland. Alan Napier as Dr. Scott.

28. *Thirty Seconds Over Tokyo* (Metro-Goldwyn-Mayer, 1944)
Directed by Mervyn LeRoy; Screenplay by Dalton Trumbo; Based on the
book by Captain Ted W. Lawson. Produced by Sam Zimbalist, Star: Spen-
cer Tracy. Alan Napier as Mr. Parker.

29. *Dark Waters* (United Artists, 1944)
Directed by Andre De Toth; Original story by Frank Cockrell and Marian
Cockrell; Screenplay by Joan Harrison and Marian Cockrell; Produced by
Benedict Bogeaus and James Nasser. Star: Merle Oberon. Alan Napier as
the doctor.

30. *The Hairy Ape* (United Artists, 1944)
Directed by Alfred Santell; from the play by Eugene O'Neill; Screenwriters:
Robert Hardy Andrews and Decla Dunning. Produced by Jules Levey and
Joseph H. Nadel. Star: William Bendix. Alan Napier as Chief Engineer
MacDougald.

31. *Mademoiselle Fifi* (RKO Radio Pictures, 1944)
Directed by Robert Wise; Screenwriters: Josef Mischel and Peter Ruric; from
short stories, "Mademoiselle Fifi" and "Boule de Suif" by Guy de Maupas-
sant; Produced by Val Lewton; Star: Simone Simon. Alan Napier as The
Count de Breville.

32. *Action in Arabia* (RKO Radio Pictures, 1944)
Directed by Léonide Moguy; Original Screenplay: Philip MacDonald and
Herbert Biberman; Produced by Maurice Geraghty; Star: George Sanders.
Alan Napier as Eric Latimer.

33. *Isle of the Dead* (RKO Radio Pictures, 1945)
Director: Mark Robson; Screenwriters: Ardel Wray (Val Lewton and Josef
Mischel- uncredited); Produced by Val Lewton and Jack J. Gross; Star:
Boris Karloff. Alan Napier as Mr. St. Aubyn.

34. *Hangover Square* (Twentieth Century Fox, 1945)
Directed by John Brahm; Screenwriter: Barré Lyndon; from the novel by Patrick Hamilton; Produced by Robert Bassler; Star: Laird Cregar. Alan Napier
as Sir Henry Chapman.

35. *House of Horrors* (Universal Pictures, 1946)
Directed by Jean Yarbrough; Screenwriter: George Bricker; Original story
by Dwight V. Babcock; Produced by Ben Pivar Star: Rondo Hatton. Alan
Napier as F. Holmes Harmon.

36. *The Strange Woman* (United Artists, 1946)
Directed by Edgar G. Ulmer (Douglas Sirk-uncredited); Screenwriter: Herb
Meadow; from the novel by Ben Ames Williams; Produced by Jack Cher-
tok and Eugen Schüfftan; Star: Hedy Lamarr. Alan Napier as Judge Henry
Saladine.

37. *Three Strangers* (Warner Brothers, 1946)

Directed by Jean Negulesco; Screenwriters: John Huston and Howard Koch; Produced by Wolfgang Reinhardt. Star: Peter Lorre. Alan Napier as David Shackleford.

38. *A Scandal in Paris* (United Artists, 1946)

Directed by Douglas Sirk; Screenwriter: Ellis St. Joseph; from the memoirs of François Eugène Vidocq (1775-1857); Produced by Arnold Pressburger; Star: George Sanders. Alan Napier as Houdon De Pierremont, Police Minister.

39. *Ivy* (Universal Pictures, 1947)

Directed by Sam Wood; Screenwriter: Charles Bennett; from the novel "The Story of Ivy" by Marie Belloc Lowndes; Produced by William Cameron Menzies; Star: Joan Fontaine. Alan Napier as Sir Jonathan Wright.

40. *Forever Amber* (Twentieth Century Fox, 1947)

Directed by Otto Preminger (John M. Stahl-uncredited); Screenwriters: Philip Dunne, Ring Lardner Jr. and Jerome Cady; from the novel by Kathleen Winsor (Mr. & Mrs. Alan Napier are credited as "Dialect directors."); Produced by William Perlberg (and Darryl F. Zanuck-uncredited); Star: Linda Darnell. Alan Napier as Landale.

41. *Unconquered* (Paramount Pictures, 1947)

Directed and Produced by Cecil B. DeMille; Screenwriters: Charles Bennett, Fredric M. Frank and Jesse Lasky Jr.; from the Neil H. Swanson novel, "The Judas Tree;" Star: Gary Cooper. Alan Napier as Sir William Johnson.

42. *Lured* (United Artists, 1947)

Directed by Douglas Sirk; Screenwriters: Jacques Companéez, Simon Gantillon, Ernst Neubach, and Leo Rosten; Produced by James Nasser; Star: George Sanders. Alan Napier as Detective Gordon.

43. *Sinbad, the Sailor* (RKO Radio Pictures, 1947)

Directed by Richard Wallace; Screenwriter: John Twist; Original story by George Worthing Yates and John Twist; Produced by Stephen Ames; Star: Douglas Fairbanks Jr. Alan Napier as Aga.

44. *Driftwood* (Republic Pictures, 1947)

Directed and Produced by Allan Dwan; Screenwriters: Mary Loos and Richard Sale; Stars: Ruth Warrick. Alan Napier as Dr. Nicholas Adams.

45. *Fiesta* (Metro-Goldwyn-Mayer, 1947)

Directed by Richard Thorpe; Screenwriters: George Bruce and Lester Cole; Produced by Jack Cummings; Star: Esther Williams. Alan Napier as the Tourist.

46. *Adventure Island* (Paramount Pictures, 1947)

Directed by Sam Newfield; Screenwriters: Maxwell Shane; from the Robert Louis Stevenson novel, "The Ebb Tide;" and from the Lloyd Osbourne novel, "Ebb-Tide." Produced by William H. Pine. Star: Rory Calhoun. Alan Napier as Attwater.

47. *High Conquest* (Monogram Pictures, 1947)

Directed and Produced by Irving Allen; Screenwriters: Max Trell and Aben Kandel; from the novel by James Ramsey Ullman; Star: Anna Lee. Alan Napier as Tommy Donlin.

48. *The Lone Wolf in London* (Columbia Pictures, 1947)
Directed by Leslie Goodwins; Screenwriters: Brenda Weisberg and Arthur
   E. Orloff; Based on "Lone Wolf" characters by author Louis Joseph Vance;
   Produced by Ted Richmond and Robert Cohn; Star: Gerald Mohr. Alan
   Napier as Monty Beresford.

49. *Macbeth* (Republic Pictures, 1948)
Directed and Produced by Orson Welles; Associate producer: Richard Wil-
   son; Executive Producer: Charles K. Feldman. Screen Adaptation: Orson
   Welles; from the play by William Shakespeare; Star: Orson Welles. Alan
   Napier as A Holy Father.

50. *Joan of Arc* (RKO Radio Pictures, 1948)
Directed by Victor Fleming; Screenwriters: from the play "Joan of Lorraine"
   by Maxwell Anderson, Andrew Solt and Maxwell Anderson; Produced by
   Walter Wanger; Star: Ingrid Bergman. Alan Napier as Earl of Warwick.

51. *Hills of Home* (Metro-Goldwyn-Mayer, 1948)
Directed by Fred M. Wilcox; Screenwriters: William Ludwig and Ian Maclaren
   (suggested by his sketches "Doctor of the Old School"); Produced by Robert Sisk; Star: Edmund Gwenn. Alan Napier as Sir George.

52. *Johnny Belinda* (Warner Brothers, 1948)
Directed by Jean Negulesco; Screenwriters: Irmgard von Cube and Allen Vin-
   cent; from the stage play by Elmer Harris; Produced by Jerry Wald; Star:
   Jane Wyman, Lew Ayres, Charles Bickford, Agnes Moorehead

53. *Criss Cross* (Universal Pictures, 1949)
Directed by Robert Siodmak; Screenwriters: Daniel Fuchs; from the novel by
   Don Tracy; Produced by Michel Kraike; Star: Burt Lancaster. Alan Napier as
   Finchley.

54. *A Connecticut Yankee in King Arthur's Court* (Paramount, 1949)
Directed by Tay Garnett; Screenwriter: Edmund Beloin; from the novel by
   Mark Twain; Produced by Robert Fellows; Star: Bing Crosby. Alan Napier as
   High Executioner.

55. *Manhandled* (Paramount, 1949)
Directed by Lewis R. Foster; Screenwriters Lewis R. Foster, Whitman Cham-
   bers; from the story by L.S. Goldsmith; Produced by William C. Thomas;
   Star: Dan Duryea. Alan Napier as Alton Bennet.

56. *The Red Danube* (Metro-Goldwyn-Mayer, 1949)
Directed by George Sidney; Screenwriters: Gina Kaus and Arthur Wimperis;
   from the novel "Vespers in Vienna" by Bruce Marshall; Produced by Carey
   Wilson; Star: Walter Pidgeon. Alan Napier as The General.

57. *Challenge to Lassie* (Metro-Goldwyn-Mayer, 1949)
Directed by Richard Thorpe; Screenwriter: William Ludwig; based on the
   novel, "Greyfriar's Bobby" by Eleanor Atkinson; Produced by Robert Sisk;
   Star: Edmund Gwenn. Alan Napier as Lord Provost.

58. *Tarzan's Magic Fountain* (RKO Radio Pictures, 1949)

Directed by Lee Sholem; Screenwriters: Curt Siodmak and Harry Chandlee; based on the Edgar Rice Burroughs character; Produced by Sol Lesser. Star: Lex Barker. Alan Napier as Douglas Jessup.

59. *My Own True Love* (Paramount, 1949)
Directed by Compton Bennett; Screenwriters: Arthur Kober, Josef Mischel and Theodore Strauss; from the novel "Make You a Fine Wife" by Yolanda Foldes; Produced by Val Lewton; Star: Phyllis Calvert. Alan Napier as Kittredge.

60. *Master Minds* (Monogram, 1949)
Directed by Jean Yarbrough; Screenwriters: Charles R. Marion (story) and Bert Lawrence; Produced by Jan Grippo. Star: Leo Gorcey. Alan Napier as Dr. Druzik.

61. *Tripoli* (Paramount, 1950)
Directed by Will Price; Screenwriters: Winston Miller and Will Price; Produced by William H. Pine and William C. Thomas; Star: John Payne. Alan Napier as Khalil.

62. *The Great Caruso* (Metro-Goldwyn-Mayer, 1951)
Directed by Richard Thorpe; Screenwriters: William Ludwig (from Dorothy Caruso's biography of her husband); Produced by Joe Pasternak and Jesse L. Lasky; Star: Mario Lanza. Alan Napier as Jean de Reszke.

63. *Across the Wide Missouri* (Metro-Goldwyn-Mayer, 1951)
Directed by William A. Wellman; Screenwriters: Talbot Jennings, Frank Cavett; from the book by Bernard DeVoto; Produced by Robert Sisk; Star: Clark Gable. Alan Napier as Captain Humberstone Lyon.

64. *The Blue Veil* (RKO Radio Pictures, 1951)
Directed by Curtis Bernhardt; Screenwriters: Norman Corwin and François Campaux (story); Produced by Jerry Wald, Norman Krasna and Raymond Hakim; Stars: Jane Wyman. Alan Napier as Professor George Carter.

65. *The Strange Door* (Universal Pictures, 1951)
Directed by Joseph Pevney; Screenwriters: Jerry Sackheim; from the Robert Louis Stevenson story "The Sire de Maletroit's Door"); Produced by Ted Richmond; Star: Charles Laughton. Alan Napier as Count Grassin.

66. *Double Crossbones* (Universal Pictures, 1951)
Directed by Charles Barton; Screenwriters: Oscar Brodney (story) and John Grant; Produced by Leonard Goldstein; Star: Donald O'Connor. Alan Napier as Captain Kidd.

67. *Tarzan's Peril* (RKO Radio Pictures, 1951)
Directed by Byron Haskin; Screenwriters: Samuel Newman, Francis Swann and John Cousins; based on the characters of Edgar Rice Burroughs; Produced by Sol Lesser; Star: Lex Barker. Alan Napier as Commissioner Peters.

68. *The Highwayman* (Allied Artists Pictures, 1951)
Directed Lesley Selander; Screenwriters: Jack DeWitt, Duncan Renaldo, Henry Blankfort; from a poem by Alfred Noyes; Produced by Hal E. Ches-

ter, Jack Dietz and Bernard W. Burton; Star: Philip Friend. Alan Napier as Barton.

69. *Big Jim McLain* (Warner Brothers, 1952)
Directed by Edward Ludwig; Screenwriters: James Edward Grant, Richard English and Eric Taylor; quotes from "The Devil and Daniel Webster" by Stephen Vincent Benet; Produced by Robert Fellows; Star: John Wayne. Alan Napier as Sturak.

70. *Julius Caesar* (Metro-Goldwyn-Mayer, 1953)
Directed by Joseph L. Mankiewicz; from the play by William Shakespeare; Produced by John Houseman; Star: Louis Calhern. Alan Napier as Cicero.

71. *Young Bess* (Metro-Goldwyn-Mayer, 1953)
Directed by George Sidney; Screenwriters: Jan Lustig and Arthur Wimperis; based on the novel by Margaret Irwin; Produced by Sidney Franklin. Star: Jean Simmons. Alan Napier as Robert Tyrwhitt.

72. *Désirée* (Twentieth Century Fox, 1954)
Directed by Henry Koster; Screenwriters: Daniel Taradash; based on the novel by Annemarie Selinko; Produced by Julian Blaustein; Star: Marlon Brando. Alan Napier as Despereaux.

73. *The Court Jester* (Paramount, 1955)
Directed by Melvin Frank; Screenwriters: Norman Panama and Melvin Frank; Produced by Norman Panama and Melvin Frank; Star: Danny Kaye. Alan Napier as Sir Brockhurst.

74. *Moonfleet* (Metro-Goldwyn-Mayer, 1955)
Directed by Fritz Lang; Screenwriters: Jan Lustig and Margaret Fitts; based on the novel by J. Meade Falkner; Produced by John Houseman; Star: Stewart Granger. Alan Napier as Parson Glennie.

75. *The Mole People* (Universal-International Pictures, 1956)
Directed by Virgil W. Vogel; Screenwriter: Laszlo Gorog; Produced by William Alland; Star: John Agar. Alan Napier as Elinu, the High Priest.

76. *Miami Exposé* (Columbia Pictures, 1956)
Directed by Fred F. Sears; Screenwriter: Robert E. Kent; from his story; Produced by Sam Katzman; Star: Lee J. Cobb. Alan Napier as Raymond Sheridan.

77. *Until They Sail* (Metro-Goldwyn-Mayer, 1957)
Directed by Robert Wise; Screenwriter: Robert Anderson (from a story by James A. Michenor); Produced by Charles Schnee and James E. Newcom; Star: Jean Simmons. Alan Napier as Prosecution Attorney.

78. *Journey to the Center of the Earth* (Twentieth Century Fox, 1959)
Directed by Henry Levin; Screenwriters: Walter Reisch and Charles Brackett; from the novel by Jules Verne; Produced by Charles Brackett; Star: James Mason. Alan Napier as Dean.

79. *Island of Lost Women* (Warner Brothers, 1959)
Directed by Frank Tuttle; Screenwriters: Ray Buffum and Prescott Chaplin (story); Produced by Albert J. Cohen; Star: Jeff Richards. Alan Napier as Dr. Paul Lujan.

80. *Wild in the Country* (Twentieth Century Fox, 1961)
Directed by Philip Dunne; Screenwriters: Clifford Odets; from the novel "The
 Lost Country" by J. R. Salamanca; Produced by Jerry Wald and Peter Nel-
 son; Star: Elvis Presley. Alan Napier as Professor Joe B. Larson.
81. *Tender Is the Night* (Twentieth Century Fox, 1962)
Directed by Henry King; Screenwriter: Ivan Moffat; from novel by F. Scott
 Fitzgerald; Produced by Henry T. Weinstein; Star: Jennifer Jones. Alan
 Napier as Señor Pardo.
82. *Premature Burial* (American International Pictures, 1962)
Directed by Roger Corman; Screenwriters: Charles Beaumont, Ray Russell;
 from the story by Edgar Allan Poe; Produced by Samuel Z. Arkoff; Star: Ray
 Milland. Alan Napier as Dr. Gideon Gault.
83. *The Sword in the Stone* (Buena Vista Pictures, 1963)
Directed by Wolfgang Reitherman; Screenwriter: Bill Peet; based on the book
 by T.H. White; Produced by Walt Disney; Star: Rickie Sorensen. Alan Napier
 as the voice of Sir Pellinore.
84. *Mary Poppins* (Buena Vista, 1964)
Directed by Robert Stevenson; Screenwriters: Bill Walsh and Don DaGradi;
 based on the books "Mary Poppins" by P.L. Travers); Producers: Bill Walosh
 and Walt Disney; Star: Julie Andrews. Alan Napier (varied voices-Hunts-
 man, Hound and Reporter # 3).
85. *My Fair Lady* (Warner Brothers, 1964)
Directed by George Cukor; Screenwriters: Writers: Alan Jay Lerner; from a
 play ["Pygmalion"] by George Bernard Shaw; Produced by Jack L. Warner;
 Star: Audrey Hepburn. Alan Napier as Eliza's escort to the Queen.
86. *Marnie* (Universal Pictures, 1964)
Directed and Produced by Alfred Hitchcock; Screenwriter: Jay Presson Allen; from the novel by Winston Graham; Star: Tippi Hedren. Alan Napier as
 Mr. Rutland.
87. *36 Hours* (Metro-Goldwyn-Mayer, 1964)
Directed by George Seaton; Screenwriters: George Seaton, Luis H. Vance
 (story), Carl K. Hittleman and Roald Dahl (from his story "Beware of the
 Dog"); Produced by William Perlberg; Star: James Garner. Alan Napier as
 General Allison.
88. *Signpost to Murder* (Metro-Goldwyn-Mayer, 1964)
Directed by George Englund; Screenwriters: Sally Benson; from the play by
 Monte Doyle; Produced by Lawrence Weingarten; Star: Joanne Woodward.
 Alan Napier as The Vicar.
89. *The Loved One* (Metro-Goldwyn-Mayer, 1965)
Directed by Tony Richardson; Screenwriters: Christopher Isherwood and
 Terry Southern; from the novel by Evelyn Waugh; Produced by John Cal-
 ley, Haskell Wexler and Neil Hartley; Star: Robert Morse. Alan Napier as
 English Club Official.
90. *Batman: The Movie* (Twentieth Century Fox, 1966)

Directed by Leslie H. Martinson; Screenwriters: Lorenzo Semple, Jr; from the characters created by Bob Kane; Produced by William Dozier and Charles B. Fitzsimons (Associate producer); Stars: Adam West and Burt Ward. Alan Napier as Alfred.

Miscellaneous credit for Alan Napier:

Enchantment (RKO Radio Pictures, 1948; Directed by Irving Reis; Produced by Samuel Goldwyn.) Writers: John Patrick, Rumer Godden; Alan Napier was hired behind the scenes as a dialogue director for various people in this film. He did not appear in this drama. The romantic lead was played by David Niven and co-starred Teresa Wright. The large cast featured Evelyn Keyes and Farley Granger.

Alan Napier - Complete listing of 120 episode titles from TVs *Batman* with their original aired dates from 1966 until 1968.

1. Hi Diddle Riddle
January 12, 1966
Director – Robert Butler
2. Smack in the Middle
January 13, 1966
Director – Robert Butler
3. Fine Feathered Finks
January 19, 1966
Director – Robert Butler
4. The Penguin's a Jinx
January 20, 1966
Director – Robert Butler
5. The Joker Is Wild
January 26, 1966
Director – Don Weis
6. Batman Is Riled
January 27, 1966
Director – Don Weis
7. Instant Freeze
February 2, 1966
Director – Robert Butler
8. Rats Like Cheese
February 3, 1966
Director – Robert Butler
9. Zelda the Great
February 9, 1966
Director – Norman Foster
10. A Death Worse Than Fate
February 10, 1966
Director – Norman Foster
11. A Riddle a Day Keeps the Riddler Away
February 16, 1966

Director – Tom Gries
12. When the Rat's Away, the Mice Will Play
February 17, 1966
Director – Tom Gries
13. The Thirteenth Hat
February 23, 1966
Director Norman Foster
14. Batman Stands Pat
February 24, 1966
Director – Norman Foster
15. The Joker Goes To School
March 2, 1966
Director – Murray Golden
16. He Meets His Match, the Grisly Ghoul
March 3, 1966
Director – Murray Golden
17. True or False Face
March 9, 1966
Director – William Graham
18. Holy Rat Race
March 10, 1966
Director – William Graham
19. The Purr-fect Crime
March 16, 1966
Director – James Sheldon
20. Better Luck Next Time
March 17, 1966
Director – James Sheldon
21. The Penguin Goes Straight
March 23, 1966
Director – Leslie H. Martinson
22. Not Yet, He Ain't
March 24, 1966
Director – Leslie H. Martinson
23. The Ring of Wax
March 30, 1966
Director – James B. Clark
24. Give 'Em The Axe
March 31, 1966
Director – James B. Clark
25. The Joker Trumps An Ace
April 6, 1966
Director – Richard C. Sarafian
26. Batman Sets The Pace
April 7, 1966

Director - Richard C. Sarafian
27. The Curse Of Tut
April 13, 1966
Director - Charles R. Rondeau
28. The Pharaoh's In a Rut
April 14, 1966
Director - Charles R. Rondeau
29. The Bookworm Turns
April 20, 1966
Director - Larry Peerce
30. While Gotham City Burns
April 21, 1966
Director - Larry Peerce
31. Death In Slow Motion
April 27, 1966
Director - Charles R. Rondeau
32. The Riddler's False Notion
April 28, 1966
Director - Charles R. Rondeau
33. Fine Finny Fiends
May 4, 1966
Director - Tom Gries
34. Batman Makes the Scenes
May 5, 1966
Director - Tom Gries
35. Shoot a Crooked Arrow
September 7, 1966)
Director - Sherman Marks
36. Walk the Straight And Narrow
September 8, 1966)
Director - Sherman Marks
37. Hot Off the Griddle
September 14, 1966
Director - Don Weis
38. The Cat and the Fiddle
September 15, 1966
Director - Don Weis
39. The Minstrel's Shakedown
September 21, 1966
Director - Murray Golden
40. Barbecued Batman?
September 22, 1966
Director - Murray Golden
41. The Spell of Tut
September 28, 1966

Director - Larry Peerce
42. Tut's Case Is Shut
September 29, 1966
Director - Larry Peerce
43. The Greatest Mother of Them All
October 5, 1966
Director - Oscar Rudolph
44. Ma Parker
October 6, 1966
Director - Oscar Rudolph
45. The Clock King's Crazy Crimes
October 12, 1966
Director - James Neilson
46. The Clock King Gets Crowned
October 13, 1966
Director - James Neilson
47. An Egg Grows In Gotham
October 19, 1966
Director - George Waggner
48. The Yegg Foes in Gotham
October 20, 1966
Director - George Waggner
49. The Devil's Fingers
October 26, 1966
Director - Larry Peerce
50. The Dead Ringers
October 27, 1966
Director - Larry Peerce
51. Hizzonner the Penguin
November 2, 1966
Director - Oscar Rudolph
52. Dizzoner the Penguin
November 3, 1966
Director - Oscar Rudolph
53. Green Ice
November 9, 1966
Director - George Waggner
54. Deep Freeze
November 10, 1966
Director - George Waggner
55. The Impractical Joker
November 16, 1966
Director - James B. Clark
56. The Joker's Provokers
November 17, 1966

Director - James B. Clark
57. Marsha, Queen of Diamonds
November 23, 1966
Director - James B. Clark
58. Marsha's Scheme of Diamonds
November 24, 1966
Director - James B. Clark
59. Come Back, Shame
November 30, 1966
Director - Oscar Rudolph
60. It's How You Play the Game
December 1, 1966
Director - Oscar Rudolph
61. The Penguin's Nest
December 7, 1966
Director - Murray Golden
62. The Bird's Last Jest
December 8, 1966
Director - Murray Golden
63. The Cat's Meow
December 14, 1966
Director - James B. Clark
64. The Bat's Kow Tow
December 15, 1966
Director - James B. Clark
65. The Puzzles Are Coming
December 21, 1966
Director - Jeffrey Hayden
66. The Duo Is Slumming
December 22, 1966
Director - Jeffrey Hayden
67. The Sandman Cometh
December 28, 1966
Director - George Waggner
68. The Catwoman Goeth
December 29, 1966
Director - George Waggner
69. The Contaminated Cowl
January 4, 1967
Director - Oscar Rudolph
70. The Mad Hatter Runs Afoul
January 5, 1967
Director - Oscar Rudolph
71. The Zodiac Crimes
January 11, 1967

Director - Oscar Rudolph
72. The Joker's Hard Times
January 12, 1967
Director - Oscar Rudolph
73. The Penguin Declines
January 18, 1967
Director - Oscar Rudolph
74. That Darn Catwoman
January 19, 1967
Director - Oscar Rudolph
75. Scat! Darn Catwoman
January 25, 1967
Director - Oscar Rudolph
76. Penguin Is a Girl's Best Friend
January 26, 1967
Director - James B. Clark
77. Penguin Sets a Trend
February 1, 1967
Director - James B. Clark
78. Penguin's Disastrous End
February 2, 1967
Director - James B. Clark
79. Batman's Anniversary
February 8, 1967
Director - James B. Clark
80. A Riddling Controversy
February 9, 1967
Director - James B. Clark
81. The Joker's Last Laugh
February 15, 1967
Director - Oscar Rudolph
82. The Joker's Epitaph
February 16, 1967
Director - Oscar Rudolph
83. Catwoman Goes to College
February 22, 1967
Director - Robert Sparr
84. Batman Displays His Knowledge
February 23, 1967
Director - Robert Sparr
85. A Piece of the Action
March 1, 1967
Director - Oscar Rudolph
86. Batman's Satisfaction
March 2, 1967

Director - Oscar Rudolph
87. King Tut's Coup
March 8, 1967
Director - James B. Clark
88. Batman's Waterloo
March 9, 1967
Director - James B. Clark
89. Black Widow Strikes Again
March 15, 1967
Director - Oscar Rudolph
90. Caught in the Spider's Den
March 16, 1967
Director - Oscar Rudolph
91. Pop Goes the Joker
March 22, 1967
Director - George Waggner
92. Flop Goes the Joker
March 23, 1967
Director - George Waggner
93. Ice Spy
March 29, 1967
Director - Oscar Rudolph
94. The Duo Defy
March 30, 1967
Director - Oscar Rudolph
95. Enter Batgirl, Exit Penguin
September 14, 1967
Director - Oscar Rudolph
96. Ring Around the Riddler
September 21, 1967
Director - Sam Strangis
97. The Wail of the Siren
September 28, 1967
Director - George Waggner
98. The Sport of Penguins
October 5, 1967
Director - Sam Strangis
99. A Horse of Another Color
October 12, 1967
Director - Sam Strangis
100. The Unkindest Tut Of All
October 19, 1967
Director - Sam Strangis
101. Louie, the Lilac
October 26, 1967

Director – George Waggner
102. The Ogg and I
November 2, 1967
Director – Oscar Rudolph
103. How to Hatch a Dinosaur
November 9, 1967
Director – Oscar Rudolph
104. Surf's Up! Joker's Under!
November 16, 1967
Director – Oscar Rudolph
105. The Londinium Larcenies
November 23, 1967
Director – Oscar Rudolph
106. The Foggiest Notion
November 30, 1967
Director – Oscar Rudolph
107. The Bloody Tower
December 7, 1967)
Director – Oscar Rudolph
108. Catwoman's Dressed To Kill
December 14, 1967
Director – Sam Strangis
109. The Ogg Couple
December 21, 1967
Director – Oscar Rudolph
110. The Funny Feline Felonies
December 28, 1967
Director – Oscar Rudolph
111. The Joke's On Catwoman
January 4, 1968
Director – Oscar Rudolph
112. Louie's Lethal Lilac Time
January 11, 1968
Director – Sam Strangis
113. Nora Clavicle and the Ladies' Crime Club
January 18, 1968
Director – Oscar Rudolph
114. Penguin's Clean Sweep
January 25, 1968
Director – Oscar Rudolph
115. The Great Escape
February 1, 1968
Director – Oscar Rudolph
116. The Great Train Robbery
February 8, 1968

Director – Oscar Rudolph
117. I'll Be a Mummy's Uncle
February 22, 1968
Director – Oscar Rudolph
118. The Joker's Flying Saucer
February 29, 1968
Director – Sam Strangis
119. The Entrancing Dr. Cassandra
March 7, 1968
Director – Sam Strangis
120. Minerva, Mayhem and Millionaires
March 14, 1968
Director – Oscar Rudolph
Alan Napier – Stage Credits (USA)
Lady in Waiting (1940)
McCarter Theatre (Princeton University)
Princeton, New Jersey
One night only- March 16th 1940
The National Theatre
Washington, D.C.
March 18 through March 23, 1940
Martin Beck Theatre
New York City
March 27, 1940 – June 8, 1940   (87 Performances)
Staged by Antoinette Perry.
Written by Margery Sharp
Scenic Design by John Root
Produced by Brock Pemberton
Staged by Antoinette Perry
Cast:
Alan Napier. . . . . Sir William Warring
Albert Allen. . . . . Bert Genocchio
Stephen Ker Appleby. . . . . Bryan Relton
Anita Bolster. . . . . Griffin
Michelette Burani . . . . Anthelmine
Lenore Chippendale . . . . . Mrs. Packett
Carol Curtis-Brown . . . . . . Susan Packett
James Decker. . . . . Joe Genocchio
Paul Foley . . . . Burns
Gladys George. . . . . Julia Packett
Mary Heberden . . . . Esme Bellingham
Walter Moore. . . . . Willie Genocchio
Ethel Morrison . . . . "Ma" Genocchio
Leonard Penn. . . . . Fred Genocchio
Guy Spaull. . . . . Rogers

Lady in Waiting continued as a road tour through December 30, 1940 in the
  following cities: Hartford, Connecticut; Boston, Chicago; Buffalo, New York,
  and Cleveland Ohio.
And So to Bed (1948)
Las Palmas Theatre
Los Angeles, California
"James B. Fagan's Production of His Own Comedy –Based on the Diary of
  Samuel Pepys"
Alan Napier as Charles II
Various productions staged in U.S. cities by Eugenie Leontovich
With:
Eugenie Leontovich
Rollo Peters
Katherine Wick Kelly
Yvonne Arnaud,
Walter Meade
Emlyn Williams
Walter Kingsford
Claude Rains
Mary Robson.
Gertie (1952)
Plymouth Theatre
New York City
January 30, 1952 – February 2, 1952 (5 performances)
Written by Enid Bagnold
Scenic Design by William and Jean Eckart
Costume Design by Hazel Roy
Staged by Herman Shumlin
Produced by Herman Shumlin
Cast:
Alan Napier as Mr. Ritchie
Anita Cooper . . . . . . .Bianca
Albert Dekker. . . . . . .Rex
Robert Duke . . . . .James
Glynis Johns . . . . .Gertie
Polly Rowles . . . . .Mrs. Candida Kaufman
Patricia Wheel . . . . . .Sarah
Dial M For Murder (1952 Road engagement)
Premiere: Wilbur Theatre
Boston, Massachusetts - December 26, 1952
Chicago, Illinois - January 25, 1953 – May 24, 1953
From the play written by Frederick Knott
Sets and Lighting by Peter Larkin
Costumes by Neel Taylor
Presented by James F. Sherwood

Staged by Reginald Denham
Cast:
Alan Napier as Inspector Hubbard
J. Pat O'Malley (closing week replacement for Alan Napier)
Faith Brook .... Margot Wendice
Mark Roberts .... Max Halliday
Richard Greene ..... Tony Wendice
Ralph Clanton ...... Captain Lengale
Bruce Jewell........ Thompson
Coriolanus
Phoenix Theatre
New York City
January 19, 1954 – February 28, 1954 (48 performances)
Playwright – William Shakespeare
Music by Alex North
Costume designer – Alvin Colt
Produced by T. Edward Hambleton and Norris Óoughton
Directed by John Houseman
Cast:
Alan Napier as Menenius Agrippa
Norman Beim .... Senator/ Soldier/ Citizen
Peter Benzoni........ Senator / Soldier / Citizen
Jack Bittner.......... 3rd Citizen
Peter Buchan .... Senator/ Soldier/ Citizen
Nat Burns............ Senator/ Soldier/ Citizen
David Clarke......... 2nd Citizen
Donald Draper .... Senator/ Soldier/ Citizen
Nora Dunfee......... Gentlewoman
Joseph Elic .... Senator/ Soldier/ Citizen
John Emery.......... Tullus Aufidius
George Fells .... 2nd Senator
Mel Fillini........... Senator/ Soldier/ Citizen
Jack Friend .... Senator/ Soldier/ Citizen
Will Geer............ Sicinius
Erle Hall............. Senator/ Soldier/ Citizen
Joseph Holland ...... Cominius
Carl Jacobs.......... 4th Citizen/ 2nd Aedile/ 2nd Sentinel/ 1st Conspirator
Jack Klugman .... 6th Citizen/ 2nd Volscian Servant
Paula Laurence ...... Valeria
Richard Lederer...... Senator/ Soldier/ Citizen
J. Frank Lucas........ Senator/ Soldier/ Citizen
Paul Lukather .... Senator/ Soldier/ Citizen
Joseph Macaulay..... 1st Senator
Lori March.......... Virgilia
Richard Marr......... Senator/ Soldier/ Citizen

Hugh Mosher . . . . Senator/ Soldier/ Citizen
Terry Nardin . . . . Son to Coriolanus
Joseph Nathan. . . . . . . Senator/ Soldier/ Citizen
Mildred Natwick . . . . . Volumnia
Jim Oyster. . . . . Senator/ Soldier/ Citizen
Lou Polan. . . . . Titus Lartius/ 1st Lord
Lou Polan. . . . . 1st Lord
John Randolph. . . . . . . Junius Brutus
Frederick Rolf. . . . . 1st Citizen
Robert Ryan . . . . Caius Martius Coriolanus
Gene Saks . . . . 7th Citizen/ 1st Volscian Servant
Richard Shull. . . . . Senator/ Soldier/ Citizen
Jamie Smith . . . . 1st Aedile/ Lieutenant to Aufidius
Tim Squires . . . . Senator/ Soldier/ Citizen
Jerry Stiller . . . . 5th Citizen/ 3rd Volscian Servant
Michael Tolan . . . . Senatorial Messenger
Laurence Vide . . . . Senator/ Soldier/ Citizen
Too Late the Phalarope (1956)
Belasco Theatre
New York City
October 11, 1956 – November 10, 1956
Based on the novel by Alan Paton
Written by Robert Yale Libott
Incidental music by Joseph Marais
Directed by John Stix
Scenic Design by George Jenkins
Costume Design by Dorothy Jeakins
Lighting Design by George Jenkins
Company Manager: Ben Rosenberg
Stage Managers: Seymour Milbert, Kurt Cerf and Paul Leaf
Produced by Mary K. Frank
Cast:
Alan Napier as Captain Massingham
Rudolph Adler . . . . . . Party Guest
Roy Barba . . . . Frikkie Van Vlaanderen
Laurinda Barrett . . . . Nekia Van Vlaanderen
Lindsey Bergen . . . . . Party Guest
Joe Biviano . . . . Party Guest
Adelaide Boatner . . . Native
Josephe Boatner . . . Native
Joseph Boley . . . . Matthew Kaplan ("Kappie")
Kurt Cerf . . . . Johannes Maartens
Grant Code . . . . Dominee Stander
Finlay Currie . . . . Jakob Van Vlaanderen
Bill Glover . . . . Native

Marvin Goodis . . . . . . Party Guest
Estelle Hemsley . . . . . Esther
Robert Henson. . . . . . Native
Ellen Holly . . . . Stephanie
Geoffrey Horne . . . . . Dick Vorster
Wesley Lau . . . . Party Guest
Janine Manatis . . . . . . Anna Van Aardt
Paul Mann . . . . Japie Grobler
Bruce Peyton . . . . Party Guest
Byron Russell . . . . Herman Geyer
Bronia Stefan . . . . Veronica Massingham
Barry Sullivan . . . . Lieutenant Pieter Van Vlaanderen
Ralph Sumpter . . . . . . Captain Jooste
Roy Thompson   . . . . Native Policeman
. . . . Native
Cherokee Thornton . Isak
George Tyne . . . . Sergeant Steyn

Alan Napier - Radio Credits
(From the CBS network unless specified otherwise)
November 12, 1939 – The Campbell Playhouse
"The Murder of Roger Ackroyd" by Agatha Christie
Scripted by Herman J. Mankiewicz
Announcers - Niles Welch and Ernest Chappell
Produced by John Houseman
Directed by Orson Welles
Music by Bernard Herrmann
Cast: Orson Welles (Hercule Poirot, Dr. James Sheppard), Edna May Oliver
    (Caroline Sheppard), Alan Napier (Roger Ackroyd), Brenda Forbes (Mrs.
    Ackroyd), Mary Taylor (Flora), George Coulouris (Inspector Hempstead),
    Ray Collins (Mr. Raymond), Everett Sloane (Parker, the butler).
November 20, 1939 – The Lux Radio Theatre
"Goodbye, Mr. Chips" by James Hilton (Intermission guest, author)
Adaptation - George Wells
Announcer - Melville Ruick
Directed by Sanford Barnett
Music director - Louis Silvers
Cast: Laurence Olivier, Edna Best, Cecil B. DeMille, Alan Napier, Bill Martin,
    Bob Stevens, Bobby Mauch, Bobby Winkler, Montague Shaw, Cliff Oland,
    Clifford Severn Sr., Douglas Scott, Edwin Mills, Eric Snowden, Ernest Carl-
    son, Frederic Worlock, Harry Duff, Ian MacLaren.
November 27, 1939 – The Lux Radio Theatre
"Pygmalion" George Bernard Shaw (author)
Adaptation – George Wells
Host - Cecil B. DeMille

Announcer – Melville Ruick
Directed by Sanford Barnett
Music director - Louis Silvers
Cast: Jean Arthur, Brian Aherne, Alan Napier, Jack Lewis, Eric Snowden, Mary Gordon, Thomas Freebairn-Smith, Evelyn Beresford, Mary Taylor, Lou Merrill, Margaret Brayton, Janet Young, Thomas Mills, and Gloria Gordon.
July 7, 1941 – The Lux Radio Theatre
"Algiers" (The classic love story of Pepe Le Moko in the Casbah.)
Author - Roger D'Ashelbe
Adaptation by George Wells
Screenwriters – Roger D'Ashelbe, John Howard Lawson, James M. Cain, Henri Jeanson.
Directed by Sanford Barnett
Announcer – Melville Ruick
Music director – Louis Silvers
Cast: Cecil B. DeMille, Hedy Lamarr (her radio debut), Charles Boyer, Bea Benaderet, Bruce Payne, Frederic Worlock, Charles Seel, Noreen Gammill, Paul Dubov, Virginia Gordon, Alan Napier, Howard McNear, Jeff Corey, Leo Cleary, Lou Merrill, Hans Conried.
Fifth War Loan Drive (June 12, 1944 - July 8, 1944)
"Radio Almanac" (broadcast of June 14, 1944)
Orson Welles originally started this broadcast about the states of Texas and Arkansas going to war against each other. Instead, the President makes a statement. Welles was placed on the U.S. Treasury payroll as an expert consultant during the duration of WWII to sell what became known as War Bonds devoting an hour-long program to the cause.
Cast: Agnes Moorehead, Keenan Wynn, Franklin Roosevelt, Henry Morgenthau, Lois Andrews, Edgar Barrier, Walter Huston, Gloria Jean, Alan Napier, and Natalie Darby. Orson Welles is actor, writer and director.
April 10, 1945 – "This Is My Best" (Radio series, 1944-1946)
"The Master of Ballantrae" by Robert Louis Stevenson
Produced by Orson Welles
Announcer – Vern Smith
Adaptation by Robert Tallman
Composer – Bernard Katz
Cast: Orson Welles, Agnes Moorehead, Ray Collins, and Alan Napier
November 19, 1945 – The Lux Radio Theatre
"The Keys of the Kingdom"
Directed by Sanford Barnett
Author - A. J. Cronin
Adaptation by Fred MacKaye
Screenwriters - Joseph Mankiewicz and Nunnally Johnson
Host – William Keighley
Announcers – John Milton Kennedy and Thomas Hanlon
Music – Louis Silvers

Sound effects by Charlie Forsyth
Cast: Joseph Kearns, Colin Campbell, Eric Snowden, Alan Napier, Ramsay Hill, Charlie Lung, Lal Chand Mehra, H. T. Tsang, Ronald Colman, Ann Harding, Barbara Jean Wong, Peter Chong, Charles Seel, and Duane Thompson.
July 9, 1961 – Heartbeat Theatre
"Honor Among Thieves" (Salvation Army syndication to 500 U.S. radio stations)
Sponsored by the Salvation Army fund appeal
Produced by C.P. MacGregor
Host – C. P. MacGregor
With: Alan Napier.

David Manners - Filmography
1. *The Sky Hawk* (Fox Film Corporation, 1929)
Directed by John G. Blystone
David Manners as a Pilot (uncredited)
2. *Journey's End* (Tiffany-Gainsborough Pictures, Ltd., 1930)
Directed by James Whale
David Manners as Second Lieutenant Raleigh
3. *He Knew Women* (RKO Productions, Inc., 1930)
Directed by Hugh Herbert
David Manners as Austin Lowe
4. *Sweet Mama* (First National Pictures, Inc., 1930)
Directed by Edward Cline
David Manners as Jimmy
5. *Kismet* (First National Pictures, Inc., 1930)
Directed by John Francis Dillon
David Manners as Caliph Abdallah
6. *The Truth About Youth* (First National Pictures, Inc., 1930)
Directed by William Seiter
David Manners as Richard Dane, the Imp
7. *Mothers Cry* (First National Pictures, Inc., 1930)
Directed by Hobart Henley
David Manners as Artie
8. *The Right to Love* (Paramount Publix Corporation, 1930)
Directed by Richard Wallace
David Manners as Joe Copeland
9. *Dracula* (Universal Pictures Corporation, 1931)
Directed by Tod Browning
David Manners as John Harker
10. *The Millionaire* (Warner Bros. Pictures, Inc., 1931)
Directed by John G. Adolfi
David Manners as Bill Merrick
11. *The Miracle Woman* (Columbia Pictures Corporation, 1931)
Directed by Frank Capra

David Manners as John Carson
12. *The Last Flight* (First National Pictures, Inc., 1931)
Directed by William Dieterle
David Manners as Shep Lambert
13. *The Ruling Voice* (First National Pictures, Inc., 1931)
Directed by Rowland V. Lee
David Manners as Dick Cheney
14. *The Greeks Had a Word for Them* (United Artists Corporation, 1932)
Directed by Lowell Sherman
David Manners as Dey Emery
15. *Lady With a Past* (RKO Pathé Pictures, Inc., 1932)
Directed by Edward H. Griffith
David Manners as Donnie Wainwright
16. *Beauty and the Boss* (Warner Bros. Pictures, Inc., 1932)
Directed by Roy Del Ruth
David Manners as Paul
17. *Man Wanted* (Warner Bros. Pictures, Inc., 1932)
Directed by William Dieterle
David Manners as Tom Sheridan
18. *Stranger in Town* (Warner Bros. Pictures, Inc., 1932)
Directed by Erle C. Kenton
David Manners as Jerry
19. *Crooner* (Warner Bros. Pictures, Inc., 1932)
Directed by Lloyd Bacon
David Manners as Teddy Taylor
20. *A Bill of Divorcement* (RKO Radio Pictures, Inc., 1932)
Directed by George Cukor
David Manners as Kit (Humphrey)
21. *They Call It Sin* (First National Pictures, Inc., 1932)
Directed by Thornton Freeland
David Manners as Jimmy Decker
22. *The Mummy* (Universal Pictures Corporation, 1932)
Directed by Karl Freund
David Manners as Frank Whemple
23. *The Death Kiss* (World Wide Pictures, Inc. & Fox Film Corp., 1933)
Directed by Edwin L. Marin
David Manners as Franklyn Drew
24. *From Hell to Heaven* (Paramount Productions, Inc., 1933)
Directed by Erle C. Kenton
David Manners as Wesley Burt
25. *The Warrior's Husband* (Fox Film Corporation, 1933)
Directed by Walter Lang
David Manners as Theseus, commander of the Greek army
26. *The Girl in 419* (Paramount Productions, Inc., 1933)
Directed by Alexander Hall

David Manners as Dr. Martin Nichols
27. *The Devil's in Love* (Fox Film Corporation, 1933)
Directed by Wilhelm Dieterle
David Manners as [Captain] Jean [Fabien]
28. *Torch Singer* (Paramount Productions, Inc., 1933)
Directed by Alexander Hall
David Manners as Michael Gardner
29. *Roman Scandals* (United Artists Corporation, 1933)
Directed by Frank Tuttle
David Manners as Josephus
30. *The Black Cat* (Universal Pictures Corporation, 1934)
Directed by Edgar G. Ulmer
David Manners as Peter Alison
31. *The Luck of a Sailor* (Wardour Films, UK, 1934)
Directed by Robert Milton
David Manners as Captain Colin
32. *The Great Flirtation* (Paramount Productions, Inc., 1934)
Directed by Ralph Murphy
David Manners as Larry Kenyon
33. *The Moonstone* (Monogram Pictures Corporation, 1934)
Directed by Reginald Barker
David Manners as Franklin Blake
34. *Mystery of Edwin Drood* (Universal Pictures Corporation, 1935)
Directed by Stuart Walker
David Manners as Edwin [Ned] Drood
35. *The Perfect Clue* (Majestic Producing Corporation, 1934)
Directed by Robert G. Vignola
David Manners as David Mannering
36. *Jalna* (RKO Radio Pictures, Inc., 1935)
Directed by John Cromwell
David Manners as Eden Whiteoaks
37. *Hearts in Bondage* (Republic Pictures Corporation, 1936)
Directed by Lew Ayres
David Manners as Raymond Jordan
38. *A Woman Rebels* (RKO Radio Pictures, Inc., 1936)
Directed by Mark Sandrich
David Manners as Lieutenant Alan Craig Freeland
39. *Lucky Fugitives* (Canada) (Columbia Pictures Corporation, 1936)
Directed by Nick Grinde
David Manners as Jack Wycoff (Cy King)

David Manners - Broadway Credits (USA)
Dancing Mothers (1924)
Booth Theatre (New York)
Opened: August 11, 1924

Closed: May 1925 (312 performances)
A play in four acts
Written by Edmund Goulding and Edgar Selwyn
Produced by Edgar Selwyn
Staged by Edgar Selwyn
With a cast of twenty-two that included:
Helen Hayes, Rodolfo Badaloni and Michael Dawn (later known as David
    Manners) played Kenneth Cobb.
Lady Windermere's Fan (1946)
Cort Theatre (New York and on tour for several months)
Opened: October 14, 1946
Closed: April 26, 1947 (228 performances)
A play in four acts
Written by Oscar Wilde
Directed by Jack Minster
Stage managers: Robert Linden and assistant Guy Blake
Scenic design, costume design and lighting design by Cecil Beaton
The cast of twenty-five included:
Cecil Beaton, Stanley Bell, Penelope Ward, Sally Cooper, Cornelia Otis
    Skinner, John Buckmaster, Estelle Winwood and Henry Daniell, who was
    replaced by David Manners in the part of Lord Windermere.
Hidden Horizon (1946)
Plymouth Theatre (New York)
Opened: September 19, 1946
Closed: September 28m, 1946 (12 performances)
Produced by Messrs. (Lee and J.J.) Shubert
Written by Agatha Christie
Staged by Albert De Courville
The cast of fifteen included: Charles Alexander, Diana Barrymore, Blair Da-
    vies, Halliwell Hobbes, and David Manners as Smith.
Truckline Café (1948)
Belasco Theatre (New York)
Opened: February 27, 1948
Closed: March 9, 1948 (13 performances)
Produced by Harold Clurman and Elia Kazan (in association with The Play-
    wright's Company (Maxwell Anderson, S.N. Behrman, Elmer Rice, Robert E.
    Sherwood and Sidney Howard.)
Directed by Harold Clurman
Written by Maxwell Anderson
Scenic design by Boris Aronson
Costume design by Millia Davenport
Stage manager: James Gelb
The cast of thirty-one included newcomer Marlon Brando in addition to the
    talents of:

Joseph Adams, Irene Dailey, Karl Malden, Kevin McCarthy and David Manners as Wing Commander Hern.

INDEX